MICROSOFT WINDOWS 95

EDWARD G. MARTIN
CHARLES S. PARKER
CHARLES E. KEE

This manual contains numerous features that help you master the material quickl[y] reinforce your learning:

- *A Table of Contents.* A list of the manual's contents appears on the first pag[e] the manual. Each chapter starts with an *outline,* a list of learning *objectives,* and *overview* that summarizes the skills you will learn.

- *Bold Key Terms.* Important terms appear in bold type as they are introduced. The[y] are also conveniently listed at the end of each chapter, with page references for further review.

- *Color as a Learning Tool.* In this manual, color has been used to help you work through each chapter. Each step is numbered in green for easy identification. Within each step, text or commands that you should type appear in orange. Single keys to be pressed are shown in yellow boxes. For example,

  1 Type **WIN** and press ↵

- *Step-by-Step Mouse Approach.* This manual stresses the mouse approach. Each action is numbered consecutively in green to make it easy to locate and follow. Where appropriate, a mouse shortcut (toolbar icon) is shown in the left margin; a keyboard shortcut may be shown in brackets at the right, as follows:

  1 Click *Edit, Cut*   [**Ctrl** + **X**]

As your skills increase, the "click this item" approach slowly gives way to a less-detailed list of goals and operations so that you do not mindlessly follow steps, but truly master software skills.

- *Screen Figures.* Full-color annotated screens provide overviews of operations that let you monitor your work as you progress through the tutorial.

- *Tips.* Each chapter contains numerous short tips in bold type at strategic points to provide hints, warnings, or insights. Read these carefully.

- *Checkpoints.* At the end of each major section is a list of checkpoints, highlighted in red, which you can use to test your mastery of the material. Do not proceed further unless you can perform the checkpoint tasks.

- *Summary and Quiz.* At the end of each chapter is a bulleted summary of the chapter's content and a 30-question quiz with true/false, multiple-choice, and matching questions.

- *Exercises.* Each chapter ends with two sets of written exercises (Operations and Commands) and six guided hands-on computer applications that measure and reinforce mastery of the chapter's concepts and skills. Each pair of applications present problems relating to school, personal, and business use.

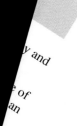

astery Cases. The final page of each chapter presents three unguided cases that allow you to demonstrate your personal mastery of the chapter material.

- *A Note about the Manual's Organization.* The topics in this manual are arranged in order of increasing difficulty. Chapters 1 and 2 present beginning and intermediate techniques and should be completed in sequence, for each skill builds upon the previous one. However, Chapter 3 includes several *independent* modules that present advanced skills. These modules may be followed in any order or omitted, as time and interest allow.

- *End-of-Manual Material.* The manual also provides a comprehensive reference *appendix* that summarizes commands and provides alphabetical listings of critical operations, a *glossary* that defines all key terms (with page references), and an *index* to all important topics.

WHAT'S NEW FOR MICROSOFT WINDOWS 95

1. *Simpler Look:* Only two major components to the main Windows 95 screen—a taskbar (bottom of screen) and the desktop (area above taskbar).

2. *Launching Programs:* Programs can be easily launched (started) from the Windows *Start* menu. This menu is accessible through the taskbar.

3. *Closing Windows:* A Close button, resembling an "X," has been added to every Window's title bar. This feature allows for quick closing of a window (exiting) by mouse.

4. *File and Folder Names:* File (program or document) and folder (groups of files) names are no longer restricted to eight characters plus an optional three-character extension. These names can contain up to 255 characters.

5. *Easier Multitasking:* The taskbar can be used to quickly switch between running programs.

6. *File Management:* Windows offers two programs for file management: My Computer displays the parts of a computer in a window, and Explorer displays the parts of a computer in a tree form. Files can be copied or cut and pasted in the same way as other selected (marked) data in the Windows environment.

MICROSOFT WINDOWS 95

CHAPTER 1
THE WINDOWS
ENVIRONMENT   WIN1

OVERVIEW   WIN1

GETTING STARTED   WIN2
Handling Disks and Hardware
   WIN2
Starting Windows   WIN3
The Windows Screen   WIN5
Mouse and Keyboard Operations
   WIN6
Shutting Down Windows   WIN13

**COMMON WINDOWS FEATURES
WIN14**
Launching a Program   WIN15
Types of Windows   WIN17
Title Bar   WIN17
Menu Bar   WIN22
Menu Indicators   WIN26
Command Buttons and Drop-Down
   Boxes   WIN27
Shortcut Menus   WIN29
Workspace   WIN30

**BASIC DOCUMENT
MANAGEMENT   WIN31**
Using the Default Document   WIN32
Saving a Document   WIN32
Printing a Document   WIN35
Creating a New Document   WIN35
Opening a Document   WIN36

BASIC MULTITASKING   WIN37
Launching Multiple Programs   WIN37
Switching between Programs   WIN38
Standard Window Displays   WIN38
Custom Window Displays   WIN41
Sharing Data   WIN42
Alternative Window Closing
   Techniques   WIN45

THE HELP FEATURE   WIN46
Using Windows Main Help   WIN47
Getting Help within a Dialog Box
   WIN50
Getting Help within a Program
   Window   WIN51

**OTHER START MENU
COMMANDS   WIN52**
Documents Menu   WIN52
Settings Menu   WIN53
Find Menu   WIN55
Run Dialog Box   WIN55

CHAPTER 2
MANAGING YOUR
COMPUTER   WIN67

OVERVIEW   WIN67

**UNDERSTANDING MY
COMPUTER   WIN68**
Launching My Computer   WIN68
Storing Programs and Documents
   WIN68
Disk Operations   WIN70
Finding a File   WIN70
Looking in a Folder   WIN73
Viewing Options   WIN76

MANAGING YOUR FILES WIN78
Folders   WIN79
Document Approach   WIN82
Selecting Multiple Files   WIN83
Opening Files   WIN83
Renaming Files   WIN85
Printing Files   WIN86

**SHARING AND REMOVING
YOUR FILES   WIN87**
Copying and Moving   WIN87
Creating a Shortcut   WIN93
Using Undo   WIN96
Deleting and Recycling   WIN97

**CONTROLLING YOUR
ENVIRONMENT   WIN99**
Changing Properties   WIN99
Using the Control Panel   WIN102
Using Printers   WIN106

**UNDERSTANDING EXPLORER
WIN107**
Launching Explorer   WIN108
Operating Explorer   WIN110

CHAPTER 3
OTHER WINDOWS
FEATURES   WIN123

OVERVIEW   WIN123

WORDPAD   WIN124
Getting Started   WIN124
Inserting New Text   WIN128
Selecting Text   WIN131
Deleting Text   WIN132
Undoing an Action   WIN132
Changing Text Appearance   WIN133
Changing Text Layout   WIN136
Moving and Copying a Selection
   WIN142

PAINT   WIN144
Getting Started   WIN144
Selecting a Drawing Tool   WIN146
Drawing Objects   WIN149
Moving and Copying Objects WIN152
Inserting Text   WIN154
Capturing a Screen   WIN156

**LINKING AND EMBEDDING
WIN157**
Linking   WIN158
Embedding   WIN158

**OTHER WINDOWS PROGRAMS
WIN163**
Accessibility Options   WIN163
Accessories   WIN164
Communications   WIN164

**APPENDIX: MICROSOFT
WINDOWS 95 FEATURES
AND OPERATION REFERENCE
WIN175**

GLOSSARY   WIN219

INDEX   WIN223

1

THE WINDOWS ENVIRONMENT

OUTLINE

GETTING STARTED
Handling Disks and Hardware
Starting Windows
The Windows Screen
Mouse and Keyboard
  Operations
Shutting Down Windows

COMMON WINDOWS FEATURES
Launching a Program
Types of Windows
Title Bar
Menu Bar
Menu Indicators
Command Buttons and Drop-Down
  Boxes

Shortcut Menus
Workspace

BASIC DOCUMENT MANAGEMENT
Using the Default Document
Saving a Document
Printing a Document
Creating a New Document
Opening a Document

BASIC MULTITASKING
Launching Multiple Programs
Switching between Programs
Standard Window Displays
Custom Window Displays
Sharing Data

Alternative Window Closing
  Techniques

THE HELP FEATURE
Using Windows Main Help
Getting Help within a Dialog Box
Getting Help within a Program
  Window

OTHER START MENU COMMANDS
Documents Menu
Settings Menu
Find Menu
Run Dialog Box

OBJECTIVES

After completing this chapter, you will be able to

1 Explain the difference between a character-based and a graphical-user-interface (GUI) environment.

2 Describe the procedures to start and shut down Windows.

3 Describe the components of the Windows screen.

4 Operate common Windows features including launching and closing programs and using window components.

5 Operate more than one program at a time—multitasking.

6 Describe how to access on-line help and use dialog boxes.

7 Explain the operations of other *Start* menu commands.

OVERVIEW

This chapter introduces you to the basics of Microsoft Windows 95—a *graphical user interface,* or *GUI* (pronounced "gooey"), operating environment that uses symbols (pictures) and menus instead of typewritten commands. You will learn how to start and shut down Windows 95, read the Windows 95 screen, operate common Windows features, use basic document management techniques, use multiple programs (multitasking), use the on-line help feature, and operate other options of the *Start* menu.

Although you can sit at a microcomputer and try each action presented in the tutorials, it is best to read the text first and examine the screens in preparation for the hands-on sessions and as a review. This text assumes that you have a mouse. However, keyboard actions are presented where available.

As you operate Windows, the items on your Windows screen may differ from the figures presented in this module. What you see depends on how Windows was set up on your system. However, many of Windows' key components, such as the taskbar, *Start* menu, and *Close* button, operate the same way.

Each set of tutorials is followed by a "Checkpoint"—a set of questions or tasks that quickly tests your mastery of the skills presented in that section. Do not proceed to the next section if you cannot successfully answer the Checkpoint questions. Review the material and try again.

GETTING STARTED

Embarking on any new learning experience is both exhilarating and frightening. This is especially true (and perhaps mysterious) when you are using technology. Some experiences may frustrate you, especially when your commands seem to be ignored or misunderstood. Remember, however, that the computer is only a tool that responds to *your* instructions.

Today, a **graphical user interface,** or **GUI** (pronounced "gooey"), operating system can simplify communication with your computer by using common symbols (called **icons**) and menus instead of typewritten commands. To begin a program, you simply select its symbol and name from a menu instead of typing its name. It is similar to when a company displays a picture of a phone instead of using the word "phone" to identify a phone booth. The GUI operating system presented in this text is called **Microsoft Windows 95.**

In the Windows environment, much of your work is done in rectangular boxes called windows. A **window** may contain a **program** (set of computer instructions) or **document** (a file with data). It is also used to request or give information about a task or feature. **Data** may include text and objects. **Objects** are graphic images (pictures or symbols) that may include text. Icons and windows are also considered objects.

The Windows environment also offers a variety of other features that are normally unavailable in a character-based environment (one that requires the use of typewritten commands). These features include the ability to operate several programs at once (called *multitasking*) and to easily and quickly share or link (dynamically connect) data among programs.

Although Windows provides a dynamic GUI operating environment, it requires more processing time than a character-based environment. If you are operating Windows on a less than state-of-the-art computer system, the time it takes to process your information may be intolerably slow.

Having said all this, relax. Normally, you cannot hurt the computer, nor can it hurt you. Do not be afraid to experiment with commands and techniques as you gain confidence in how they are used. As the old adage says, practice makes perfect.

HANDLING DISKS AND HARDWARE

Like automobiles, microcomputers can provide reliable service for years if they are used and maintained properly. Careful handling of your hardware and disks can significantly extend their life and reduce maintenance costs and down time. **Hardware** is any physical computer equipment. **Disks** are storage media that can be used to hold computer generated files. A **file** may contain a program or document. A *program,* as mentioned earlier, is simply a set of instructions. A *document* is a file that contains data. It is similar to paper documents. Files may also be organized into folders on a disk or other storage media. A **folder** is a group of related files.

When operating your computer system, avoid such obvious risks as hitting the hardware (such as banging on the keyboard). You should also keep the work environment clean.

To complete this tutorial, you will need a blank disk and a hard disk or network system that contains Windows 95. This text assumes that your computer hardware is configured with at least one disk drive (called Drive A) and a hard-disk drive (called Drive C). If you have a second drive, it is typically labeled as Drive B, and a CD ROM drive is identified as Drive D. Your actual configuration may differ.

As you read the rest of this chapter, pay particular attention to the number of steps in each section and follow them while sitting at your computer. This module refers to Windows 95 as simply "Windows."

STARTING WINDOWS

The procedure to starting Windows on a system with a hard-disk drive is easy. Simply turn on your computer system (called **booting up**) and wait for the Windows screen to appear as in Figure WIN1-1. Your screen may differ slightly.

FIGURE WIN1-1 ■ THE WINDOWS SCREEN

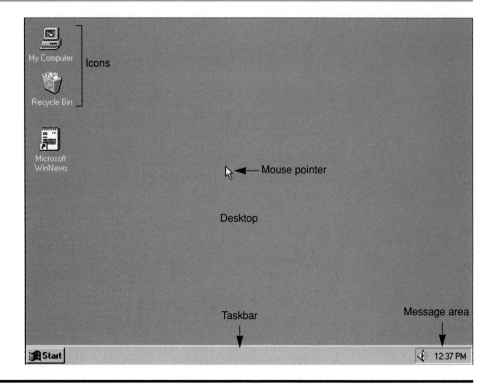

USING A NETWORK.   Windows may be available to you through a local network. In this case, Windows is kept on the hard disk of another computer that is shared by many users. So many network configurations are used today that it is difficult to predict which one you will use. Check with your instructor or network administrator for specific instructions. In general, if you use a Windows 95 network, you start your system the same way as you do when using a hard-disk drive system. If you are using a network in which Windows 95 is available through a network menu, in general, you might do the following:

STEPS

1 Boot the network operating system (perhaps with your own disk)

2 Type any command needed to access the network menu

In many networks, you do this by typing **LAN** and pressing the Enter key

3 Select (or type) the appropriate command on your screen to access Windows

4 Go to Step 3 in the following section—"Using a Hard-Disk Drive"

USING A HARD-DISK DRIVE.   This text assumes that Windows is on your hard disk (Drive C). To start Windows,

STEPS

1 Turn on your system unit

2 Turn on the monitor's separate power switch, if necessary

Tip: If you programmed Windows to start in MS-DOS mode, at the C:\ prompt, simply type WIN and press Enter.

3 Wait for the Windows screen

As Windows is booting up, you may see a variety of self-tests being performed. A screen briefly appears with the caption "Microsoft Windows 95" and finally the Windows screen as in Figure WIN1-1 appears. If a "Welcome to Windows 95" screen appears in the center of your screen,

4 Press **Esc** or **Alt** + **F4** or click the *Close* button to remove the "Welcome to Windows 95" screen

The "Welcome to Windows 95" screen is a **dialog box** (a window that requests or gives information). It provides a different tip on using Windows each time you start the program. You may also get information about what is new in this version of Windows.

> **Tip:** Clicking the *Show this Welcome Screen next time you start Windows* check box at the bottom of the dialog box and then clicking the *Close* button will remove the *Welcome to Windows 95* dialog box from the opening screen.

THE WINDOWS SCREEN

Your screen should now resemble Figure WIN1-1. (Note: The contents of your screen may differ depending on how it was programmed.) The **Windows screen** has two primary parts: the taskbar and the desktop. The **taskbar** is the bar at the bottom of the screen with a *Start* button on its left side. The **desktop** is the large area above the taskbar. Occupying the upper left side of the desktop are several icons, starting with *My Computer.*

Another object that should currently appear on your screen is a small graphic resembling an arrow. This is called the **mouse pointer** or **pointer.** You control its movements by using a **pointing device.** The most common pointing device is a **mouse.** Other pointing devices include a trackball, pointing stick, track pad, or electronic pen. These pointing devices are more commonly used with portable computers.

THE TASKBAR.   As you will soon see, the taskbar's **Start button** (left side) can be used to access the *Start* menu (the Windows main menu) by mouse. You can use the **Start menu** to start programs, find documents, adjust system settings, open a document (file), access help, or shut down Windows. Each option on the *Start* menu is listed with its corresponding icon to its left.

The taskbar can also be used to switch quickly between opened (running) programs or other windows by mouse. As you open each item, a corresponding button appears on the taskbar. These buttons will be used later in the "Basic Multitasking" section to switch among open programs.

The button on the right side of the taskbar displays the system time and other messages. These messages are generally displayed as icons. For instance, the taskbar in Figure WIN1-1 displays an icon of a speaker indicating that the system has sound features. If you are using a portable computer on battery power, an icon displaying the battery level would appear. The display on your taskbar may differ.

THE DESKTOP.   The desktop is the electronic version of the top of an office desk. Objects that may occupy the desktop include icons and windows. Remember, icons are symbols that represent a program, document, or other features. The icons on the desktop are similar to a closed book or notepad. If opened, their contents are viewed through windows (rectangular boxes) on the desktop. All programs and documents are displayed through windows on the desktop. Later, you will practice moving and resizing icons and windows on the desktop.

WIN

MOUSE AND KEYBOARD OPERATIONS

Two common input devices used today are the mouse and the keyboard. An *input device* is a piece of equipment (hardware) that allows you to communicate with a computer. This text assumes that you have both a mouse and a keyboard.

In Windows, the primary input device for accessing *commands* is a mouse or other pointing device. As such, most command steps presented in this manual refer to mouse operations. Keyboard commands, where available as *shortcut keys,* are presented in brackets [ ] to the right of a mouse command. For example (do not invoke this command!),

STEPS

 1 Click the *Start* button on the taskbar for the *Start* menu   [**Ctrl** + **Esc**]

(Note also that, where available, an icon is placed in the left margin of a command as a visual aid.)

To invoke this command you either use the mouse instructions on the left or the keys in brackets on the right.

Shortcut keys provide quick keyboard access to specific commands. They may involve pressing a function key alone or in conjunction with the Ctrl, Alt, or Shift keys. **Function keys** are labeled F1 through F12, and they may be located at the extreme left of your keyboard or across the top in one horizontal row. The Ctrl, Alt, or Shift keys may also be used in conjunction with other keys.

Windows also offers a feature called **MouseKeys** to invoke the common mouse actions by keyboard. The procedures to activate this feature are discussed under the "MouseKeys" portion of this section.

In the following exercises, you will practice basic mouse techniques as summarized in Figure WIN1-2a. You will also learn how to turn on the MouseKeys feature if you desire to use the keyboard to invoke the same mouse actions. MouseKey commands are summarized in Figure WIN1-2b.

POINTING. Often, the mouse pointer resembles a small arrow on your screen. You control its movements by using a pointing device. In Windows, the mouse pointer may appear in the forms displayed in Figure WIN1-2c. A mouse or other pointing device generally has at least two buttons-left and right. You can use a mouse to perform several actions. The most basic is pointing. This involves moving your mouse on a flat surface, which moves the mouse pointer on your screen to a desired item or area. If you are using a pointing device other than a mouse, refer to its manual for operating instructions.

To **point** (move) your mouse pointer:

STEPS

 1 Slowly move your mouse on a flat surface or mouse pad (a small rubber pad) and notice the direction in which the mouse moves on your screen

Note: If you run out of space, simply lift your mouse, place it in the original position, and start again.

FIGURE WIN1-2 ■ MOUSE POINTERS AND ACTIONS

(a) Common mouse actions.
(b) Mouse actions by keyboard.

(a)

Mouse Action	Description
Pointing	Moving the mouse, and thus the mouse pointer, to the desired item.
Clicking	Pressing and quickly releasing the left mouse button.
Right-Clicking	Pressing and quickly releasing the right mouse button.
Dragging	Pressing and holding the left mouse button while moving the mouse to the desired location with the object pointed to.
Dropping	Releasing the mouse, and thus releasing the object pointed to after dragging.
Double-Clicking	Rapidly pressing and releasing the left mouse button twice.

In order to use the numeric keypad for mouse actions, the *Use MouseKeys* feature and NumLock must be on. When on, a Mouse icon will appear in the message area of the taskbar. Double-clicking this icon will open the Accessibility Options Properties dialog box for adjusting or turning off the *Use MouseKey* features.

(b)

Mouse Icon Appearance	Operation	Numeric KeyPad Keys
	Horizontally, Vertically (1)	[←], [→], [↑], [↓]
	Diagonally (1)	[Home], [End], [PgUp], [PgDn]
	Click	[5]
	Double-Click	[+]
	Switch to Right Click (2)	[−], [5] or [+]
	Switch to Both Click (2)	[*], [5] or [+]
	Switch Back to Normal (Left) Click	[/]
	Drag Turn On Mouse Button Hold Down	[Ins] (Do Not Hold)
	Drag Mouse (1)	[←], [→], [↑], [↓], [Home], [End], [PgUp], [PgDn]
	Turn Off Mouse Button Hold Down	[Del] (Do Not Hold)

(1) Pressing and holding the Ctrl key with these keys will speed up the pointer movement. Pressing and holding the Shift key with these keys will slow down the pointer movement.

(2) When on, pressing the [5] key will invoke their action.

continued

FIGURE WIN1-2 ■ *continued*

(c) Common mouse pointers in Windows.

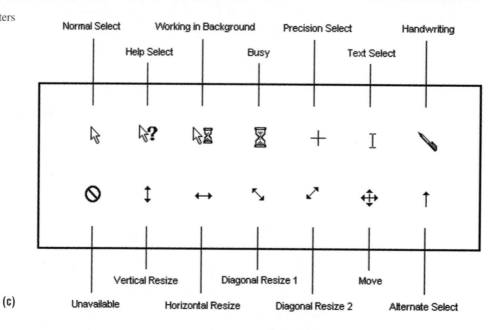

(c)

---

2 Point to the *My Computer* icon at the top left corner of your desktop

3 Slowly point to the *Start* button at the left side of the taskbar and wait

---

FIGURE WIN1-3 ■ **POINTING AND CLICKING**

(a) Pointing to a button in the Windows environment often displays its function. (b) Pointing and clicking the *Start* button opens the *Start* menu. (c) Pointing to a menu item followed by a "▶" at its right opens a submenu.

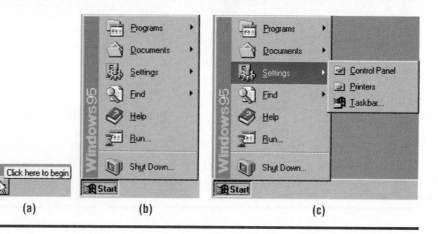

The caption "Click here to begin" should briefly appear as in Figure WIN1-3a. Many buttons in the Windows environment offer brief descriptions when you point to them.

CLICKING.   The second most common mouse action is **clicking.** This involves pointing to an item and then rapidly pressing and releasing the left mouse button.

STEPS

1 Click the *Start* button (point to the *Start button* and then rapidly press and release your left mouse button)   [Ctrl + Esc]

The *Start* menu should appear as in Figure WIN1-3b. As mentioned earlier, this is the main menu in Windows. Although the *Start* menu's operations are discussed later, use it now to further practice mouse operations. Note also that each option is listed with a corresponding icon to its left and that each option has an underlined letter. For example, the *Help* option has an icon of a book with a question mark and the letter "H" is underlined. You can tap the underlined letter to access the option by keyboard.

As you proceed with the next exercise, watch the mouse pointer as you move it within a menu. It moves with a selection highlight to each item you point to. In addition, pointing to menu items with a "▶" to its far right opens a submenu. Try this:

2 Slowly point to *Settings* and notice a submenu as in Figure WIN1-3c   [S]

Although you can select a submenu item by pointing to and then clicking it, you will practice this later. Now, to close the *Start* menu without selecting anything,

3 Click an open space on the desktop to close the menu without selecting anything
                                                                              [Esc   twice]

A menu item without a "▶" to its far right starts a feature or opens a window. For now, keep the *Start* menu opened as you proceed to the next step. Here you will practice invoking a direct command from the *Start* menu:

4 Click the *Start* button   [Ctrl + Esc]

5 Point to *Help*

As you move your mouse pointer, notice again that the selection highlight moves with it to *Help*.

6 Click *Help* to open the *Help* dialog box   [H]

Remember, to click, rapidly press and release your left mouse button.

The *Help* dialog box should now appear on your screen. Remember, a *dialog* box is a window that either provides or requests information. For example, the *Help* dialog box provides information on a desired topic. Dialog box operations will be discussed in detail later.

To close the dialog box,

7 Click the *Cancel* button at the bottom right of the box   [**Esc**]

RIGHT-CLICKING.   Pointing to an item and clicking your *right mouse button,* or **right-clicking,** generally results in opening its *Shortcut* menu. A **Shortcut menu** contains common commands that you can invoke on the related item. For example,

STEPS

1 Right-click a blank area of the desktop for its *Shortcut* menu

The desktop's *Shortcut* menu as in Figure WIN1-4a, should now appear. To select a menu item, you can either click (left mouse button) it or press its underlined letter. Menu items that appear in a lighter color are not currently available. For now, to close *Shortcut* menu without selecting a command,

2 Click (left mouse button) anywhere outside the *Shortcut* menu   [**Esc**]

You can also close a *Shortcut* menu by opening another item or another *Shortcut* menu. Try opening these *Shortcut* menus,

3 Right-click an open area of the taskbar for its *Shortcut* menu as in Figure WIN1-4b

4 Right-click the *Start* button for its *Shortcut* menu as in Figure WIN1-4c

5 Right-click the *My Computer* icon for its *Shortcut* menu as in Figure WIN1-4d

6 Click (left mouse button) anywhere outside the *Shortcut* menu to close it without selecting a command   [**Esc**]

FIGURE WIN1-4 ■   *SHORTCUT* MENUS

Pointing to certain items in the Windows environment and clicking your right mouse button will open a *Shortcut* menu.
(a) The desktop *Shortcut* menu. (b) The taskbar *Shortcut* menu. (c) The *Start* button *Shortcut* menu. (d) The *My Computer* icon *Shortcut* menu.

(a)

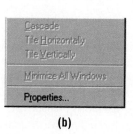
(b)

(c)

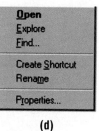
(d)

Different *Shortcut* menus are available for many items in the Windows environment. In some cases, different *Shortcut* menus are available for each part of an item. For example, in Steps 3 and 4, you received two different *Shortcut* menus from clicking your right mouse button on the two different areas of the taskbar.

DRAGGING AND DROPPING.   The next mouse action you will try is called *dragging* and *dropping*. This action is often used to move or copy icons, windows, or other objects. **Dragging** involves pointing to a desired object and then pressing and holding your left mouse button while moving your mouse and the object to a new location. **Dropping** involves releasing your mouse and thus releasing the object after dragging it to a new location. Try this:

STEPS

1 Drag the *My Computer* icon from the top left corner to the center of your screen (point to and then press and hold your left mouse button down while moving the pointer and the *My Computer* icon to the center of your screen)

2 Drop the *My Computer* icon (release your mouse and thus the *My Computer* icon)

> Tip: Pressing and holding the Ctrl key while dragging and dropping an object will copy the object in the new location.

Your screen should resemble Figure WIN1-5a. (Please note that parts of your screen may differ.)

DOUBLE-CLICKING.   Another commonly used mouse action is **double-clicking.** This involves first pointing to an item and then rapidly pressing and releasing your left mouse button twice. Double-clicking an icon on your screen resizes it to a window. Double-clicking also has a variety of other uses that will be discussed as needed.

Before beginning the next exercise, notice that the *My Computer* icon is a different color than the other icons on the desktop. This indicates that it is the **active (or current) icon.** Keyboard commands will generally affect this icon. For example (do not invoke), if you press the Enter key, the icon would open to a window. To open the *My Computer* icon to a window by mouse requires double-clicking it. Try this:

STEPS

1 Double-click the *My Computer* icon (Rapidly press and release your left mouse button twice.)

The *My Computer* icon now resizes to a Window as in Figure WIN1-5b. (The contents of your window may differ.) To close it,

FIGURE WIN1-5 ■ DRAGGING AND DROPPING, AND DOUBLE-CLICKING

(a) Dragging and dropping
the *My Computer* icon (or
any object) will move it.
(b) Double-clicking an icon
resizes it to a window.
(The content of your winow
may differ.)

(a)

(b)

 ☒ **2** Click the *Close* button (the button with an "X" in it) at the top right of the window.
  [**Alt** + **F4**]

The "X" button is referred to as the **Close button.** It is available on most windows
and is a shortcut to closing a window. It closes any window, and thus the program, document, or other feature encased in it.

3 Drag and drop the *My Computer* icon to its original position.

(Remember, point to the icon, press and hold the left mouse button while moving the pointer and icon to the top left corner of the desktop, and then release your mouse.)

MOUSEKEYS.   Although many commands can be invoked by shortcut keys, Windows offers a feature called *MouseKeys,* which enables you to use the numeric keypad to invoke the common mouse actions. These actions include clicking, right-clicking, double-clicking, and dragging and dropping. *If you do not intend to use MouseKeys to invoke mouse actions or if the feature is not available, skip this section.* Check with your instructor before activating this feature.

To use MouseKeys, you will need to turn on the *Use MouseKeys* feature. This feature is part of the Accessibility Properties, which can be accessed through the Control Panel. (Note: The Accessibility feature must be installed on your system.)

WIN

1 Click the *Start* button   [Ctrl + Esc]

2 Point to *Settings* for its submenu

3 Click *Control Panel* for its window

4 Double-click the *Accessibility Options* icon for its dialog box

5 Click the *Mouse* tab

6 Click the *Use MouseKeys* check box

A "✓" should now appear in the *Use MouseKeys* checkbox. If it does not, click again.

7 Click the *OK* button to exit the dialog box

8 Click the *Close* button of the Control Panel window (at top right corner)

When the MouseKeys feature is on, a mouse icon appears in the message area of the taskbar. The numeric keypad (NumLock = on) can be used to invoke mouse actions by using the instructions in Figure SS1-2b. When this feature is on, the numeric keypad cannot be used for number entry.

SHUTTING DOWN WINDOWS

The **shut down** command of the *Start* menu is used to exit Windows. Try this:

1 Click the *Start* button for the *Start* menu   [Ctrl + Esc]

2 Click *Shut Down* for its dialog box   [U]

As described in Figure WIN1-6, your *Shut Down Windows* dialog box has several options. Although you may have a few other options, the options in Figure WIN1-6 should be available.

3 Click the *Yes* button to accept the default option of shutting down the computer.

The mouse point briefly turns into an hourglass, and then a "Please wait…" screen briefly appears. Finally, a screen appears with the captions "It is now safe to turn off your computer."

4 You can now shut off the power switches to your computer system

☑ CHECKPOINT

✓ Describe the difference between a character-based environment and a graphical-user-interface environment.
✓ What is Windows?
✓ Describe the procedures to start and shut down Windows.
✓ What is the taskbar and desktop?
✓ Describe the following basic mouse actions: point, click, right-click, drag and drop, and double-click.

COMMON WINDOWS FEATURES

Windows provides a wealth of common features to make operating different programs easier. For example, most programs in Windows can be launched and closed the same way. **Launching** is the Windows term for starting a program. *Closing* as described earlier, is the process of closing a window and thus the program, document, or other Windows feature that is encased in it. All programs and documents are displayed in windows (rectangular boxes)

FIGURE WIN1-6 ■ THE *SHUT DOWN WINDOWS* DIALOG BOX

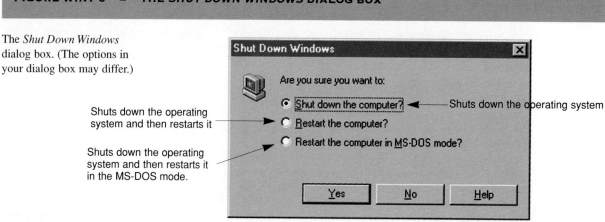

The *Shut Down Windows* dialog box. (The options in your dialog box may differ.)

Shuts down the operating system and then restarts it

Shuts down the operating system and then restarts it in the MS-DOS mode.

Shut Down Windows

Are you sure you want to:
- Shut down the computer? ◄— Shuts down the operating system
- Restart the computer?
- Restart the computer in MS-DOS mode?

Yes   No   Help

that have common components. The operations of these components will be discussed in detail shortly. **WordPad,** a simple word processor, will now be used to help you learn about these common features. WordPad is a standard accessory program that comes with Windows.

STEPS

1 Boot up your computer (turn your system on)

2 Start Windows (if needed)

3 If needed, click the *Cancel* button or press ⬛Esc to remove the "Windows Welcome" screen

LAUNCHING A PROGRAM

The most common way to launch a program in Windows is to use the *Start* menu. Although only WordPad is used to demonstrate this, the steps to launch other programs are similar. As you perform each step, take special note of the structure of the Windows main menu system.

Now, to launch WordPad (or any program):

STEPS

1 Click the Start button (taskbar) for the *Start* menu   [Ctrl + Esc]
(Remember, to click, first point to the *Start* button and then rapidly press and release your left mouse button.)

2 Point to *Programs* for its submenu   [P]

Your *Programs* submenu should now appear on your screen similar to Figure WIN1-7. (The contents of your *Programs* submenu may differ.) As with the *Start* menu, each item in the *Programs* submenu is listed with its corresponding icon at its left. An item with a "▶" to its far right opens to another submenu. In the *Programs* submenu, these items are called **program groups.** They are logical groupings of programs and files into folders by category for easier visual access. Remember, a *folder* is a group of related files.

Individual programs not grouped into a folder in the *Programs* submenu or any other menu are available for direct access. For example, the MS-DOS prompt or Windows Explorer are programs that can be launched directly from the *Programs* sub-menu.

To open the *Accessories* group submenu as in Figure WIN1-8,

3 Point to *Accessories* for its submenu   [A , ↓ if needed, →]

The *Accessories* program group menu displays several subprogram groups and accessories programs. For example, the *Games* or *System Tools* options are subprogram groups that open to their own submenus. Like the *Programs* submenu, items not followed by a

FIGURE WIN1-7 ■ THE *PROGRAMS* SUBMENU

Pointing to and clicking the *Start* button, and then pointing to *Programs* opens its submenu.

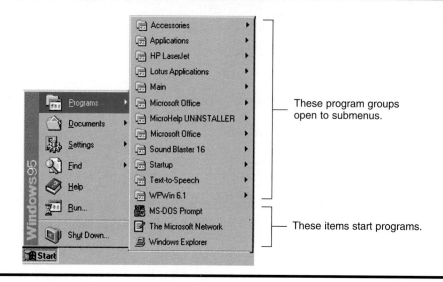

These program groups open to submenus.

These items start programs.

"▶" to their far right are programs that can be accessed directly from the *Accessories* submenu-for example, WordPad (a simple word processor), Calculator (an on-line calculator), and so on.

4   Click *WordPad* to launch it   [Arrow keys, ↵]

FIGURE WIN1-8 ■ THE *ACCESSORIES* SUBMENU

Pointing to the *Accessories* group opens its submenu.

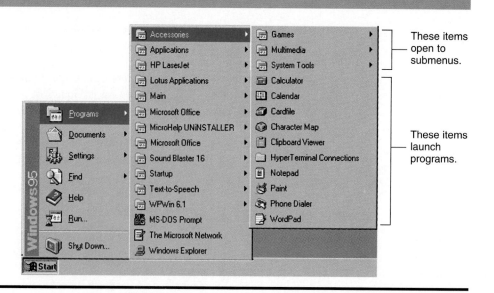

These items open to submenus.

These items launch programs.

A brief copyright message appears and is quickly replaced by the WordPad window. The size of WordPad's window when it first appears on the desktop depends on its size when last used. It may appear as a window that occupies less than the entire desktop similar to Figure WIN1-9a (the position of the window may differ on your screen). It may also appear as a window that occupies the entire desktop (when this happens, it is said that the window is **maximized**) as in Figure WIN1-9b. A maximized window is one that is enlarged to its maximum size. Sometimes a window's maximum size may be less than the entire desktop space. If your WordPad window is maximized, do the following to reduce its size for this exercise:

 5 **If needed, press** Alt + Spacebar , R

At this point examine your taskbar. A button titled "Document - WordPad" has been automatically added. Remember, as you open each program, file, or other item in Windows, a corresponding button appears on the taskbar. You can use these buttons to switch to a desired opened item. This will be further discussed later.

As demonstrated earlier with the *My Computer* icon, a program or file may also be launched (or opened) by double-clicking its icon. This method requires the program or file's icon to be available on the desktop or in a window. Procedures to create icons for programs and files are discussed later.

TYPES OF WINDOWS

As mentioned earlier, a *window* is a rectangular box that may contain a program, document, or dialog box. A window that contains a program is called a **program window.** Each program window may contain only one program. For example, the WordPad window contains only that program. Program windows also occupy the desktop.

Programs that allow you to work with multiple documents at the same time use *document windows* to display each document. A **document window** is a window within a program window. It occupies the interior space (called the **workspace**) of its program window. It may contain text and objects. Many popular programs do allow for multiple document windows.

> Note: Programs used in this manual generally allow you to work with only one document at a time. As such, the document occupies most or all of the program's workspace.

Dialog boxes, as mentioned earlier, are windows that request or give information. Dialog box operations are discussed in detail in "The Help Feature" section.

TITLE BAR

A window's *title bar* contains its name. The **title bar** is the first row in any window. For example, in Figure WIN1-9a, the title "Document - WordPad" is currently displayed in WordPad's title bar. A program or document window's title bar generally has several standard features. As in Figure WIN1-10a and b, they include (from left to right) the program or document's icon, name, two window resizing buttons, and a *Close* button. The resizing buttons that appear on a title bar depend on its window's size. For example,

FIGURE WIN1-9 ■ **STARTING A PROGRAM**

(a) When you first start a program, it may appear as a window less than the size of the entire desktop.
(b) It may also appear maximized (covering the entire desktop).

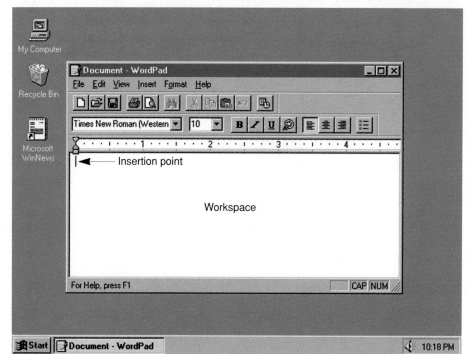

(a)

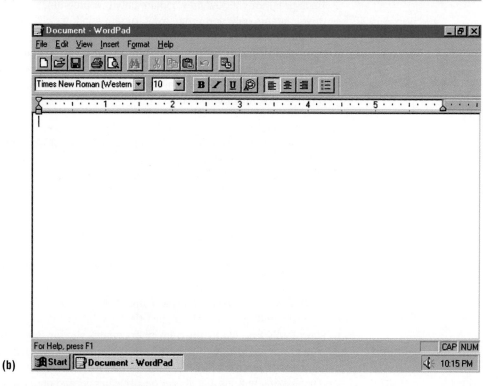

(b)

FIGURE WIN1-10 ■ TITLE BARS

(a) Title bar of a less than maximized window.
(b) Title bar of a maximized window.
(c) Description of title bar parts.
Note: Title bar parts are described in Figure WIN1-10C.

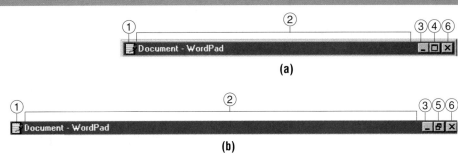

(a)

(b)

Part #	Part	Description
1	Icon	An icon that identifies the program or document. Clicking this icon opens a control-menu. Double-clicking it closes the program.
2	Name Section	The section that identifies the window. Double-clicking this section resizes the window. Right-clicking this section opens the window's control-menu.
3	Minimize Button	A resizing button that normally appears on all program and document windows. Clicking this button reduces the window to its taskbar button. Minimized windows run on less system memory and do not need to be restarted to be used.
4	Maximize Button	A resizing button that appears only on a program or document window that is not maximized. Clicking this button enlarges a window to its maximum size. Once the window is maximized, this button is replaced by a Restore button.
5	Restore Button	A resizing button that appears only on a window that is maximized. Clicking this button restores a window to its previous size. Once the window is reduced, this button is replaced by a Maximize button.
6	Close Button	Appears on all windows. Clicking this button closes the window.

(c)

a less than maximized window's title bar has a *Maximize* button. A maximized window's title bar as in Figure WIN1-10b has a *Restore* button. The functions of each of these items is discussed next.

ICON.   Each program (or document) in the Windows environment is automatically assigned an icon to represent it. These icons may appear to the left of the item's name in the *Start* menu's submenu system and in the title bar of a window. Clicking this icon on the left side of a title bar opens a **control-menu.** This menu contains commands that can be used to move, resize, or close a window. Try this:

1 Click *WordPad's* icon (left of the "Document - WordPad" on the title bar)

[**Alt** + **Spacebar**]

The window's control-menu, as in Figure WIN1-11, should now appear. At this point, you can select a command from the menu by either clicking the command or pressing its underlined letter. For now, to close the menu without selecting a command,

2 Click any area outside of the menu   [**Esc**]

You can also open Window's control-menu by right-clicking anywhere on the title bar.

> **Tip:** Although not illustrated, document windows also have control-menus. To open a document window's control-menu, click its document icon or press the Alt + − (minus) keys. The position of a document window's icon differs depending on the window's size. For example, a maximized document window's icon appears at the left end of its program's menu bar. This is because it shares its title bar with its program. Other times it appears at the left end of its title bar, as with a program window.

> **Note:** Shortcut keys presented in brackets to the right of a mouse command use the window's control-menu to demonstrate resizing and moving a window.

NAME SECTION.   In addition to identifying a window, the name section of a title bar can also be used to resize or move the window. To resize the window using its title bar,

---

FIGURE WIN1-11 ■ CONTROL-MENU

Clicking a program or document icon on a title bar opens its control-menu.

STEPS

> 📄 Document - WordPad

1 Point anywhere on the caption "Document - WordPad" on the title bar

[**Alt** + **Spacebar**]

2 Double-click it (Remember, to double-click, rapidly press and release your mouse twice.)

[**X**]

Your WordPad window should now be maximized on your screen as in Figure WIN1-9b. Now, to use the title bar to return it to its original size (that is, to **restore** it):

3 Double-click the name portion of the title bar   [**Alt** + **Spacebar** , **R**]

Your WordPad window should now be restored to its original size as in Figure WIN1-9a.

To move a window using its title bar,

4 Point to the name section of the WordPad title bar   [**Alt** + **Spacebar**]

5 Drag it to the top of your screen   [**M** , ↑ to top of screen]

(Remember, to drag, press, and hold your left mouse button while moving the mouse pointer and the object, in this case the WordPad window, to its new location.)

Notice that only an outline of the window moves with the mouse pointer. The window itself will move after you drop its outline in the new location.

6 Drop the window's outline (release your mouse)   [↵]

As you will see later, the ability to resize or move a window is helpful when using multiple windows. For now,

7 Move the WordPad window back to its original position by dragging and dropping its title bar   [**Alt** + **Spacebar** , **M** , ↓ as needed, ↵]

Again, your screen should resemble Figure WIN1-9a.

RESIZING BUTTONS.   **Resizing buttons** provide a quick way to change the size of a window. Three types of resizing buttons exist: minimize, maximize, and restore. Only one or two resizing buttons appear at a time on the right side of the title bar.

As in Figure WIN1-10, the **Minimize button** resembles a square box with a dash in it. Clicking this button will reduce the window to its taskbar button. Try this:

STEPS

1 Click WordPad's *Minimize* button   [**Alt** + **Spacebar** , **N**]

Note that after Step 2, the WordPad window shrinks to its button on the taskbar as in Figure WIN1-12. The button is also no longer depressed. When a window is minimized

FIGURE WIN1-12 ■ MINIMIZING A WINDOW

Clicking a window's
minimize button reduces it to
its taskbar button.

| 🐾 Start | 📄 Document - WordPad | | 🔊 10:39 PM |

---

it operates using less system memory. This is helpful when using more than one program at a time. A minimized window also allows you to switch to that program
quickly without having to relaunch it. For example, to restore WordPad to its former
size,

📄 Document - WordPad

2 **Click the *Document - WordPad* button on the taskbar**   [**Alt** + **Tab**]

As in Figure WIN1-10, the **Maximize button** resembles a square box with a smaller
square box in it. As mentioned earlier, maximizing a window enlarges it to its maximum size. Try this:

3 **Click WordPad's *Maximize* button**   [**Alt** + **Spacebar** , **X**]

Your WordPad window should now fill your screen, as in Figure WIN1-9b. Note that
the *Maximize* button has now been replaced by a *Restore* button. The **Restore button**
only appears on the title bar when a window is maximized. It can be used to resize a
window to its previous size. Try this:

4 **Click WordPad's *Restore* button**   [**Alt** + **Spacebar** , **R**]

Your WordPad window again should resemble Figure WIN1-9a. Note that the *Restore*
button has been replaced by a *Maximize* button.

CLOSE BUTTON.   As mentioned earlier, the *Close* button resembles an "X" and can
normally be found on the right end of a window's title bar. This button is available on all
windows. It is the quickest way to close the window.

STEPS

⌧ 1 **Click the *Close* button**   [**Alt** + **F4**]

Alternative window closing techniques are discussed later.

MENU BAR

Only program windows have menu bars. The menu bar is located just below the window's title bar, as in Figure WIN1-13. A **menu bar** provides mouse and keyboard
access to a program's features through *pull-down menus*. A **pull-down menu** is one
that drops down from its menu selection. Certain pull-down menus are standard on

WIN

FIGURE WIN1-13 ■ MENU BAR

(a) Only program windows have menu bars below their title bars. The menu bar allows mouse and keyboard access to a program's features by pull-down menus.
(b) A summary of menu bar operations.

(a)

Document - WordPad
File Edit View Insert Format Help

	Mouse Actions	Keyboard Actions
Open Pull-Down Menu	Point to and click menu bar item	Press [Alt] + [Underlined letter of menu bar item]
Select a Menu Item	Point to and click the item	Press the item's underlined letter or use arrow keys to move selection highlight to item and press Enter
Description of Menu Item's Function	Open menu and then point to item	Use arrow keys to move selection highlight to item

(b)

most windows programs, such as, the *File, Edit,* and *Help* menus. Although these pull-down menus have the same name in different programs, their options may differ. You will now take a closer look at how to operate a menu bar.

STEPS

1 Launch the WordPad program (Remember, click the *Start* button, point to *Programs, Accessories, WordPad,* and then click.)

2 Click WordPad's *Maximize* button to enlarge it to a full screen (if needed)
[**Alt** + **Spacebar** , **X**]

Note: A maximized window makes it visually easier to operate its components. You can however, operate the same components in a smaller screen.

This manual will refer to a pull-down menu as simply a *menu.*

USING MENUS.   Menus from the menu bar can be opened by clicking the desired menu bar item or pressing the Alt key and the underlined letter of the menu bar item. Try this to open the *Help* menu:

STEPS

1 Click *Help* for its menu (Remember, point to and click *Help* or press **Alt** **+ H** .)

The *Help* menu should appear as in Figure WIN1-14a. The *Help* menu of any program window provides general and specific help on operating the program. To select an option by mouse, simply click it; to select an option by keyboard, press the item's underlined letter. You can also use the arrow keys to move the highlight to the desired item and press Enter. Note that the Alt key is used with an underlined letter only when opening a menu. Try this:

2 Click *About WordPad*   [**A**]

This command opens an *About* dialog box, which displays information about the current program. This information may include the program's version, serial number, ownership, and system resources. All windows programs have an *About* dialog box that can be accessed through its *Help* menu. To close the dialog box,

3 Click the *OK* button   [**Esc**]

Now, to open the *File* menu,

4 Click *File*   [**Alt** **+ F**]

FIGURE WIN1-14 ■ COMMON MENUS

Most menu bars have *Help, File,* and *Edit* menus.
(a) The *Help* menu provides access to a program's on-line help.
(b) The *File* menu provides access to basic file management commands.
(c) The *Edit* menu provides access to a variety of document editing commands.

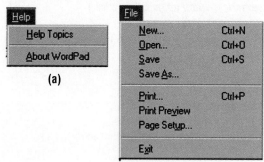

The *File* menu should now appear as in Figure WIN1-14b. This menu has file management commands that you can use to save or open (retrieve) files from disk or other storage media. A *file* may contain a program or document. (Remember, a program is simply a set of instructions and a document may contain data or objects.) These procedures will be discussed later. Again, to select a menu item, simply click it; to select an item by keyboard, press the underlined letter. For now, to close a menu without selecting a command,

5   **Click anywhere outside the menu**   [**Alt**]

Another common menu is the *Edit* menu. This menu generally provides commands to undo your last action, copy, move, or link (dynamically connect) a selection. A **selection** is data marked for editing or other operations. Data selection techniques and *Edit* menu operations are discussed in detail later. To open the *Edit* menu as in Figure WIN1-14c,

6   **Click _Edit_**   [**Alt** + **E**]

Leave this menu opened as you continue to the next steps.

Once one menu is opened, you can quickly move to another menu by pointing. Try this:

7   **Point to Insert**   [→]

8   **Point to Format**   [→]

9   **Point to Help**   [→]

10   **Click anywhere outside the menu to close it**   [**Alt**]

MENU COMMANDS.   Many programs display a brief description of a menu command when pointed to. The location of this description is often in the program's status bar (generally at the bottom of the window) or its title bar. Try this to get a brief description of the *Save As* command in the *File* menu.

STEPS

1   **Click _File_ for its menu**   [**Alt** + **F**]

2   **Point to (but do not click) _Save As_**   [↓ three times]

The message "Saves the active document with a new name." appears in WordPad's status bar as in Figure WIN1-15.

3   **Click anywhere outside the _File_ menu to close it**   [**Alt**]

WIN

FIGURE WIN1-15 ■ **COMMAND DESCRIPTION**

Pointing to a menu item will display a description of its function in the status bar.

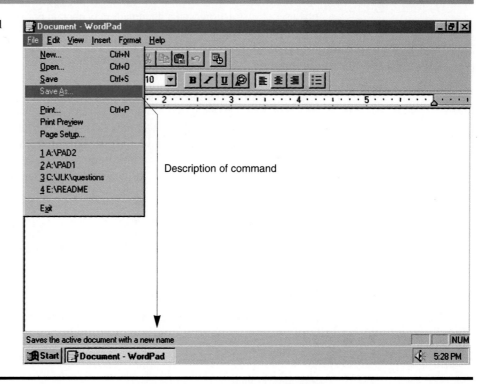

MENU INDICATORS

Menus throughout the Windows environment use standard Windows indicators or conventions. Earlier, when you used the *Start* menu, items with a "▶" at their far right open to a submenu and items with no notation invoke a command directly. This is true for any menu in the Windows environment. WordPad's *File* menu will now be used to illustrate other menu indicators.

STEPS

 Click _File_   **[Alt + F]**

The *File* menu should appear again as in Figure WIN1-16a. (Your *File* menu may differ slightly.) Menu items with neither a triangle pointer "▶" at their extreme right (not shown in Figure WIN1-16a) nor an ellipsis (...), such as *Save,* invoke a command directly. If shortcut keys can be used to invoke a menu directly, they are displayed at the extreme right of the item. For example, the Shortcut keys Ctrl + S appear to the far right of the command Save.

Figure WIN1-16b lists standard windows menu indicators.

FIGURE WIN1-16 ■ MENU INDICATORS

(a) Menus in the Windows environment use menu indicators that are standard. (b) A summary of menu indicators.

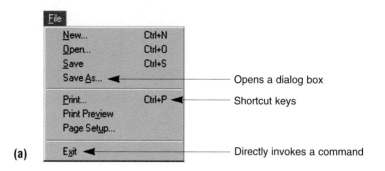

(a)

Menu Items with	Description
Ellipsis (…)	Opens to a dialog box or another window.
▶ at far right	Opens to a submenu.
No notation	Invokes a command or other feature.
Keys at far right	Short key(s) to invoke the menu item by keyboard.
✔ to left of item	A toggle (on/off) feature that has been turned on.
Dimmed (or not visible)	A menu item not currently available.

(b)

---

2   **Click anywhere outside the menu to close it**   **[Alt]**

COMMAND BUTTONS AND DROP-DOWN BOXES

Many Windows programs offer a variety of command buttons and drop-down boxes for quick mouse access to program features. A **command button,** when clicked, directly accesses a feature in a program or window. Earlier, you learned how to operate several *window command buttons* such as the Minimize, Maximize, Restore, and Close buttons. Here you will examine a few command buttons that directly access WordPad's program features.

A **drop-down box** is a rectangular box with a "▼" button on its right side. In your WordPad window, the box that contains the caption "Times New Roman" is a drop-down box. Clicking the "▼" button of a drop-down box opens a list of available options.

Most programs group command buttons and drop-down buttons into sets with related functions. As in Figure WIN1-17a, WordPad has two sets of command buttons beneath its menu bar. The first set is called the toolbar and the second is called the format bar. The format bar also contains two drop-down boxes. The **toolbar** contains buttons that affect basic file management and editing. The buttons and drop-down boxes on the **format bar** can be used to change the text appearance and alignment. Programs may use different terminology for these bars.

FIGURE WIN1-17 ■ COMMAND BUTTONS AND DROP-DOWN BOXES

(a) Many programs have bars with command buttons and drop-down boxes. WordPad's bars are called the toolbar and format bar.
(b) Pointing to a button will display a caption of its function.
(c) Pointing to a drop-down box will display a caption of its function.
(d) Clicking the ▼ button of a drop-down box opens its drop-down list.

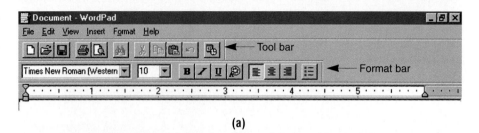

(a)

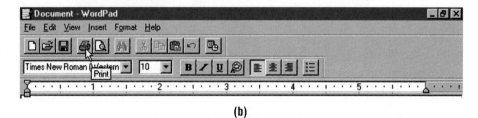

(b)

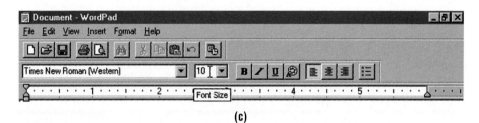

(c)

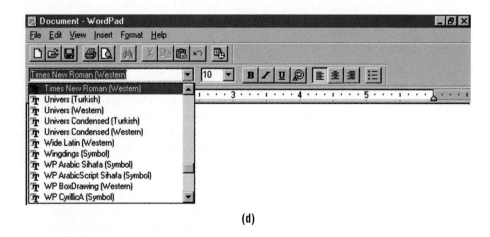

(d)

When you point to most buttons and drop-down boxes in the Windows environment, their titles will appear. A brief description of their function also appears in the status bar or title bar. Try this:

STEPS

 1 Point to the *Print* button (toolbar) and wait a moment

The caption "Print" appears on your screen and its function appears in the status bar as in Figure WIN1-17b.

 2 Point to the drop-down box that contains "10" (format bar)

The caption "Font Size" appears as in Figure WIN1-17c. A **font** is a type style. **Font size** is the size of the current font measured in points (approximately ½ inch per point). Now, to open a drop-down menu:

 3 Click the ▼ button of the *Font* drop-down box (format bar) for the *Font* drop-down list

A *Font* drop-down list should appear as in Figure WIN1-17d. The contents of your list may differ, depending on the fonts installed in your system. Now, to close the drop-down list without selecting an option,

4 Click anywhere outside the drop-down list   [Esc]

Actual operations of program command buttons and drop-down boxes will be discussed later.

SHORTCUT MENUS

Earlier, under the "Mouse Operations" section, you practiced opening *Shortcut* menus by pointing to an object and clicking your right mouse button. In most windows (program, document, or dialog box), pointing to certain areas and right-clicking will also open a *Shortcut* menu. These menus provide quick access to commands related to the area clicked. Try this:

STEPS

1 Right-click a blank area within WordPad's workspace (the large interior space of the window) (Remember, to right-click, point to and then rapidly press and release your right mouse button.)

A *Shortcut* menu as in Figure WIN1-18a appears. To select a *Shortcut* menu option, simply click it or press its underlined letter. For now, try to open another *Shortcut* menu as follows:

 2 Right-click the "10" in the *Font Size* drop-down box (format bar) for its *Shortcut* menu

The *Shortcut* menu as in Figure WIN1-18b now appears.

3 Click anywhere outside the *Shortcut* menu to close it   [Esc]

FIGURE WIN1-18 ■ *SHORTCUT* MENUS

(a) Pointing to WordPad's workspace and clicking the right mouse button will open this *Shortcut* menu.
(b) Pointing to a drop-down box on the format bar and clicking the right mouse button will open this *Shortcut* menu.

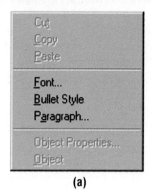

(a)

(b)

WORKSPACE

As mentioned earlier, a window's *workspace* is its large interior space. A program window's workspace may contain one or more documents. This depends on the program. For example, WordPad only allows one document to occupy its workspace at a time.

FIGURE WIN1-19 ■ **CREATING A DOCUMENT**

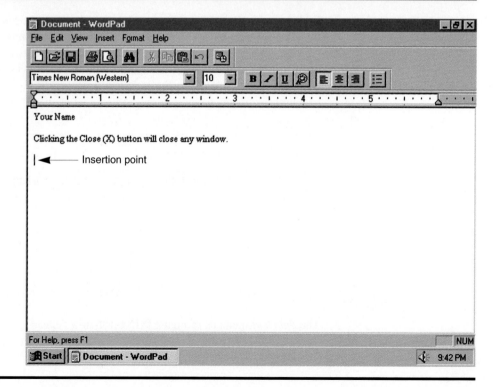

WIN

Programs such as Microsoft Word and Excel allow multiple documents to occupy their program windows' workspaces. A document window also has a workspace that may contain data or graphical images.

Currently, as in Figure WIN1-19, there is a vertical blinking line called the insertion point in WordPad's workspace. The **insertion point** is simply a placeholder. It indicates where the next character you enter will appear. The insertion point appears in any window or box that allows character entry.

To close WordPad,

STEPS

1 Click WordPad's *Close* button   [Alt + F4]

Tip: Double-clicking WordPad's program icon (located at the left end of the title bar) will also close the program quickly.

☑ CHECKPOINT

✓ Open WordPad, maximize it, and then restore it.
✓ Open WordPad's *Help* menu and then close it
✓ Describe the standard menu indicators used in the Windows environment.
✓ Open the *Font Size* drop-down box (format bar) and then close it.
✓ Close WordPad.

BASIC DOCUMENT MANAGEMENT

Many Windows programs are used to create documents that may contain text and graphic images (pictures). A *document* is simply an electronic file created with a program. When using any program to create a document, it is important to learn the basic document management commands. These commands include saving to and then opening (retrieving) from a disk, and printing a hard copy on paper.

In this section, you will create a simple document with text in WordPad as in FigureWIN1-19. You will also save, print, and open (retrieve) this document. Detailed operating instructions for other WordPad features are discussed in Chapter 3.

STEPS

1 If needed, start Windows and remove the "Welcome" screen

2 Launch WordPad (Accessories group)

□   **3** **If needed, click WordPad's *Maximize* button to enlarge it to a full screen**

[**Alt** + **Spacebar** , **X**]

USING THE DEFAULT DOCUMENT

Most programs are launched with a blank new document in their workspace. This is called the **default document.** It is like a clean sheet of paper.

To enter data into WordPad's workspace, simply type using your keyboard. If you make a mistake, use the Backspace or Delete keys to erase the incorrect data. Try this:

STEPS

1 **Type your name**

2 **Press ↵ twice**

3 **Type** Clicking the Close (X) button will close any window.

4 **Press ↵ twice**

The workspace in your WordPad should resemble Figure WIN1-19.

SAVING A DOCUMENT

In most programs, the *File* menu offers two options for saving a document. These options are *Save* and *Save As.* Invoking the **Save** command on a previously saved document will resave it under its original name. Invoking it on an unsaved document opens the *Save As* dialog box for assigning a filename. Invoking the **Save As** command allows you to save the current document under a different name and warns you if the name has already been used. This feature is helpful when updating documents because it allows you to save the updated version under a new name, thus keeping the original under its old name.

FILENAMES.   Before saving any document, you must assign it a **filename.** Filenames are used to identify a document or program. If you are using DOS-based or pre-Windows 95 programs, you are restricted to filenames of up to 8 characters with a 3-character optional extension. The programs that come with Windows 95 can accept filenames of up to 255 characters.

SAVING.   As mentioned earlier, when invoked on an unsaved document, both the Save and Save As command will open the *Save As* dialog box. Try this:

STEPS

WIN

1 Insert your data disk into Drive A

2 Click *File, Save*   [Ctrl + S]

A *Save As* dialog box should appear similar to Figure WIN1-20a. (Your dialog box's contents may differ.) Most *Save As* dialog boxes have similar features. These features are identified in Figure WIN1-20a and described in WIN1-20c. Note that the word "Document" in the *Filename* text box is highlighted. At this point you can type a filename in this text box, which will type over the highlighted text. To save this document as PAD1,

3 Type PAD1 in the Filename text box

You can also set default drive at this point before saving. The **default drive** is the drive that your program is currently pointing to. In this case, it is your hard or network drive. Because you will be saving the documents you create on your data disk in Drive A, you must first set the program to Drive A. Do this by using the *Save in* drop-down box. Note that you only need to set the default drive once during a work session. It will remain the default drive until you change it or close the program.

4 Click the "▼" button of the *Save in* drop-down box

3½ Floppy (A:)   5 Click the *3½ Floppy (A:)* drive icon

> **Tip:** Instead of using the *Save in* drop-down box in Steps 4 and 5, you could also type the drive letter and a colon with the filename (for example, A:PAD1) in Step 3 to set the default drive for the current session.

If your disk was not formatted, you will receive a dialog box that asks if you would like to format now. Before performing Steps 6 through 9 to format, check with your instructor. If your disk is already formatted, skip Steps 6 through 9.

6 Click the *Yes* button for the *Format* dialog box

7 Click the *Full* option

8 Click *Start* button to begin formatting your disk

9 Click the *Close* button and then the next *Close* button

Formatting prepares a disk for use on your computer. Every new disk that is not preformatted must be formatted (organized for your computer) before you can store anything on it. Formatting sets up the disk's directory and file allocation table and divides

FIGURE WIN1-20 ■ SAVING AND OPENING DOCUMENTS

(a) The *Save As* dialog box.
(b) The *Open* dialog box.
(c) Descriptions of dialog box components.

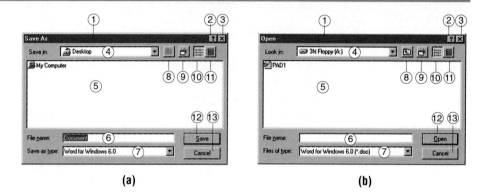

(a)　　　　　　　(b)

	Item	Description
1	Title bar	Identifies the dialog box. Right-click for control-menu. Drag to move dialog box.
2	"?" (Help) button	Click to change to help pointer and then click item for help on its operation.
3	"X" (Close) button	Click to close the dialog box.
4	Save in/Look in box	A drop-down box that is used to set the default drive and directory.
5	Files list box	A list box that displays the files in the default directory.
6	File name box	A text box that is used to enter a file's name.
7	Save as type/Files of type	A drop-down box that can be used to save a document in a specific file type or open a document of a specific file type.
8	Up One Level button	Click to display file structure up one level in the Files List box.
9	Create a New Folder button	Click to create a new folder.
10	List button	Click to list the content of the default directory in the Files List box without details. This is the default display.
11	Details button	Click to display file details in the Files List box.
12	Save/Open button	Click to save or open a document.
13	Cancel button	Click to cancel the dialog box.

(c)

the disk into addressable storage locations. It will also check for defective tracks on the disk and seal them off from further use.

Caution: A disk that was previously formatted can be reformatted; however, the process will delete the disk's files and set up a new blank directory.

WIN

To save the document,

10 Click the _Save_ button

Now, try the _Save_ command again. As you invoke the command this time, the _Save As_ dialog box does not appear. This is because the file has already been assigned a filename. Also note that the message "Saving file, Please Wait." briefly appears at the bottom of the WordPad window and your mouse pointer briefly appears as an hourglass.

 11 Click _File, Save_   [**Ctrl** + **S**]

Your document has been resaved under its previous name.

PRINTING A DOCUMENT

Most _File_ menus have a **Print** command that allows you to print a hard copy of the current document or desired selection on paper. This command, of course, requires you to have a printer that is connected and configured for your system. Each program may offer different printing options; however, most programs allow you to specify the number of copies. To print your PAD1 document,

STEPS

1 Turn on your printer (be sure that it has paper)

 2 Click _File, Print_ for the _Print_ dialog box   [**Ctrl** + **P**]

3 Click the _OK_ button   [↵]

Your printer should now produce a hard copy of PAD1.

CREATING A NEW DOCUMENT

The **New** command (_File_ menu) will clear a window's workspace so that you can begin a new document.

STEPS

 1 Click _File, New_   [**Ctrl** + **N**]

A _New_ dialog box appears with several format options. Note that some programs do not offer this dialog box. To select the default format,

2 Click the _OK_ button   [↵]

Your WordPad workspace should now be blank.

If you created a new document, but forgot to save it and invoked the New command, a dialog box will appear asking if you would like to save it. This dialog box will also appear if you invoke the New command on a modified document that was not resaved.

> **Tip:** Invoking the New command in a program that allows *multiple documents* in its workspace will open a new document window. This window will be placed on top of other opened document windows. These programs generally have a Close command in their *File* menus, which allows you to close the document windows that you are not currently using. Clicking a document window's *Close* button will also close it. Closing documents or programs not in use will free some of your system's memory. This will allow your system to operate more efficiently.

OPENING A DOCUMENT

The **Open** command (*File* menu) retrieves a saved document from a disk and places it into a window. Opening a document can be done by typing its filename or selecting it from a list. Only the latter is discussed here. Try this to open PAD1:

STEPS

1 Click *File, Open* for the *Open* dialog box   [**Ctrl** + **O**]

The *Open* dialog box should again appear as in Figure WIN1-20b. As described in Figure 1-20c, this dialog box has features and operations similar to those in the *Save As* dialog box. At this point you can also set the default drive if needed. For example, click the "▼" button of the *Look in* drop-down box and then click the *3½ Floppy (A:)* drive icon.

2 Click *PAD1* in the *Files* list box

3 Click the *Open* button   [↵]

> **Tip:** You can also double-click a document's name in the *Files* list box instead of Steps 2 and 3 to open it.

4 Click *File, New, OK* to clear your workspace

> **Tip:** Programs that allow multiple documents in their workspace will require clicking *File, Close* or pressing [Ctrl] + [F4] to clear your workspace before Step 4. Some programs automatically open a new document when you invoke the Close command (*File* menu). In this case, skip Step 4.

Note also that in most programs, the *File* menu lists the last few documents used. To open one, simply click it.

CHECKPOINT

Note: You may want to save your Checkpoint files on another disk. Figures in this manual will not display check point files.

✓ Launch WordPad and create your own letterhead.
✓ Save the document as LETTERHEAD. (Be sure to set your default drive to A, if needed.)
✓ Use the New command to clear WordPad's workspace and then close the program.
✓ Launch WordPad again and open your LETTERHEAD document.
✓ Resave your LETTERHEAD document and then close the program.

BASIC MULTITASKING

Multitasking is the ability to work with two or more programs at the same time. As seen earlier, you can launch more than one program during a work session in Windows. You can also quickly switch to an opened program by clicking its button on the taskbar. Here you will learn how to manipulate program windows on the desktop, custom resize them, and share data between them.

LAUNCHING MULTIPLE PROGRAMS

In Windows, you may launch as many programs as your system's memory can handle. The procedures to launch more that one program are the same as those for launching a single program. Just repeat the procedure until each program you desire is launched. To practice launching more than one program in a session, launch WordPad, open your PAD1 document, and then launch Notepad.

STEPS

1 If needed, start Windows and remove the "Welcome" screen

 2 Click the *Start* button   [Ctrl + Esc]

3 Point to *Programs* for its submenu

4 Point to *Accessories* for its submenu

5 Click *WordPad*

 6 Click *File, Open* for its dialog box   [Ctrl + O]

▼ 7 Click the "▼" button of the *Look in* drop-down box

💾 3½ Floppy (A:) 8 Click *3½ Floppy (A:)* drive icon

9 Click *PAD1* and then the *Open* button

10 **Launch Notepad (Accessories group)**

At this point there should be two program windows on the desktop with corresponding buttons on the taskbar. The size of each window may vary.

You should note several other things at this point. Windows automatically added a button for each program opened on the taskbar. The button that is currently depressed—in this case, Notepad—is the **active window.** On the desktop, generally, only one program window, dialog box, or icon can be active at a time. The active window or icon is the one on which you are currently working. It is also the window or icon that will accept most keyboard commands. Note also that the active window's title bar (top row of window), is in a darker color than that of other open windows.

SWITCHING BETWEEN PROGRAMS

To switch back to WordPad as the active window using its taskbar button,

STEPS

| Pad1 - WordPad |

1 Click the *PAD1-WordPad* button on the taskbar   [**Alt** + **Tab**]

> **Tip:** You can also switch between windows by clicking any area of the desired window, if visible. Remember, Windows allows you to open as many programs, documents, or dialog boxes as your system's memory can handle. Again, as you open each program or dialog box, a button is added to the taskbar. You can use these buttons to switch to a desired program or another window.

STANDARD WINDOW DISPLAYS

The ability to rearrange multiple windows makes them visually easier to work with. Windows has several standard multiple window displays: Cascade, Tile Horizontally, Tile Vertically, and Minimize All Windows. The **Cascade** display makes multiple windows of equal size overlap each other, as in Figure WIN1-21a. The **Tile** display places multiple windows beside each other, either horizontally (FigureWIN1-21b) or vertically (Figure WIN1-21c). The **Minimize All Windows** command reduces all windows to their taskbar button, as in Figure WIN1-21d.

CASCADING WINDOWS.   To cascade the program windows on the desktop,

STEPS

1 Point to the space between the Notepad and *System time* button (or any space between buttons) on the taskbar similar to Figure WIN1-22

2 Right-click it for the *Shortcut* menu in Figure WIN1-22b

FIGURE WIN1-21   ■   STANDARD WINDOWS DISPLAYS

(a) Cascaded windows.
(b) Tiled horizontally
windows.

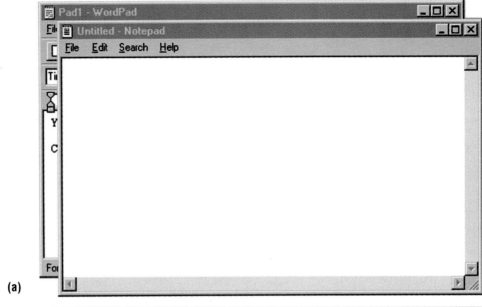

(a)

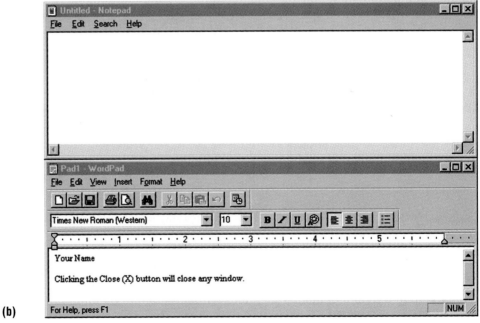

(b)

continued

3   Click _Cascade_

Your windows should appear as in Figure WIN1-21a. To switch to a window, simply
click its taskbar button or click anywhere on the desired window.

WIN

FIGURE WIN1-21 ■ *continued*

(c) Tiled vertically windows.
(d) Minimized all windows.

(c)

(d)

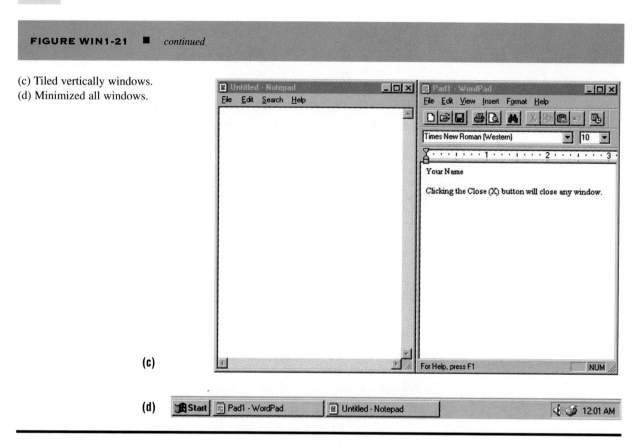

Tip: As you perform each display command, note that an Undo Cascade command appears on the *Shortcut* menu to undo your last display command.

FIGURE WIN1-22 ■ **OPENING THE TASKBAR'S *SHORTCUT* MENU**

(a) Position your pointer on
an open area of the taskbar.
(b) Right-click to open the
taskbar's *Shortcut* menu.

(a)

(b)

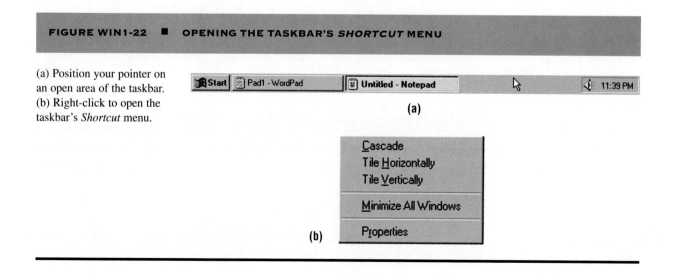

TILING WINDOWS.   To tile the windows horizontally and then vertically,

1 **Right-click the space between the Notepad and *System time* button (or any space between buttons) on the taskbar for the *Shortcut* menu**

2 **Click *Tile Horizontally***

Your windows should now appear as in Figure WIN1-21b. Again, to switch to a window, simply click its taskbar button or click anywhere on the desired window. Now, to change the display to tile vertically,

3 **Right-click the space between the Notepad and *System time* button (or any space between buttons) on the taskbar for the *Shortcut* menu**

4 **Click *Tile Vertically***

Your windows should now appear as in Figure WIN1-21c.

MINIMIZING ALL WINDOWS.   To minimize all window in the desktop,

1 **Right click the space between the Notepad and *System time* button for the *Shortcut* menu**

2 **Click *Minimize All Windows***

All windows in the desktop are now minimized as in Figure WIN1-21d.

3 **Right click the space between the Notepad and *System time* button (or any space between buttons) on the taskbar for the *Shortcut* menu**

4 **Click *Undo Minimize All***

5 **Close each program on the desktop (If needed, drag the window's title bar to reposition the window so that its *Close* button is displayed.)**

> **Tip: You can also use the *Shortcut* menu for displaying windows to change the properties of the taskbar. This will be discussed in later chapters.**

CUSTOM WINDOW DISPLAYS

Most program and document windows can be resized to meet a user's need. To custom resize a window, simply drag and drop one of its window walls. Try this:

WIN

1 **Launch WordPad**

2 **Right-click an open space on the taskbar for the *Shortcut* menu**

3 **Click *Cascade***

When the Cascade command is invoked with only a single window on the desktop, it resizes the window to a medium size window. This is done to make the next exercise visually easier.

4 **Drag the window's title bar to move it to the center of the desktop**

5 **Slowly point to the right wall until your mouse pointer resembles that in Figure 1-23a**

6 **Drag this wall to the left until you have reached the last character of the title bar's name and then drop the wall there (release your mouse)**

Your window should resemble Figure WIN1-23b.

SHARING DATA

In the Windows environment you can easily share data within the same document or between documents of the same or different programs. Remember, data may include text and objects. Sharing includes copying, moving or linking information. **Copying** is the process of duplicating data in a new location. **Moving** involves relocating data. **Linking** creates a special connection between data in different documents. The documents can be

---

FIGURE WIN1-23 ■ CUSTOM RESIZING A WINDOW

(a) Dragging a window's wall or corner will resize the window.
(b) The resized window.

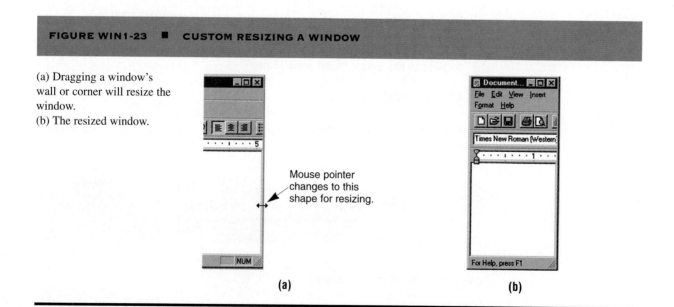

Mouse pointer changes to this shape for resizing.

(a)   (b)

from the same program or from different programs. Linking techniques are demonstrated later.

The exercises in this section provides an overview of sharing data among documents of different programs. Detailed operating instructions for sharing data within the same document and documents of other programs are provided in Chapter 3 of this manual.

STEPS

1 If needed, start Windows and remove the "Welcome" screen

2 Launch WordPad and open the PAD1 document (if needed, set the default drive to A)

3 Maximize WordPad

4 Launch Notepad

5 Switch to WordPad (click its taskbar button)

SELECTING.   Selecting is a process of marking data for editing. Selected data is called a *selection.* The selection process from one program to another may differ. Generally, however, to select text in a word processing program, simply drag your mouse pointer over the desired text. With the keyboard, press and hold the Shift key while using the arrow keys. In a graphics program, you normally have to first pick a selection tool, then drag your mouse pointer around the object. Selection techniques are discussed as they relate to an operation.

COPYING DATA.   The commands to copy a selection are called Copy and Paste (*Edit* menu). The **Copy** command duplicates the selection onto Windows **Clipboard.** This program temporarily holds a selection for future pasting. The **Paste** command involves placing a selection from Clipboard to a desired location. This location can be within the same document or another document. The other document can be a different program's document. In the next exercises, you will copy some data from your PAD1 document to a Notepad document. **Notepad** is a program that allows you to create or edit text-only files.

Try to copy the sentence "Clicking the Close (X) button will close any window." from the PAD1 document (WordPad) to the default Notepad document as in Figure WIN1-24.

STEPS

1 Use your arrow keys to move to the beginning of "Clicking the Close (X) button will close any window." as in Figure WIN1-25a

FIGURE WIN1-24 ■ COPYING DATA

Data can be copied from one program to another.

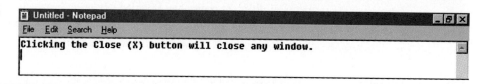

2 Slowly point to the left of the "C" in "Clicking" and wait for your pointer to change to a right pointing arrow as in Figure WIN1-25b

3 Click to select the entire line (you can also drag across to select the line) as in Figure WIN1-25c

FIGURE WIN1-25 ■ SELECTING DATA

(a) Move your insertion point to the beginning of the selection.
(b) Point to the left of "Clicking."
(c) Click to select the entire sentence.

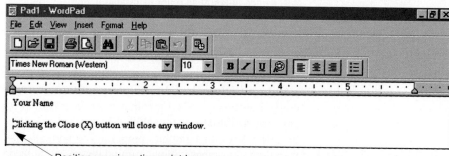

(a)

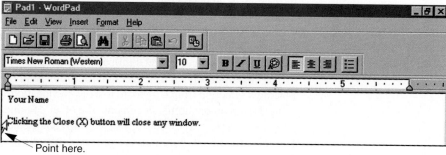

(b)

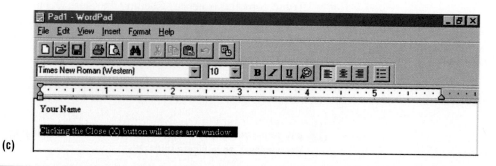

(c)

Tip: To select by keyboard, press and hold your Shift key while using your arrow keys.

  4 Click *Edit, Copy* to copy the selection to the Clipboard   [**Ctrl** + **C**]

  5 Click the *Untitled-Notepad* button on the taskbar to switch to it   [**Alt** + **Tab**]

  6 Click *Edit, Paste* to paste the selection   [**Ctrl** + **V**]

Your screen should resemble WIN1-24. The Paste command will place the selection at the insertion point. Now save the Notepad document as NOTE1 and then close it.

  7 Click *File, Save*   [**Ctrl** + **S**]

Remember, since this is the first time that your are saving the document, the Save command will open the *Save As* dialog box before saving.

8 Type **NOTE1**

Now change the default drive to A before saving.

9 Click the ▼ button of the *Save in* drop-down box

10 Click the *3½ Floppy (A:)* drive icon

11 Click the *Save* button   [↵]

Your document has now been saved as NOTE1. Notice that the caption NOTE1 appears in Notepad's title bar.

12 Click Notepad's *Close* button to close the program   [**Alt** + **F4**]

13 Close WordPad without saving   [**Alt** + **F4**]

  MOVING DATA.   To move a selection, use the same commands as with copying; however, instead of clicking *Edit, Copy* (or pressing Ctrl + C) in Step 4 earlier, click *Edit, Cut* (or press Ctrl + X). The **Cut** command moves a selection from a document to the Clipboard for future pasting.

ALTERNATIVE WINDOW CLOSING TECHNIQUES

Until now, you have been using a window's *Close* button (or the Alt+F4 shortcut keys) to exit a program. Other techniques to close a program window include using its **File** menu or control-menu, or its program icon. Each one of these techniques will be demonstrated.

> **1** **Launch WordPad, Paint, and then Notepad**

> **2** **Cascade the windows (remember to use the taskbar *Shortcut* menu)**

To close Notepad using its *File* menu,

> **3** **Click *File***   [Alt + F]

> **4** **Click *Exit***   [X]

To close Paint using its control-menu,

> **5** **Point anywhere on Paint's title bar and click your right mouse button**
>   [Alt + Spacebar]

> **Tip: You can also click (left mouse button) the program's icon on the title bar to open the control-menu.**

> **6** **Click *Close***   [C]

To close WordPad using its program icon,

> **7** **Point to WordPad's program icon to the left of "Document - WordPad" on the title bar**

> **8** **Double-click WordPad's program icon**

A summary of closing techniques displayed in Figure WIN1-26.

☑ CHECKPOINT

✓ Launch WordPad and NotePad.
✓ Cascade and then tile the windows. Next, switch to WordPad.
✓ Open your LETTERHEAD document and copy your letterhead to the default NotePad document.
✓ Save the NotePad document as NOTEHEAD.
✓ Close each program using a different closing technique.

THE HELP FEATURE

Windows offers an extensive main on-line help feature. Many dialog boxes and program windows also have help features. Procedures to access these help features are discussed next.

FIGURE WIN1-26 ■ ALTERNATIVE PROGRAM CLOSING TECHNIQUES

Method	By Mouse	By Keyboard
Shortcut	Click *Close (X)* button or double-click program icon (title bar)	Press [Alt] + [F4]
Control-Menu	Click program icon (title bar) or right-click title bar and then click *Close*	Press [Alt] + [Spacebar], [C]
File Menu	Click *File, Exit*	Press [Alt] + [F], [X]

WIN

USING WINDOWS MAIN HELP

Windows Main Help can be opened through the *Start* menu.

STEPS

1 Start Windows and remove the "Welcome" screen (if needed)

 2 Click the *Start* button   [Ctrl + Esc]

3 Click *Help*   [H]

The *Help Topics: Windows Help* dialog box should appear. This dialog box has three tabs: Contents, Index, and Find. A **tab** is a section of a dialog box, similar to tabs used in a manual file system. The *Contents* tab lets you access help topics by category. The *Index* tab allows you to access help topics by typing a word or phrase, or by selecting from a list. The *Find* tab allows you to search for all help topics related to a specific word or phrase. Only the *Index* tab is demonstrated here. See the appendix for instructions on using the other tabs.

Note: The techniques used in this section to operate and select help features are common to most dialog boxes and windows.

REQUESTING HELP BY TYPING.   The *Index* tab can be used to search for help by either typing the desired topic's name or selecting it from the index's list. To request help on the filenames by typing,

STEPS

Index   **1** Click the *Index* tab (if needed)

Your dialog box should resemble Figure WIN1-27a. The insertion point should now be in the text box just below "1. Type the first few letters of the word you're looking for." As you type each letter in the next steps, watch the *Index* list box.

2 **Type** **f**

A selection highlight appears in the lower list box and scrolls (moves) to "Faster ways to work with Windows." This is the first topic that starts with an "f."

3 **Type** **ilenames**

Now, as in Figure WIN1-27b, the selection highlight moves to "filenames." This topic also has a variety of subtopics listed below it. To select the subtopic "about longer filenames,"

4 **Double-click** *about longer filenames*   [↓ , ↵]

FIGURE WIN1-27   ■   REQUESTING HELP

(a) The Help *Index* tab.
(b) Typing a topic's name or clicking the topic in the list box will select it.
(c) Help on long filenames.

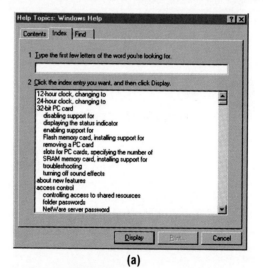

(a)

(b)   **(c)**

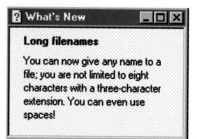

A Help window appears with the topic "A new look and feel" and a list of topics. To receive help on "Longer filenames,"

 Click *Longer filenames*

A window displaying help on longer filenames appears as in Figure WIN 1-27c. Now to close both windows,

☒ **6 Click the *Close* button of the *What's New* window**   [**Alt** + **F4**]

7 Click the Close button of the Windows Help window   [**Alt** + **F4**]

WIN

REQUESTING HELP BY SELECTING. To access help on longer filenames by selecting from the *Index* list box,

STEPS

 1 Click the *Start* button for the *Start* menu   [**Ctrl** + **Esc**]

2 Click *Help* for its dialog box

Index **3 Click the *Index* tab, if needed**

Again, your dialog box should resemble Figure WIN1-27a. Items listed in a list box are normally displayed in numeric and then alphabetical order. This list box has a scroll bar on its right wall. A **scroll bar** allows you to move (scroll) vertically or horizontally through a list box or window's contents by mouse. Clicking the arrow button on either end of a scroll bar or dragging the small box (called the *scroll box*) on the scroll bar will quickly move through the contents of a list box or window. Scroll bars generally appear in a list box or window when its contents is larger than its display area. They may appear either on the list box or window's right and/or bottom wall. Try this to locate the topic "filenames" in the *Index* list box:

Scroll box ——→  **4 Point to the scroll box just beneath the up arrow scroll button**

5 Slowly drag the scroll box down until topics that begin with the letter "f" appear in the list box

6 Click either arrow scroll button until "filenames" appears

Note that the selection highlight does not move from its position when using the scroll bar. To move the selection highlight to "filenames,"

7 Double-click *about long filenames* in the list box

8 Click *Long filenames*

A window displaying help on long filenames appears as in Figure WIN 1-27c. Leave these windows open as you proceed to the next section.

> **Tip:** To scroll to a desired item quickly, type the item's first letter and then use the scroll bar to locate the item.

PRINTING HELP INFORMATION.   Help topics can be printed by using a *Short-cut* menu. To print the information on the *Long filenames,*

STEPS

1 Turn on your printer

2 Right-click anywhere within the *What's New* Help window for its *Shortcut* menu

3 Click *Print Topic* for the *Print* dialog box

4 Click *OK*

5 Click the *What's New* window's *Close* button

At this point you can return to the *Help Topics: Windows Help* dialog box by clicking the *Help Topics* button (do not click) or exit help. To exit help,

6 Click Windows Help's *Close* button

> **Tip:** To copy a help topic to the Clipboard for pasting into a program, click *Copy* in-stead of *Print Topic* in Step 3.

GETTING HELP WITHIN A DIALOG BOX

Many dialog boxes have a [?] button to the left of the *Close* button that can be used to access help on a specific area of a dialog box. Try this:

STEPS

1 Click the *Start* button for the *Start* menu

2 Click *Help* for its dialog box

3 **Click the *Find* tab**

4 **Click the [?] button (left of the *Close* button)**

Your mouse pointer changes to an arrow with a question mark. Pointing to and clicking a desired area of the dialog box will open a caption box describing the area's operations. For example,

5 **Click the text box below the caption "1. Type the word(s) you want to find"**

A caption box appears with a brief description of the text box's operation as in Figure WIN1-28.

6 **Click anywhere outside the caption box to close it**

7 **Click the dialog box's *Close* button**

> **Tip: In general, to access help in dialog boxes that do not have a help [?] button, simply press [F1].**

GETTING HELP WITHIN A PROGRAM WINDOW

Most Windows programs have a *Help* menu that can be accessed through its menu bar. You can also press F1 to access a program's main help. Although each program's help features may differ, their general dialog box and window operations are similar to the Windows main help. In addition, most programs offer both general and specific help. You may want to try the Help feature in a few different programs to get a feel for its operations.

FIGURE WIN1-28 ■ DIALOG BOX HELP

Clicking the *Help* button and then a desired item on a dialog box will display a caption on its operation.

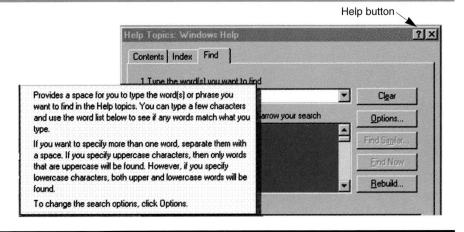

WIN

CHECKPOINT

✓ Access Windows main *Help* dialog box.
✓ Use the *Index* tab to search for help on "dialog boxes, using."
✓ Print the information on dialog boxes.
✓ Close the Help window.
✓ How can you access help on a specific dialog box component operation?

OTHER START MENU COMMANDS

The *Start* menu, as in Figure WIN1-29, offers several other commands in addition to Programs and Help. These commands include Documents, Settings, Find, and Run. The first three open submenus and the Run command opens a dialog box. The operation of each option is discussed next.

DOCUMENTS MENU

The **Documents menu** can be used to open any of the last 15 documents used with its related program. To use the *Documents* menu,

STEPS

  ⬚ **Click the *Start* button**   [**Ctrl** + **Esc**]

FIGURE WIN1-29 ■ **START MENU COMMANDS**

2 **Point to** *Documents* **to open its submenu**

3 **Click any document listed to open it**

Windows will now open the document you selected and its related program.

 4 **Click the program window's** *Close* **button**

> **Tip:** To clear the Documents menu, click the *Start* button, point to *Settings*, click *Taskbar*, the *Start Menu Programs* tab, the *Clear* button, OK.

SETTINGS MENU

The **Settings menu** contains commands to launch the Control Panel program, Printers program, and open the *Taskbar Properties* dialog box. Each of these items will be discussed next.

CONTROL PANEL. The **Control Panel** program can be used to change the settings of your computer. Many of these settings are automatically set when Windows was installed on your system. However, sometimes these settings may require adjustment (for example, when adding new hardware or changing the system's time).

STEPS

 1 **Click the** *Start* **button**   [**Ctrl** + **Esc**]

2 **Point to** *Settings* **to open its submenu**

3 **Click** *Control Panel*

The Control Panel window should appear similar to Figure WIN1-30. (Your Control Panel contents may differ.) At this point you can access any of its items by clicking the item, clicking *File,* and then *Open.* Try this to open the *Date/Time* dialog box as in Figure WIN1-31,

 4 **Click the** *Date/Time* **icon**

5 **Click** *File* **(on the menu bar),** *Open*   [↵]

This dialog box has two tabs: *Date & Time* and *Time Zone.* The *Date & Time* tab is used to set the system date and time. The *Time Zone* tab is used to set your own time zone. For now,

FIGURE WIN1-30 ■ THE CONTROL PANEL

The Control Panel can be used to adjust the computer's settings.

<table>
<tr><td>6</td><td>Click the Cancel button to return to the Control Panel window</td><td>[Esc]</td></tr>
<tr><td>[X] 7</td><td>Click the Control Panel's Close button</td><td>[Alt + F4]</td></tr>
</table>

FIGURE WIN1-31 ■ THE DATE/TIME PROPERTIES DIALOG BOX

This dialog box can be used to adjust the system's date and time.

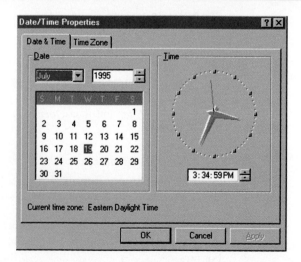

Tip: Instead of Steps 4 and 5, you can double-click an icon to open it.

PRINTERS.   **Printers** is a program that displays the current printers installed on your system. You can use this window to add another printer or open a window displaying the activity of a printer.

TASKBAR.   The Taskbar command opens a **Taskbar Properties dialog box.** This dialog box can be used to change the taskbar's display settings and add or remove programs from the *Programs* menu. The operations of this dialog box will be examined in detail later.

FIND MENU

The **Find menu** opens to a menu that displays at least the command *Files or Folders.* This command is used to locate files or folders within your system quickly. A *folder* is a set of related files. Its operation will be discussed in Chapter 2.

RUN DIALOG BOX

The **Run dialog box** as in Figure WIN1-32, allows you to launch a program, or to open a folder or document by typing its command line. This dialog box is often used to install new programs. To open the *Run* dialog box,

STEPS

1 Click the *Start* button   [Ctrl + Esc]

2 Click *Run* for its dialog box

The *Run* dialog box should appear as in Figure WIN1-32. The Browse feature of this dialog box is helpful to locate files. Try this:

3 If needed, insert your data disk

4 Click the *Browse* button for its dialog box

As in Figure WIN1-32, the *Browse* dialog box resembles an *Open* dialog box. In fact, its components operate the same way. For now, close all windows and shut down Windows.

5 Click the *Browse* dialog box's *Close* button

6 Click the *Run* dialog box's *Close* button

7 Click the *Start* button and then *Shut Down*

FIGURE WIN1-32 ■ THE RUN COMMAND

(a) Clicking the Run command (*Start* menu) opens its dialog box.
(b) Clicking the *Browse* button opens a dialog box that can be used to look in a particular directory of a disk.

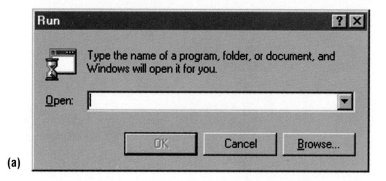

(a)

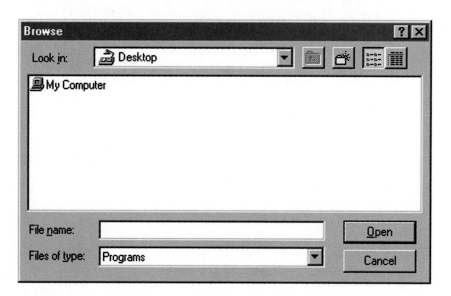

(b)

☑ **CHECKPOINT**

✓ What does the Document command of the *Start* menu allow you to do?
✓ Which *Setting* menu command can be used to change system settings?
✓ Which dialog box can be used to add new programs to the taskbar?
✓ How do you access it?
✓ Describe the function(s) of the Run command.
✓ For what reason is the Find command (*Start* menu) used?

SUMMARY

■ Windows is a graphical user interface, or GUI (pronounced "gooey"), operating system that simplifies communication with your computer by using common symbols (called icons) and menus instead of typewritten commands.

- A window is a rectangular box that may contain a program (set of computer instructions) called a program window or document (a file with data, information, or graphics) called a document window. It may also be used to request or give information about a task or feature called a dialog box.

- Booting up is the process of starting Windows on a system with a hard-disk drive. This generally involves turning on your computer system and waiting for the Windows screen.

- The Windows screen has two main parts: the taskbar (bottom of screen) and the desktop (large area above the taskbar). The desktop also has several icons, starting with the *My Computer* icon. Icons are small graphical images or symbols (pictures) that may represent programs, documents, and other features.

- The mouse pointer, or pointer, is a small graphical image resembling an arrow on the screen. You control it by using a pointing device such as a mouse (most common), trackball, pointing stick, track pad, or electronic pen.

- Pointing involves moving the mouse pointer on your screen to a desired item. Clicking involves pointing to a desired item and then rapidly pressing and releasing your left mouse button. Clicking will invoke an item's feature. Right-clicking involves pointing to a desired item and then pressing and releasing the right mouse button. Right-clicking will open an item's *Shortcut* menu.

- Dragging and dropping can be used to move or copy icons, windows, or other objects. Dragging involves pointing to a desired object and then pressing and holding the left mouse button while moving the mouse and the object to a new location. Dropping involves releasing the mouse and thus the object after dragging it to a new location.

- Double-clicking (pointing to and then rapidly pressing and releasing the left mouse button twice) is generally used to open an icon directly to a window or other feature.

- Shortcut keys provide a quick way to invoke certain commands by pressing a function key alone or in conjunction with the Ctrl, Alt, or Shift keys. The Ctrl, Alt, and Shift keys may also be used in conjunction with other keys.

- Clicking the taskbar's *Start* button (left side) or pressing Ctrl + Esc will open the Windows main menu called the *Start* menu. It is used to start programs, find documents, adjust system settings, find a document (file), access help, or shut down Windows. Each option on the *Start* menu is listed with its corresponding icon to its left.

- To shut down (exit) Windows, click the *Start* button, *Shut Down,* and then the *Yes* button.

- *Launching* is the Windows term for starting a program. The *Programs* menu of the *Start* menu is normally used to launch a program. It contains a list of program groups and certain primary programs. Program groups open to submenus. They are logical groupings of programs and files into categories for easier visual access.

- Closing is the process of closing a window and thus exiting the program, document, or other Windows feature that is encased in it. To close any window, click its *Close* button (a button with an "X" at the right end of the title bar).

- The title bar is the first row in any window and is used to identify the window. It can be used to resize, move, or close a window. It may include the program or document's icon, name, two window resizing buttons, and a *Close* button. The title bars in dialog boxes may include a *Help* (?) button instead of resizing buttons.

- A menu bar provides mouse and keyboard access to a program's features through pull-down menus. Only program windows can have a menu bar. Most Windows programs have *File, Edit,* and *Help* menus. To open a pull-down menu from a bar, click the desired menu bar item or press the Alt key and the underlined letter of the menu bar item.

■   Standard Windows menu indicators include (1) items with a "▶" open a submenu, (2) no notation directly invokes a command, (3) items with an ellipsis (…) open another window, and (4) dimmed items are currently not available.

■   A command button directly accesses a program or window's feature when clicked. Command buttons that can be used to manipulate a window are located on the title bar. They include the program or document icon, *Minimize, Maximize, Restore,* and *Close* buttons. Command buttons that activate a program feature are generally grouped in functional sets below the menu bar. These sets are often called a toolbar or format bar.

■   A drop-down box resembles a one-line rectangular box that has a "▼" button on its right side. They may be found with command button sets or in dialog boxes. Clicking the "▼" button of a drop-down box opens a drop-down list of available options.

■   Basic document management includes procedures to use the default document to create documents with data and objects and then save, print, and open those documents. It also includes using the New command to clear the current workspace for a new document. These commands are generally located in a program's file menu.

■   Filenames are used to identify a document or program and can have up to 255 characters.

■   Formatting prepares a disk for use on the computer. Every new disk that is not preformatted must be formatted (organized for your computer system) before you can store anything on it. Formatting sets up the disk's directory and file allocation table and divides the disk into addressable storage locations. It also checks for defective tracks on the disk and seals them off from further use.

■   Multitasking is the computer's ability to work with two or more programs at the same time. For each program launched, a corresponding button is added to the taskbar. To switch to a program, click its taskbar button.

■   The active window is the one currently in use. Its title bar is highlighted and taskbar button depressed. Most keyboard commands affect the active window.

■   The ability to rearrange the display of multiple windows makes them visually easier to work with. Standard multiple window displays available through the taskbar's *Shortcut* menu include Cascade (overlapping each other), Tile Horizontally (on top of each other), Tile Vertically (next to each other), and Minimize All Windows (reduced to the taskbar button). You can also custom resize a window by dragging one of its walls or corners.

■   Information can be easily copied, moved, or linked within the same document or among documents of the same or different programs. These commands are located in the *Edit* menu and include *Copy, Cut, Paste,* and *Paste Link.* The Copy command duplicates a selection (marked data or objects) onto the Clipboard (a temporary holding program) for future pasting. The Cut command moves the selection to the Clipboard. The Paste command copies a selection from the Clipboard to a desired location.

■   Windows main *Help* dialog box can be opened through the *Start* menu. It has three tabs: Contents, Index, and Find. A tab is a section of a dialog box, similar to tabs used in a manual file system. The *Contents* tab lets you access help topics by category. The *Index* tab allows you to access help topics by typing a word or phrase or selecting from a list. The *Find* tab allows you to search for all help topics related to a specific word or phrase.

- ■ To get help on a specific operation of a dialog box, click the [?] button (title bar) and then the desired item or press F1. To get help in a program window, click *Help* for the *Help* menu and then click the desired help item or press F1.
- ■ Other *Start* menu commands include Documents (opens to a menu that can be used to open any of the last 15 documents used), Settings (opens to a menu that can be used to open the Control Panel window, Printers window, and *Taskbar Properties* dialog box), Find (used to locate files or folders quickly), and Run (used to open a program, folder, or document by typing its command line). The Run command is often used to install new programs.

KEY TERMS

Active (or current) icon (WIN11)
Active window (WIN38)
Booting up (WIN3)
Cascade (WIN38)
Clicking (WIN9)
Clipboard (WIN43)
Close button (WIN12)
Command button (WIN27)
Control Panel (WIN53)
Control-menu (WIN20)
Copy (WIN43)
Copying (WIN42)
Cut (WIN45)
Data (WIN2)
Default document (WIN32)
Default drive (WIN33)
Desktop (WIN5)
Dialog box (WIN5)
Disks (WIN3)
Document (WIN2)
Document window (WIN17)
Documents menu (WIN52)
Double-clicking (WIN11)
Dragging (WIN11)
Drop-down box (WIN27)
Dropping (WIN11)
File (WIN3)
Filename (WIN32)
Find menu (WIN55)
Folder (WIN3)
Font (WIN29)

Font size (WIN29)
Format bar (WIN27)
Formatting (WIN33)
Function keys (WIN6)
Graphical user interface, or GUI (WIN2)
Hardware (WIN2)
Icons (WIN2)
Insertion point (WIN31)
Launching (WIN14)
Linking (WIN42)
Maximize button (WIN22)
Maximized (WIN17)
Menu bar (WIN22)
Microsoft Windows 95 (WIN2)
Minimize all windows (WIN38)
Minimize button (WIN21)
Mouse (WIN5)
Mouse pointer (WIN5)
MouseKeys (WIN6)
Moving (WIN42)
Multitasking (WIN37)
New (WIN35)
Notepad (WIN43)
Objects (WIN2)
Open (WIN36)
Paste (WIN43)
Pointer (WIN5)
Pointing (WIN6)
Pointing device (WIN5)
Print (WIN35)
Printers (WIN55)

Program (WIN2)
Program groups (WIN15)
Program window (WIN17)
Pull-down menu (WIN22)
Resizing buttons (WIN21)
Restore (WIN21)
Restore button (WIN22)
Right-click (WIN10)
Run dialog box (WIN55)
Save (WIN32)
Save as (WIN32)
Scroll bar (WIN49)
Selection (WIN25)
Settings menu (WIN53)
Shortcut keys (WIN6)
Shortcut menu (WIN10)
Shut down (WIN13)
Start button (WIN5)
Start menu (WIN5)
Tab (WIN47)
Taskbar (WIN5)
Taskbar properties dialog box (WIN55)
Tile (WIN38)
Title bar (WIN17)
Toolbar (WIN27)
Window (WIN2)
Windows screen (WIN5)
WordPad (WIN15)
Workspace (WIN17)

WIN

QUIZ

TRUE/FALSE

____ 1. A graphical user interface operating system uses symbols and menus instead of typewritten commands.

____ 2. Launching is the process of starting a program.

____ 3. Double-clicking an object opens its *Shortcut* menu.

____ 4. The desktop is the interior space of a window.

____ 5. Pressing the **Ctrl** + **Esc** keys opens the *Start* menu.

____ 6. The *File* menu in most programs contains commands to save, open, or print a document.

____ 7. Only program windows have a *Close* button.

____ 8. Pressing the **Alt** + **F4** keys will close a program window.

____ 9. Multitasking is the computer's ability to work with more than one program at the same time.

____ 10. The *Run* dialog box can be used to install programs.

MULTIPLE CHOICE

____ 11. The bar at the bottom of the Windows screen is called the
   a. Status bar
   b. Menu bar
   c. Taskbar
   d. Desktop

____ 12. The main portion of the Windows screen is called the
   a. Desktop
   b. Workspace
   c. Taskbar
   d. Title bar

____ 13. All of the following are mouse actions except
   a. Point
   b. Click
   c. Press
   d. Right Click

____ 14. A program window's title bar has all of the following except
   a. Name section
   b. Resizing buttons
   c. *Close* button
   d. *Help* button

____ 15. A program window can be closed by all of the following except
   a. Press **Alt** + **F4**
   b. Click *File, Close*
   c. Click the *Close* button
   d. Click *File, Exit*

___ 16. To open an item's *Shortcut* menu,
   a. Click *File, Shortcut*
   b. Click *Start, Shortcut*
   c. Right Click the item
   d. Press **Alt** + **S**

___ 17. Dragging a corner of a nonmaximized window will _____ it.
   a. resize
   b. move
   c. cascade
   d. tile

___ 18. The process of marking data for editing is called
   a. Copying
   b. Coloring
   c. Selecting
   d. Right Clicking

___ 19. Clicking the ? button of a dialog box will
   a. Close it
   b. Open its menu
   c. Start its function
   d. Access help

___ 20. The Copy command places a copy of a selection in the _____ for future pasting.
   a. Desktop
   b. Clipboard
   c. taskbar
   d. dialog box

MATCHING

Select the lettered item from the figure that best matches each phrase below.

___ 21. Controlled by a pointing device.

___ 22. Clicking this item opens the Windows main menu.

___ 23. Right clicking this item will open a *Shortcut* menu with the Cascade command.

___ 24. Clicking this item will open a menu with document Saving, Opening, and Printing commands.

___ 25. Clicking this item will open a control-menu.

___ 26. Dragging this item will move a window.

___ 27. Clicking this item maximizes a window.

___ 28. Clicking this item will close a window.

___ 29. Pressing **Ctrl** + **Esc** will open this menu.

___ 30. Clicking this item will open a menu with Copying, Cutting, and Pasting commands.

ANSWERS

True/False: 1. T; 2. T; 3. F; 4. F; 5. T; 6. T; 7. F; 8. T; 9. T; 10. T
Multiple Choice: 11. c; 12. a; 13. c; 14. d; 15. b; 16. c; 17. a; 18. c; 19; d; 20. b
Matching: 21. k; 22. l; 23. m; 24. f; 25. b; 26. c; 27. d; 28. i; 29. j; 30. e

WIN

FIGURE WIN1-33 ■ CHAPTER 1 MATCHING FIGURE

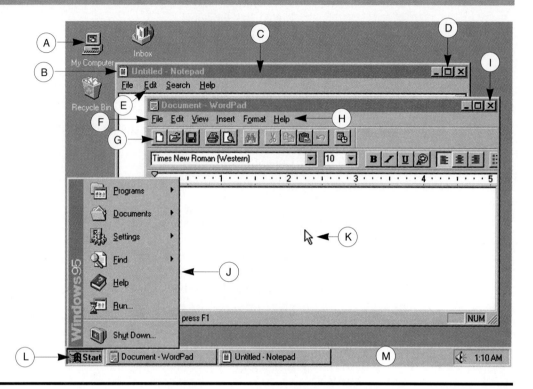

EXERCISE

I. OPERATIONS

Provide the Windows commands to do each of the following operations. For each operation, assume a hard-disk system with a disk in Drive A. You may want to verify each command by trying it on your computer.

1. Start Windows and open the *Start* menu.

2. Launch the WordPad and Notepad programs.

3. Vertically tile and then cascade the windows.

4. Switch to WordPad and maximize it.

5. Type the second item from the chapter's summary.

6. Save this file as SUMMARY1.

7. Select the entire paragraph and copy it to the Clipboard.

8. Switch to Notepad and maximize it.

9. Paste the paragraph into Notepad's default document and save it as SUMMARY2.

10. Close all windows and then shut down Windows.

II. COMMANDS

Describe fully, using as few words as possible, what command is initiated, or what is accomplished, in Windows by the actions described below. Assume that each exercise part is independent of any previous parts.

1. Pressing **Ctrl** + **Esc** keys.

2. Clicking the *Start* button.

3. Pointing to a *Start* menu item that has a "▶" at its right.

4. Double-clicking a program window's title bar.

5. Pressing the **Alt** + **F4** keys when using a program.

6. Clicking the "X" button of a window.

7. Pointing to a WordPad toolbar button.

8. Clicking a program's taskbar button.

9. Pressing the **Ctrl** + **X** keys on a selection.

10. Pressing the **Ctrl** + **V** keys.

III. APPLICATIONS

Perform the following operations, briefly tell how you accomplished each operation, and describe its results.

APPLICATION 1: GETTING STARTED

1. Boot your computer and start Windows.

2. Point to the *Start* button on the taskbar and wait for its caption.

3. Click the *Start* button for the *Start* menu.

4. Point to *Programs* for its submenu.

5. Point to *Accessories* for its submenu.

6. Click *WordPad* to launch it.

7. Click WordPad's *Close* button.

8. Drag and drop the *Recycle Bin* icon in the center of the desktop.

9. Double-click the *Recycle Bin* icon to launch it.

10. Click the Recycle Bin's *Close* button.

11. Shut down Windows.

APPLICATION 2: COMMON WINDOWS FEATURES

1. Boot your computer and start Windows.

2. Launch WordPad.

3. Use the *WordPad* control-menu to minimize it. (Hint: Click its icon on the title bar or right click the tile bar.)

4. Resize the WordPad to a window and then maximize it.

5. Point to a few of the toolbar and format bar buttons for their titles.

6. Use the keyboard to open the *Edit* menu and then move the highlight to a few of the commands and review their descriptions as they display on the status bar.

7. Close the menu without selecting a command.

8. Open the toolbar's *Shortcut* menu and then close it.

9. Close WordPad.

10. Shut down Windows.

APPLICATION 3: BASIC DOCUMENT MANAGEMENT

1. Boot your computer and start Windows.

2. Start WordPad.

3. Type your name.

4. Save the document as MYNAME.

5. Use the new command (*File* menu) to clear the workspace an open a new document.

6. Open MYNAME.

7. Type your address below your name (use two lines).

8. Resave the document as MYNAME.

9. Print the MYNAME document.

10. Close WordPad and the shut down Windows.

APPLICATION 4: BASIC MULTITASKING

1. Boot your computer and start Windows.

2. Launch WordPad and Notepad.

3. Switch to WordPad and open the MYNAME document created in Application 3.

4. Select the data in the MYNAME document.

5. Use the Copy command to copy the selection to the Clipboard.

6. Switch to Notepad.

7. Use the Paste command to place the selection in the default Notepad document.

8. Tile horizontally and then cascade the windows.

9. Minimize all windows.

10. Close all windows and shut down Windows.

APPLICATION 5: THE HELP FEATURE

1. Boot your computer and start Windows.

2. Open the main *Help* dialog box.

3. Click the *Index* tab.

4. Use the *Index* list to access help on multitasking.

5. Print the contents of the Help window.

6. Click the *Find* tab.

7. Locate topics related to windows.

8. Close all Help windows.

9. Launch Paint and use its *Help* menu to access help on toolbox.
10. Close any windows and shut down Windows.

APPLICATION 6: OTHER START MENU COMMANDS

1. Boot your computer and start Windows.
2. Use the *Documents* menu to open your last document (or any document).
3. Close the window.
4. Use the *Settings* menu to launch the Control Panel.
5. Examine the settings options in the Control Panel window.
6. Close the window.
7. Use the *Find* menu to locate the PAD1 file on your disk.
8. Close the window.
9. Open the *Run* dialog box and browse through the contents of your data disk.
10. Close any opened window and shut down Windows.

MASTERY CASES

The following mastery cases allow you to demonstrate how much you have learned about this software. Each case describes a fictitious problem or need that can be solved using the skills that you have learned in this chapter. Although minimum acceptable outcomes are specified, you are expected and encouraged to design your own response (files, data, lists) in ways that display your personal mastery of the software. Feel free to show off your skills. Use real data from your own experience in your solution, although you may also fabricate data if needed.

These mastery cases allow you to display your ability to

- Start and shut down Windows.
- Use common windows features.
- Operate basic document management commands.
- Perform basic multitasking operations.
- Use on-line help.

CASE 1: USING WINDOWS AT SCHOOL

You have been asked to prepare a small presentation describing the common components of a window. Use WordPad to prepare a list of common window parts and their operations. Save the document and print it. Close the program and shut down Windows.

CASE 2: USING WINDOWS AT HOME

Members of your home have asked you to prepare instructions on how to launch a program and access on-line help. Use WordPad to prepare these instructions. Save the document and print it. Close the program and shut down Windows.

CASE 3: USING WINDOWS AT WORK

You have been asked to prepare a small presentation on the benefits of multitasking. Use WordPad to create a document listing a few benefits of multitasking and save the document. Next, launch Notepad and copy the data from your WordPad document to it. Save and print the Notepad document. Close both programs and shut down Windows.

2

MANAGING YOUR COMPUTER

OUTLINE

UNDERSTANDING MY COMPUTER
Launching My Computer
Storing Programs and Documents
Disk Operations
Finding a File
Looking in a Folder
Viewing Options

MANAGING YOUR FILES
Folders
Document Approach
Selecting Multiple Files

Opening Files
Renaming Files
Printing Files

SHARING AND REMOVING YOUR FILES
Copying and Moving
Creating Shortcuts
Using Undo
Deleting and Recycling

CONTROLLING YOUR ENVIRONMENT
Changing Properties

Using the Control Panel
Using Printers

UNDERSTANDING EXPLORER
Launching Explorer
Operating Explorer

OBJECTIVES

After completing this chapter, you will be able to

1. Describe how to launch and use My Computer to view and find your computer's components.
2. Explain how your computer stores programs and documents.
3. Use My Computer for formatting a disk and performing disk diagnostics.
4. Create folders and documents using My Computer and Folder windows.

5. Rename a file and open or print multiple files.
6. Copy, move, and create *Shortcut* icons for single and multiple files.
7. Use the Undo command and recycle bin.
8. Change properties of various components of your system.
9. Launch and operate Windows Explorer.

OVERVIEW

This chapter introduces a variety of techniques to help you to better manage your computer. It focuses on using My Computer, a program that allows you to view and manage every part of your computer. First, you will review how to launch My Computer. You will then learn how your computer stores files, as well as how to format and diagnose a disk, look in a folder (group of files), create new folders, and open, rename, and print single and multiple files or folders. You will also practice single and multiple file sharing and removing techniques that include copying, moving, creating shortcuts, deleting, and recycling.

Next, you will learn how to control your computer environment by changing an item's properties (characteristics), changing the computer's default settings, and managing your printing.

This chapter concludes with a look at Windows Explorer, another program that you can use to manage your computer. In Explorer, folders and other components of your system are listed in a hierarchal tree. Selecting (marking) a folder (or other item) on the tree will display its contents (files and folders). Commands used with the My Computer program are also available through Explorer.

UNDERSTANDING MY COMPUTER

My Computer is a program that can be used to browse (view) and access all of the components of your computer. You can also use it to access features that will help you manage your files and control your computer settings and printing. As you will soon see, system components are displayed as icons in My Computer's workspace.

LAUNCHING MY COMPUTER

As demonstrated in Chapter 1, the My Computer program is normally launched directly from the desktop, not the *Start* menu. To launch the My Computer program,

STEPS

1 Double-click the *My Computer* icon at the top left corner of the desktop

To resize the window to resemble the Figure WIN2-1,

2 Right-click an empty area of the taskbar for its *Shortcut* menu

3 Click *Cascade*

Your My Computer window should resemble Figure WIN2-1 (the contents of your window may differ).

Although you can work with a window in a variety of sizes and places on the desktop, it is recommended that you resize your window(s) as indicated in the tutorials. This will make it easier to relate them to the corresponding figures.

The My Computer window contains a variety of common Windows features, including a title bar (with a *Program* icon, resizing buttons, and a *Close* button), a menu bar, workspace, and status bar. These items operate the same as in other program windows. Currently occupying its workspace are several drive icons, the *Control Panel* folder and the *Printers* folder.

STORING PROGRAMS AND DOCUMENTS

Before learning how to use My Computer, you should understand how your computer stores programs and documents. Storage media includes disks (hard disk and 3½" or 5¼"

FIGURE WIN2-1 ■ THE MY COMPUTER WINDOW

Double-clicking a *Drive* or *Folder* icon will open its Folder window.

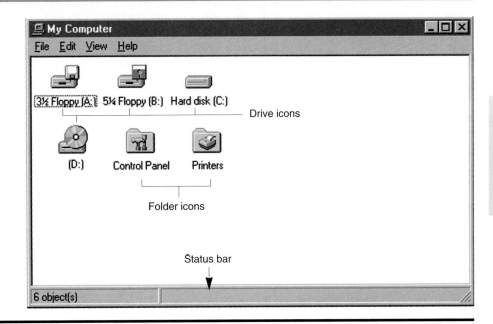

WIN

disks), CD-ROM (a special disk that has *read only memory*), tape, and system memory (RAM or ROM). This text assumes that you are using a hard disk and a 3½″ disk for data. (Note: Windows often refers to 3½″ or 5¼″ disks as floppies.) In addition, any disk can be assigned a **label** (name). Disk labeling is discussed in the "Changing Properties" section of this chapter.

FILES AND FOLDERS.   A *file* is a program or document that is saved on a disk or other storage media. Files are represented by icons and titles (filenames). The number of files that can be stored on a particular storage media depends on its capacity.

A *folder* is a group of related files. Folders may also contain other folders called **subfolders.** In Windows, a disk (or other storage media) is considered a folder. In this manual, the disk will be referred to as the *main folder.* In pre-Windows 95 systems, a folder was called a *directory* and a subfolder was called a *subdirectory.* The main folder was called the *root (or main) directory.*

Note: Throughout this manual, file operations often relate to both files and folders.

FILE AND FOLDER NAMES.   As mentioned earlier, filenames are used to identify documents or programs. Folder names are used to identify groups of files. If you are using DOS-based or pre-Windows 95 programs, you are restricted to filenames with up to 8 characters and an optional 3-character extension. The programs that come with Windows 95 can accept filenames of up to 255 characters.

STORAGE TERMINOLOGY.   Your computer defines the storage volume of a disk in terms of bytes. A **byte** is equivalent to one alphanumeric character (A–Z, 0–9, and so forth). A kilobyte (KB) is one thousand bytes, a megabyte (MB) is one million bytes, and a gigabyte (GB) is one billion bytes.

DRIVES.   A **drive** is a device that reads and/or writes to a storage medium (such as a disk or CD-ROM). As displayed in the My Computer window (Figure WIN2-1), drive icons and letter titles are used to identify each drive in your system. The letter C is normally used to represent the hard drive, the letters A and B represent disk drives, and the letter D is generally used for a CD-ROM. Other letters may be used to identify a network. Your actual configurations may differ.

DISK OPERATIONS

My Computer can be used to perform some basic disk operations including formatting and diagnosing a disk. *Formatting* prepares a disk for use on your computer. Disk diagnostics features can examine a disk for a variety of problems and repair them.

FORMATTING.   Every new disk that is not preformatted must be formatted (organized for your computer) before you can store anything on it. Formatting sets up the disk's folder and file allocation table and divides the disk into addressable storage locations. It will also check for defective tracks on the disk and seal them off from further use. A disk that has been previously formatted can be reformatted. This will, however, delete the disk's files and set up a new blank main folder.

   The data disk that you are currently using is already formatted and should not be reformatted. (Remember, reformatting will erase the entire contents of your disk.) Disk formatting procedures and options have been provided in Figure WIN2-2. Use them only as needed.

> **Tip: When first saving a document on an unformatted disk, Windows will ask if you desire to format the disk.**

DISK DIAGNOSTICS.   Windows offers several disk diagnostic tools to locate and repair a variety of disk problems. These tools are accessible through the *Disk Properties* dialog box and should only be used when needed. See the "Changing Properties" section of this chapter for information on accessing these tools.

FINDING A FILE

The **Find** feature can be used to locate any file in a folder. (Remember, a disk is considered a main folder.) Once located, you can open the file from the lower section of the *Find* dialog box.

FIGURE WIN2-2 ■ FORMATTING A DISK

(a) Procedures to format a disk.
(b) The *Format* dialog box.

Procedures to Format a Disk

Caution: Formatting a disk will erase all of its contents!

1. Launch My Computer

By *Shortcut* Menu

2. Right-click the *3½ Floppy (A:)* drive icon for its *Shortcut* menu
3. Click *Format* for its dialog box

By *File* Menu

2. Click the *3½ Floppy (A:)* drive icon to select it
3. Click *File, Format* for its dialog box

At this point you can select any of the options of the dialog box as indicated in Figure WIN2-2b. In general,

Reformat a Formatted Disk

4. Click *Start* to perform a quick format (the default setting)

Format a New Unformatted Disk

4. Click a *Full* option and then *Start*

A *Format Results* dialog box will appear when the formatting process is completed. This dialog box provides information about the disk. To remove it and return to the *Format* dialog box,

5. Click *Close* (*Format Results* dialog box)

You can now either format another disk by removing the current disk, inserting a new one, and repeating Steps 4 and 5, or you can exit the dialog box. To exit,

6. Click *Close* (*Format* dialog box)

(a)

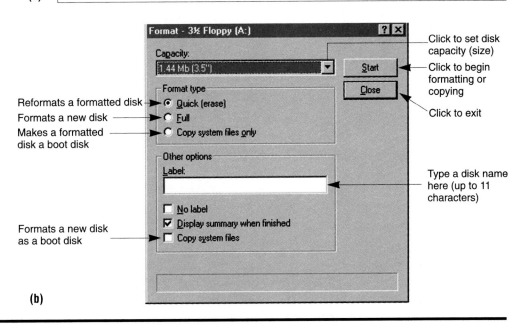

(b)

WIN

INITIAL SEARCH.   To locate the NOTE1 file in the main folder of your data disk,

1 Insert your data disk into Drive A

BY *SHORTCUT* MENU	BY *FILE* MENU
2 Right-click the *3½ Floppy (A:)* drive icon	**2** Click the *3½ Floppy (A:)* drive icon
3 Click (left mouse button) *Find* for its dialog box	**3** Click *File, Find*

The *Find* dialog box should appear as in Figure WIN2-3a. To search for the NOTE1 document,

---

FIGURE WIN2-3 ■ THE *FIND* DIALOG BOX

(a) The *Find* dialog box can be accessed from a *Shortcut* menu or the *File* menu.
(b) The Search results appear at the bottom of the dialog box.

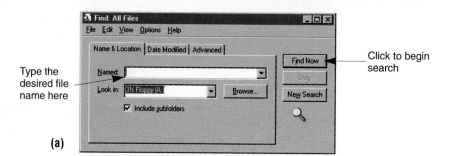

(a)

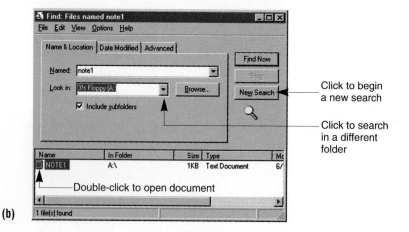

(b)

4   Type **NOTE1** in the *Find* text box

5   Click the *Find Now* button   [↵]

The results of your search will appear at the bottom of the dialog box as in Figure WIN2-3b. To access the file,

 6   Double-click *NOTE1*   [↵]

Your NOTE1 document now appears on your screen in Notepad.

 7   Close Notepad   [Alt + F4]

NEW SEARCH.   To perform another search using the *Find* dialog box you need to first click the *New Search* button. The command will remove the results of the previous search prior to your entering a new find request. Try this to locate the PAD1 file on your data disk:

STEPS

1   Click the *New Search* button

 2   Click the "▼" button of the *Look in* drop-down box

💾 3½ Floppy (A:)   3   Click *3½ Floppy (A:)* in the *Look in* drop-down list

4   Click the *Named* drop-down box to place the insertion point there

(Remember, the insertion point is a vertical blinking line that indicates when the next character you type will appear.)

5   Type **PAD1** in the *Find* text box

6   Click the *Find Now* button   [↵]

The results of your search should appear at the bottom of the dialog box. If desired, you can now open the document by double-clicking it. For now,

 7   Close the *Find* dialog box

LOOKING IN A FOLDER

The *Drive* and *Folder* icons can be used to open Folder windows. **Folder windows** display the contents of a disk (or other storage media) or folders within the disk. Remember, a disk is also considered a folder and will be referred to as the *main folder.*

FOLDER DISPLAY OPTIONS. The My Computer program offers two ways to browse through folders: separate windows for each folder (the default) or a single window that changes to display each folder that is opened. The text assumes that your system is set to the default browse option. Try this to open the Folder window that displays your data disk's main contents:

STEPS

1. If needed, insert your data disk into Drive A

 2. Double-click the *3½ Floppy (A:)* drive icon

 3. If needed, click the *Maximize* button of the 3½ Floppy (A:) window

A 3½ Floppy (A:) window should appear maximized as in Figure WIN2-4a. (The contents of your window may differ.) As you will shortly see, Folder windows can also perform a variety of file management operations.
To check the browse settings of My Computer,

4. Click *View, Options* for its dialog box

Folder 5. If needed, click the *Folder* tab

6. If the *Browse folders using a separate window for each folder* option is selected (black dot in option circle), click the *Cancel* button and skip Step 7

7. If the *Browse folders using a separate window for each folder* option is not selected, click it, and then click *OK*

 Tip: When viewing folders through a single window that changes to display each folder that is opened, you can click the *Up One Level* (see left margin for button) toolbar button to go back one level. The Toolbar must, of course, be on.

TOOLBAR. Like other Windows programs, many menu commands can be accessed through a toolbar. Currently, the My Computer toolbar may not be displayed in your window. If needed, to display the toolbar,

STEPS

1. Click *View, Toolbar*

FIGURE WIN2-4 ■ THE 3½″ FLOPPY (A:) WINDOW

(a) The 3½″ floppy (A:) window is the main folder window of your data disk. (b) Clicking *View, Toolbar* will turn on/off the toolbar. This toolbar is the same for all folder windows, the My Computer window, and the Explorer window. Pointing to a toolbar button displays its title.

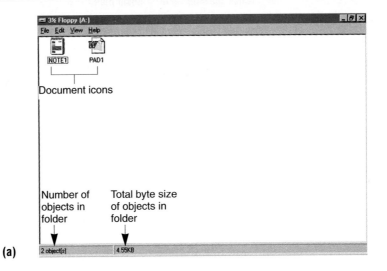

(a)

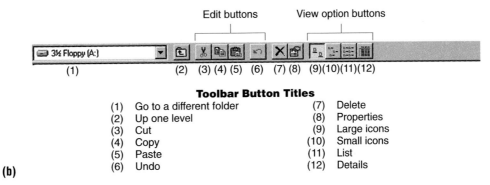

(b)

Toolbar Button Titles

(1) Go to a different folder	(7) Delete
(2) Up one level	(8) Properties
(3) Cut	(9) Large icons
(4) Copy	(10) Small icons
(5) Paste	(11) List
(6) Undo	(12) Details

A toolbar similar to Figure WIN2-4b should appear below your menu bar. The Toolbar command (*View* menu) can be used to turn on/off any folder window's toolbar. This toolbar contains the same features in the My Computer window, Folder windows, and the Explorer window. As with many buttons and drop-down boxes in the Windows environment, pointing to a toolbar item will display its title.

THE STATUS BAR.   The status bar (bottom of window) displays the number of objects (*drive, file,* and *folder* icons) in the workspace and the amount of bytes that those objects occupy on the disk. (The objects and bytes information in your window may differ.) All items in a folder or the My Computer window are referred to as *objects*. The status bar is also used for other messages when using this program. For example, if you open a pull-down menu and point to any of its choices, a brief description of its function will appear in the status bar. Try this:

| 1 | Click *View* for its drop-down menu | [**Alt** + **V**] |

| 2 | Point to (do not click) *Details* | [Do not press **D** ; use arrow keys] |

The message "Displays information about each item in the window." appears in the status bar.

As you use this program or any other program that has a status bar, you will find its brief messages helpful.

VIEWING OPTIONS

The workspace in a Folder window (or My Computer window) can be adjusted to display the icons in a smaller size, in a list, and with more or less detail. These *View* options are available through the *View* menu or toolbar.

1 If needed, click *View, Toolbar* to turn it on

As with many buttons and drop-down boxes in the Windows environment, pointing to a toolbar item will display its title. For example,

2 Point to the last toolbar button on the right and wait (do not click)

The title "Details" should appear.

3 Either click the *Details* toolbar button or click *View, Details* (*Menu* bar)

Your Folder window should now display detailed information on each object similar to Figure WIN2-5a. A *Details bar* appears below the toolbar. Each object's name, size, type, and date and time last modified or created is displayed below this button bar.

Any *Details bar* buttons can be used to switch the display order from ascending to descending (or vice versa) by clicking the button's title. For example,

Name

4 Click the *Name* button on the Details bar

Your objects are now displayed in a reverse alphabetical order by name. To return the display to the original ascending order,

5 Click the *Name* button again

The *Size* button will reverse the order of the display by object size, the *Type* button by object document type, and the *Modified* button by object date and time.

Now try a few other view options:

FIGURE WIN2-5 ■ VIEW OPTIONS

(a) The *Details view* option displays each object's name, size, type, and date and time created or last modified.
(b) The *List view* option lists objects in vertical columns.
(c) The *Small Icons view* option displays objects as small icons in horizontal rows.
(d) The *Large Icons view* option (the default) displays objects as large icons in horizontal rows.

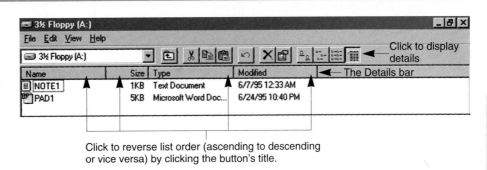

(a)

(b)

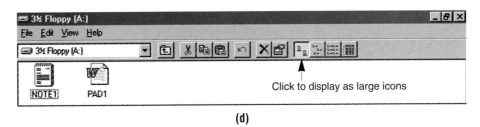

(c)

(d)

WIN

---

6   Click *View, List* to list objects vertically as small icons as in Figure WIN2-5b

7   Click *View, Small Icons* to display objects as small icons horizontally as in Figure WIN2-5c

8   Click *View, Large Icons* to return objects to their original size as in Figure WIN2-5d

View menu options are listed and described in Figure WIN2-6. More advanced *View* options such as *Folder browsing* options, displaying hidden files and MS-DOS file extensions, and file association settings can be controlled by using the *Options* dialog box. Refer to the dialog box's on-line help for these operations.

FIGURE WIN2-6 ■ THE *VIEW* MENU

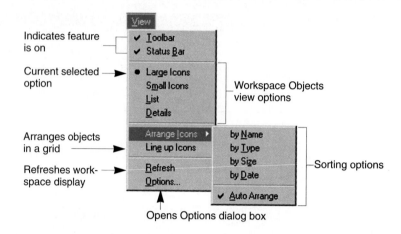

Indicates feature is on

Current selected option

Workspace Objects view options

Arranges objects in a grid

Refreshes work-space display

Sorting options

Opens Options dialog box

☒   9   **Close the 3½ Floppy window**

☒   10   **Close the My Computer window**

☑   CHECKPOINT

✓   Launch My Computer and describe the components of its workspace.
✓   Open a window displaying the contents of your hard-disk drive or network drive.
✓   Turn on the toolbar and change the display to show all details.
✓   Describe the meaning of the details of the first object in the window.
✓   Reset the display to large icons and close the drive and My Computer windows.

MANAGING YOUR FILES

My Computer can be used to perform a variety of file management tasks. **File management** involves organizing and maintaining files (including folders) within your computer environment. This section explores some of the fundamental file management commands. First, you will learn how to create new folders in the main folder and then within other folders. This allows you to group your documents into subgroups (subfolders) within the same disk. Next, you will examine and apply single and multiple selection techniques to open files and folders from a Folder window. You will then practice several object-renaming techniques and print a selection.

1   **Start Windows and remove the "Welcome" window if necessary**

2   **Launch My Computer**

3 Insert your data disk into Drive A if needed

4 Double-click the *3½ Floppy (A:)* drive icon

5 Click the *Maximize* button of the *3½Floppy (A:)*

FOLDERS

Folders are used to group files. A *Folder* icon is used to represent each folder created on a disk. Double-clicking a *Drive* icon in the My Computer window opens a Folder window that displays the main contents of the disk in its drive. (Remember, this text also refers to this folder as the *main folder.*)

Folders can also be created within folders. Double-clicking a folder within a Folder window displays its contents in another Folder window.

CREATING A NEW FOLDER.   To create the folders *Database, WIN 95, Word Processing,* and *Spreadsheets* as in Figure WIN2-7:

STEPS

1 Click *File* for its menu as in Figure WIN2-8a

This *File* menu appears when no objects are selected (marked) in the window.

2 Point to *New* for its submenu and then click *Folder*

A new folder appears in the 3½ Floppy window. Note that its title is highlighted, indicating that whatever you enter next will type over the text in the highlighted area.

3 Type Database and then press ↵

4 Click *File* for its menu as in Figure WIN2-8b

Tip: If desired, pressing an arrow key when text is highlighted (selected) will remove the highlight.

FIGURE WIN2-7 ■ CREATING FOLDERS

You can use the *File* menu or the workspace *Shortcut* menu to create new folders.

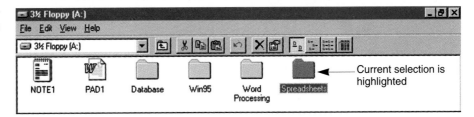

FIGURE WIN2-8 ■ *FILE* **MENUS AND** *WORKSPACE SHORTCUT* **MENU**

(a) The *File* menu when no objects are selected.
(b) The *File* menu when at least one object is selected.
(c) The *Workspace Shortcut* menu.

(a)

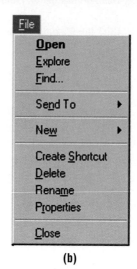

(b)

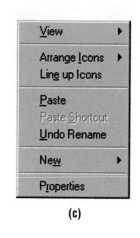

(c)

This *File* menu appears when at least one object is selected in the window's workspace. It offers a few more commands that you can invoke on the selected object(s). Currently, the *Database* folder is selected (notice that its title and icon are highlighted).

5 Point to *New*, and then click *Folder* to create another new folder

6 Type   WIN 95   and then press ↵

Now try using a *Shortcut* menu to create the next folder.

7 Right-click an empty area of the 3½ Floppy window's workspace for its *Shortcut* menu as in Figure WIN2-8c

8 Point to *New*, and then click *Folder* to create another new folder

9 Type   Word Processing   and then press ↵

10 Create the *Spreadsheets* folder using either the *File* menu or a *Shortcut* menu

These new *Folder* icons should now occupy the workspace of the 3½ Floppy window similar to Figure WIN2-7. Again, your workspace may differ depending on the objects you have on your disk.

FOLDERS WITHIN FOLDERS.   To create a subfolder (folder within a folder), first open the folder that you would like to contain the subfolder. Opening a folder displays its contents in a window. You will now create the folders *Roster* and *Consult* within the *Database* folder as in Figure WIN2-9a.

FIGURE WIN2-9 ■ CREATING FOLDERS WITHIN FOLDERS

(a) and (b) To create a folder within a folder, first open the folder that is to contain the subfolder(s) and then use the *File* menu or *Shortcut* menu to create the subfolders.

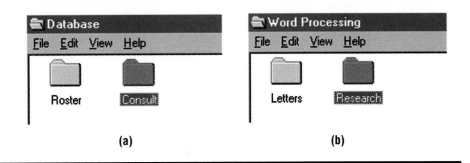

(a)   (b)

STEPS

Database

1 Double-click the *Database* folder

> **Tip:** You can also open a folder by clicking it and then clicking *File*, *Open* or by right-clicking it and then clicking *Open*.

2 Click the *Maximize* button of the Database window

The Database window opens with a blank workspace. This window operates the same way as any other Folder window.

3 Click *File*, point to *New*, and then click *Folder*

4 Type Roster and then press ↵

Now use the workspace *Shortcut* menu to create the folder *Consult*.

5 Right-click an empty area of the Database window's workspace for its *Shortcut* menu

6 Point to *New* and then click *Folder*

7 Type Consult and then press ↵

The new folders in the Database window should now resemble Figure WIN2-9a.

8 Close the Database window

Next, you will create the folders *Letters* and *Research* in the Word Processing folder as in Figure WIN2-9b.

Word
Processing

NOTE2

9 Double-click the *Word Processing* folder and then maximize it

10 Create the folders *Letters* and *Research* within the Word Processing folder

11 Close the Word Processing window

Before continuing, rearrange the objects in alphabetical order by name.

12 Click *View*, point to *Arrange Icon* for its submenu

The *Arrange Icon* submenu has a variety of sorting options. For now,

13 Click *by Name* to rearrange icons in alphabetical order

Note that Windows displays folder icons first.

DOCUMENT APPROACH

To create a new saved document without first launching its program, use the *New* submenu that you just used to create folders. (Note: The related program or document type must be listed in the submenu.) Try this to create a new text (Notepad) document:

BY *SHORTCUT* MENU

1 Right-click an empty area of the workspace for its *Shortcut* menu

2 Point to *New* and then click *Text Document*

BY *FILE* MENU

1 Click *File*

A *New Text Document* icon appears in the 3½ Floppy window workspace. This document is already saved, however, it is blank. To name this document NOTE2 and then open it,

NOTE2

3 Type NOTE2 and press ↵

4 Double-click the *NOTE2* icon

Note that text documents generally open in the Notepad program. Next you will enter the following text and then save and close the document.

5 Type The New submenu can be used to create a new saved document without first launching its program.

6 Click *File*, *Save*

7 Close the Notepad window

SELECTING MULTIPLE FILES

Selecting, as defined earlier, is the process of marking items. Once marked, you can invoke a variety of commands on them. Remember, file selection techniques apply to both files and folders. To select a file, simply click it. To select additional files, press and hold the Ctrl key while clicking each additional file (or other objects). You may also select files in a block. A **block** is a set of contiguous files (or other objects). To select a block of files, click the first file and then press and hold the Shift key while clicking the last file in the block. A block can be selected alone or with other selected files. Figure WIN2-10 summarizes object selection techniques used in the next section.

> **Tip:** Clicking *Edit, Invert Selection* reverses the items selected with those that are not. Clicking *Edit, Select All* or press Ctrl + A selects all files in a window.

OPENING FILES

In general, a document created and saved with a Window program is automatically **associated** (has a special connection) to its program. As such, you directly open such documents

---

FIGURE WIN2-10 ■ OBJECT SELECTION TECHNIQUES

(a) Selecting one object.
(b) Selecting a group of objects.
(c) Selecting a block of objects.

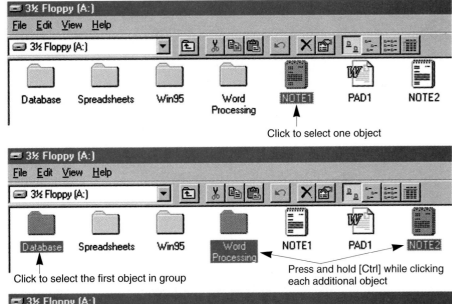

(a)

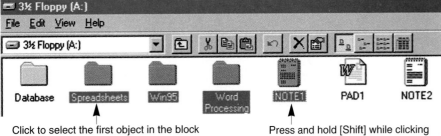

(b)

(c)

(along with their programs) from a Folder window without first launching their programs. This method provides quicker access to your document if you know the folder in which it was stored. The open techniques discussed in this section can be applied to single or multiple files (a group or block). Files include documents, programs, and folders. Like opening a folder, opening a document or launching a program involves double-clicking its icon or using its *Shortcut* menu or the *File* menu. To open (or launch) folders or multiple documents and programs, select their icons and then click *File, Open* (from the menu bar).

SINGLE FILE.   The quickest way to open any object in a window is to double-click it. However, you can also use the object's *Shortcut* menu or the *File* menu. To open the NOTE1 document using either of these techniques:

STEPS

NOTE1

BY *SHORTCUT* MENU

1 Right click *NOTE1*

2 Click *Open*

BY *FILE* MENU

1 Click the *NOTE1* icon to select it as in Figure WIN2-10a

2 Click *File, Open*

Your NOTE1 document now appears in the Notepad window (its program).

3 Close Notepad

GROUP OF FILES.   To open (or launch) a group of files at once, first select the group and then use the Open command of the *File* menu. Try this to open the *Database* folder, *Word Processing* folder, and NOTE2 document.

STEPS

Database

1 Click the *Database* folder (the first object in the group)

2 Press and hold Ctrl while clicking the *Word Processing* folder icon and then the *NOTE2* file icon

Your selected group should resemble Figure WIN2-10b.

3 Click *File, Open* to open the objects

All three objects are now open.

4 Close the Database, Word Processing, and NOTE2 (Notepad) windows

BLOCK OF FILES.   Like opening a group of files, opening a block of files involves first selecting the block and then clicking *File, Open.* To open the *Spreadsheet, Win95, Word Processing* folders, and NOTE1 document:

STEPS

Spreadsheets

1 Click the *Spreadsheets* folder icon

2 Press and hold   Shift   while clicking the *NOTE1* icon

Your block selection should resemble Figure WIN2-10c. Now, to open the objects,

3 Click *File, Open*   [↵]

All four objects should now be open on your screen.

4 Close all windows except the My Computer and 3½ Floppy windows

RENAMING FILES

Any file or folder can be easily renamed using the same techniques. You can use an object's *Shortcut* menu or *File* menu to rename it. When using the *File* menu, you must first select the object. Try this to rename the *Spreadsheets* folder to *Worksheets:*

BY *SHORTCUT* MENU	BY *FILE* MENU
Spreadsheets	
1 Right-click the *Spreadsheets* folder icon for its *Shortcut* menu	**1** Click the *Spreadsheets* folder icon to select it
2 Click *Rename*	**2** Click *File, Rename*

Note that the folder's title is now highlighted (selected). The first alphanumeric character you type will delete the old title.

3 Type   Worksheets   and then press ↵

A more direct technique to rename an object is to click its title after it has been selected. Try this to change the *Win95* folder to *Windows 95:*

Win95

4 Click the *Win95* folder icon to select it

5 Click the *Win95* title

The folder's title is now selected and ready to be changed.

WIN

FIGURE WIN2-11 ■ RENAMING FILES

The *Spreadsheet* and *Win95* folders have been renamed *Worksheet* and *Windows 95,* respectively.

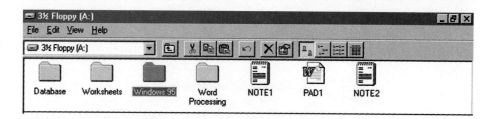

The icons in your 3½ Floppy window should resemble Figure WIN2-11.

PRINTING FILES

Document files can be printed using a Folder window. Simply select the desired file icon(s) and then invoke the print command from the *File* menu. Try this to print the NOTE1 and NOTE2 documents:

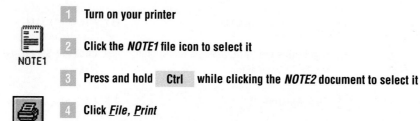

1 Turn on your printer

2 Click the *NOTE1* file icon to select it

3 Press and hold ``Ctrl`` while clicking the *NOTE2* document to select it

4 Click *File, Print*

As you wait, Windows first opens each document with its program, prints them, and then closes the document and its program.

To print a single document, it is generally quicker to use its *Shortcut* menu. For example, to print the NOTE2 document,

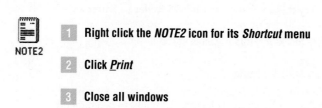

1 Right click the *NOTE2* icon for its *Shortcut* menu

2 Click *Print*

3 Close all windows

CHECKPOINT

 ✓ Launch My Computer and open the 3½ Floppy window.
 ✓ Print the NOTE1 document.
 ✓ Create a folder with your name on it.
 ✓ Open the folder and create two more folders named *Computers* and *Accounting*.
 ✓ Rename the *Accounting* folder *Art*. Close all windows.

WIN

SHARING AND REMOVING YOUR FILES

Sharing files involves copying or moving documents, programs, and folders within the same folder or between folders. Remember, *copying* is the process of duplicating a selection into a new location and *moving* relocates it there. In Windows, you can also create an icon (called a **Shortcut icon**) that has a link (special connection) to the original file or folder. This allows you to open the original document or folder or to launch the original program from the desktop or another folder.

 After practicing sharing techniques you will learn how to use the Undo command to undo your last action, and the Delete command to remove unwanted files. You will then learn about Windows **Recycle Bin,** a program that stores references to files deleted from other places on your hard disk and desktop.

STEPS

 1 **If needed, start Windows and remove the "Welcome" screen**

 2 **Launch My Computer**

 3 **Insert your data disk into Drive A**

 4 **Double-click the *3½ Floppy (A:)* drive icon for its Folder window**

 5 **If needed, maximize the window and turn on the toolbar (*View, Toolbar*)**

 6 **Click *View*, point to *Arrange Icons*, and then click *by Name* to sort by name**

COPYING AND MOVING

The exercises in this section explore a variety of techniques used to copy or move files and folders. They include using the Copy, Cut, and Paste commands of the *Edit* menu or *Shortcut* menus as well as drag and drop techniques. The folder from which a selection is copied or cut (moved) will be called the *source folder*. The folder in which it is

FIGURE WIN2-12 ■ SHARING FILES SUMMARY

The following techniques assume that you have already launched My Computer and your source folder is opened.

With the Same Folder

Edit Menu	Drag and Drop
1. Select objects 2. Click *Edit, Cut* (to move), or *Copy* 3. Click *Edit, Paste*	1. Select the objects 2. Press and hold [Ctrl] while dragging and dropping the selection to copy it to a new location in the workspace (or simply drag and drop to move)

Between Folders in the Same Disk

Edit Menu	Drag and Drop
1. Select objects 2. Click *Edit, Cut* (to move), or *Copy* 3. Double-click the destination folder icon to open it 4. Click *Edit, Paste*	1. Open the destination folder window 2. Right-click an empty area of the taskbar for its *Shortcut* menu, and then click *Minimize All Windows* 3. Click the taskbar buttons of the source and destination folder windows 4. Right-click an empty area of the taskbar, and then click *Tile Vertically* 5. Select the objects 6. Press and hold [Ctrl] while dragging and dropping the selection from its source to its destination folder to copy (or simply drag and drop to move)

Between Folders of Different Disks

Edit Menu	Drag and Drop
1. Select objects 2. Click *Edit, Cut* (to move), or *Copy* 3. Click the *My Computer* taskbar button to switch to it 4. Open the destination folder 5. Click *Edit, Paste*	1. Click the *My Computer* taskbar button to switch to it 2. Open destination folder window 3. Right-click an empty area of the taskbar for its *Shortcut* menu, and then click *Minimize All Windows* 4. Click the taskbar buttons of the source and destination folder windows 5. Right-click an empty area of the taskbar, and then click *Tile Vertically* 6. Select objects 7. Drag and drop the selection from its source to its destination folder to copy (or press and hold [Alt] while dragging and dropping to move)

pasted (placed) in will be called the *destination folder*. Figure WIN2-12 presents a summary of sharing techniques. You should try all the techniques and then use the one that feels most comfortable to you.

WITHIN THE SAME FOLDER.   To copy or move a selection of files (and folders) within the same folder, simply copy it to the Clipboard and then paste it into your destination folder. When copying or moving within the same folder, the source and destination folders are the same.

To create a copy of the NOTE1 document on the same disk as in Figure WIN2-13,

STEPS

NOTE1

1 Click the *NOTE1* icon to select it

2 Click *Edit, Copy*

(To move the selection, click *Cut* (or **Ctrl** + **X**), instead of *Copy* (or **Ctrl** + **C**) in Step 2.) The selection is now copied to the Clipboard for future pasting. (The Cut command moves the selection onto the Clipboard.) To paste (copy the selection from the Clipboard) it within the workspace of the 3½ Floppy window,

3 Click *Edit, Paste*

A document icon appears titled *Copy of NOTE1,* as in Figure WIN2-13. At this point you can rename the copy if desired.

BETWEEN FOLDERS.   A selection of files can also be copied or moved to another folder using the Copy and Paste commands. The folder can be within the same disk or in another disk. The only difference is that the destination folder is on another disk. Only copying or moving files between folders on the same disk is demonstrated. See Figure WIN2-12 for procedures to share files between folders of different disks.

To copy the *Windows 95* folder, NOTE1, and PAD1 documents to the *Letters* folder within the *Word Processing* folder as in Figure WIN2-14:

STEPS

Windows 95

1 Click the *Windows 95* folder to select it

FIGURE WIN2-13 ■ COPYING WITHIN THE SAME FOLDER

When copying within the same folder, Windows adds the words "Copy of" before the copied file's name.

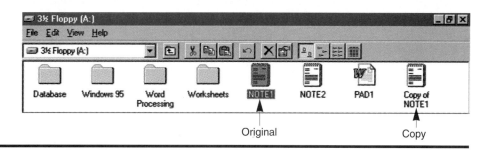

These objects have been
copied from the main folder
to the Letters subfolder.

2 **Press and hold** Ctrl **while clicking the *NOTE1* and then the *PAD1* icons to select them**

(Remember, pressing and holding the Ctrl key while clicking allows you to select additional icons.)

3 **Click *Edit, Copy*** [Ctrl + C]

(To move the selection, click *Cut* (or Ctrl + X), instead of *Copy* (or Ctrl + C)
in Step 2.)

4 **Double-click the *Word Processing* folder to open its window**

Word
Processing

5 **If desired, click *View, Toolbar***

BY *SHORTCUT* MENU

Letters

6 **Right-click the *Letters* folder for its *Short-cut* menu**

7 **Click *Paste***

BY *EDIT* MENU

6 **Double-click the *Letters* folder to open its window**

The folder must be open to paste by the *Edit* menu. Menu bar or Toolbar commands normally only affect the current window.

7 **Click *Edit, Paste*** [Ctrl + V]

The selection is now copied to the Letters directory. If you used the *Shortcut* menu to paste, you will need to perform Step 8 to view the copies in the *Letters* folder.

Letters

8 **If needed, double-click the *Letters* folder to open it**

The contents of your Letters window should resemble Figure WIN2-14 (your window size may differ). Note that the selection has been copied with its original name. Windows uses the original file or folder name when copying to a different folder.

 　9　 **Close the Letters and Word Processing windows**

BY DRAGGING AND DROPPING.   Drag and drop techniques involve copying or moving a selection by moving your pointer (with the selection) to a new location, sometimes with the use of other keys. In the next exercise you will copy a block of objects from your main folder (the 3½ Floppy window) to the *Consult* folder using the drag and drop technique. Remember, a *block* is a contiguous set of selected objects. The block you will copy to the *Consult* folder begins with the *Worksheets* folder icon and ends with the *NOTE1* file icon. When copied, it should appear in the Consult folder window as in Figure WIN2-15:

STEPS

　1　 **Open your 3½ Floppy window, if needed**

　2　 **Double-click the *Database* folder icon**

Database

Note that the source folder and destination folder windows must be in view to use the drag and drop technique. To display only the 3½ Floppy (source folder) and Database (destination folder) windows without closing the My Computer window,

　3　 **Right-click an empty space in the taskbar for its *Shortcut* menu (use the space between the *Database* taskbar button and the time message area)**

　4　 **Click *Minimize All Windows* to reduce them to their taskbar buttons**

FIGURE WIN2-15 ■ DRAGGING AND DROPPING

These objects were copied from the main folder by pressing and holding the Ctrl key while dragging and dropping.

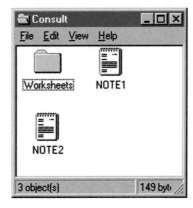

Remember, minimized windows are still running, but at a minimum state. This allows you to access them quickly without relaunching or opening. It also conserves system memory (RAM), which will make your system operate more efficiently. Now open only the 3½ Floppy and Database windows and then horizontally tile them as in Figure WIN2-16.

5 Click the *3½ Floppy (A:)* taskbar button to open its window

6 Click the *Database* taskbar button to open its window

7 Right-click an empty area of the taskbar for its *Shortcut* menu and then click *Tile Horizontally*

Your screen should resemble Figure WIN2-16. Both source and destination are in view.

8 Click the *Worksheets* folder icon (the first object in the block)

9 Press and hold   **Shift**   while clicking the *NOTE1* icon (the last object in the block)

(To select large objects in a block, they must be displayed horizontally.)

10 Point to any object in the selection

FIGURE WIN2-16 ■ TILING SOURCE AND DESTINATION FOLDERS

The taskbar *Shortcut* menu can be used to tile the source and destination folders to better view them in drag and drop sharing operations.

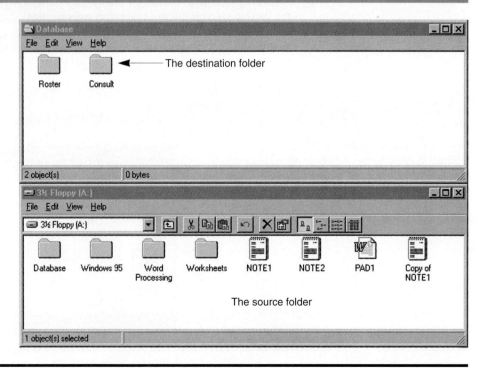

11 Press and hold **Ctrl** while dragging the selection to the *Consult* folder icon

(To move instead of copy, do not press and hold the Ctrl key while dragging in Step 11.)

12 Drop the selection into the *Consult* folder icon

Consult

13 Double-click the *Consult* folder icon to display its content as in Figure WIN2-15.

14 Close all windows

COPYING AN ENTIRE DISK.   The *Copy Disk* dialog box (Figure WIN2-17) can be used to copy the contents of an entire disk to another disk. It is accessible through the **Copy Disk** command of the *My Computer* file menu (after selecting the desired drive icon) or the desired drive icon's *Shortcut* menu. When using this command, the Copy from disk must be the same size and capacity as the Copy to disk. For example, if the original disk is a 3½″ 1.44MB disk, the Copy to disk must also be a 3½″ 1.44MB disk.

SENDING FILES.   The **Send to** submenu, as in Figure WIN2-18, can be used to copy a selection to another disk, fax, or electronic mail. To use this feature, simply select the items that you desire to send, click *File,* point to *Send to,* and click the desired destination option. The Send to menu can be customized to include destinations other than the default options. It is also available through *Shortcut* menus. Refer to your on-line help for these procedures.

CREATING A SHORTCUT

A *Shortcut icon* can be created that has a dynamic link to its original document, program, or folder. This link allows you to use the *Shortcut* icon to open (launch) the file or folder it represents from any folder or the desktop.

FIGURE WIN2-17 ■ **THE *COPY DISK* DIALOG BOX**

The *Copy Disk* dialog box can be used to copy the entire contents of one disk to another of the same capacity.

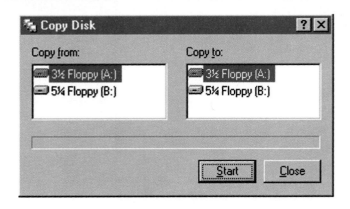

The *Send to* menu is
available in the *File* menu
after a selection is made. It
can be used to send the
selection to any of its listed
destinations.

PLACING SHORTCUTS IN A FOLDER.   To create shortcut icons for the *Windows 95* folder, place the *Copy of NOTE1* documents in the Worksheets folder as in Figure WIN2-19:

STEPS

1 **Launch My Computer**

2 **Insert your data disk and double-click the *3½ Floppy (A:)* drive icon**

Windows 95

3 **Click the *Windows 95* folder icon to select it**

4 **Press and hold Ctrl while clicking the *Copy of NOTE1* file icon to select it**

5 **Click *Edit, Copy***   [**Ctrl** + **C**]

To create a shortcut icon, use
the Copy and then the Paste
Shortcut commands.

Worksheets

6 Double-click the *Worksheets* folder to open it

7 Click *Edit, Paste Shortcut*

8 Click *View*, point to *Arrange Icons*, and then click by *Name*

Shortcut icons now appear in the Worksheets folder window as in Figure WIN2-19. You can use these icons to open the folder or files they represent from the Worksheet folder. Try this:

Shortcut to Copy of NOTE1

9 Double-click the *Copy of NOTE1* Shortcut icon to open it

10 Close the Copy of NOTE1 (Notepad) and Worksheets folder windows

PLACING SHORTCUTS ON THE DESKTOP.   If you are on a network, your system may not allow you to create a shortcut on the desktop. Check with your instructor before proceeding with the next steps.

To create a shortcut for the *Windows 95* folder on the desktop as in Figure WIN2-20,

STEPS

Windows 95

1 Click *Windows 95* to select it

2 Click *Edit, Copy*   [**Ctrl** + **C**]

3 Right-click an empty area of the taskbar for its *Shortcut* menu

4 Click *Minimize All Windows* for a better view of the desktop

5 Right click the area to the right of the *My Computer* icon (or any desired area) on the desktop

FIGURE WIN2-20 ■ **CREATING A SHORTCUT ON THE DESKTOP**

Once an object is copied to the Clipboard, it can also be pasted as a shortcut on the desktop. Simply right-click an empty area of the desktop and then click *Paste Shortcut*.

6 Click *Paste Shortcut*

Your *Shortcut* icons should now appear on your desktop (selected) similar to Figure WIN2-20. (The actual positions of your *Shortcut* icons may differ.) At this point, you can double-click the *Shortcut* icon to open its linked folder (or file). Unless deleted, *Shortcut* icons will appear on your desktop each time you start Windows. For now, to delete the *Shortcut* icon for the *Windows 95* folder:

7 If needed, select the *Windows 95* folder's *Shortcut* icon on the desktop

8 Press   Delete

9 Click *Yes*

> Note: File deletion is discussed further under the "Deleting and Recycling" section of this chapter.

10 Click the *My Computer* icon and then the *3½ Floppy* taskbar buttons to resize them to a window

USING UNDO

Most Windows programs provide an **Undo** command that can be used to undo your last action. The My Computer program also provides an undo command. Try this:

STEPS

1 Switch to the 3½ Floppy window (Click its title bar or any open area of the window.)

2 Copy the PAD1 document into the same window

(Remember, right-click PAD1, click *Copy,* and then click *Edit, Paste.*) A copy of your PAD1 document now appears. To undo this action,

3 Click *Edit, Undo Copy*   [**Ctrl** + **Z**]

A *Confirm File Delete* dialog box appears asking "Are you sure you want to delete 'Copy of PAD1'?" For now,

4 Click *Yes*

The Undo command deletes the copy of PAD1.

The Undo command is a handy tool, but it is limited as to the types of actions it will undo.

DELETING AND RECYCLING

Any selection in Windows can be deleted. The **Delete** command removes a selection from its current place and can be invoked from the *File* menu or an object's *Shortcut* menu. As seen earlier, you can also invoke the Delete command by simply pressing the Delete key. When deleting a selection from your hard disk or network disk, the file's reference is normally relocated to the *Recycle Bin* (a Windows program that stores file references as a result of invoking the Delete command) without actually deleting the file. Once there, you can either permanently delete the selection or restore it. Deleting a *Shortcut* icon will not affect the original file.

DELETING SELECTIONS   The process of deleting a selection from a data disk and hard disk is the same. Try this:

STEPS

1 Select the *Windows 95* folder, *Worksheets* folder, and *Copy of NOTE1* file icons

(Remember to press and hold the Ctrl key when selecting each additional icon.)

2 Click *File, Delete*   [**Delete**   ]

A dialog box appears asking you to confirm the deletion. To delete these objects,

3 Click *Yes*

Your 3½ Floppy window should appear as in Figure WIN2-21.

 4 Close all windows

> **Tip:** Deleting icons from the desktop requires using the Delete key or its *Shortcut* menu.

RECYCLING.   Selections deleted from a hard disk are removed from their folder, the desktop, or other location and relocated to the Recycle Bin. Once there, you can either

FIGURE WIN2-21 ■ **DELETING FILES**

The *Windows 95* folder, *Worksheets* folder, and *Copy of NOTE1* file icons have been deleted from the main folder.

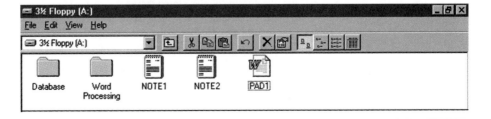

restore or permanently delete the files. See the Recycle Bin operations listed in Figure WIN2-22.

DELETED, BUT GONE FOREVER?   A final note about deleting. When you delete a file, Windows does not really remove it from the disk. It simply replaces the first character in its filename with a special initial character. This character tells the system to ignore the file and use its space allocation, even though the file is still physically left on the disk. Although its name does not appear in a folder, the file's contents are not written over until another file is saved on the disk. This opens the possibility of *undeleting* files (even those deleted from the Recycle Bin). As long as you have not copied or saved another file on the disk, Windows has a utility program called Undelete to help you identify the deleted files and put them back in their original folders—in effect *undeleting* them. The Undelete (MWUNDEL) program is located in the Applications group on the *Programs* menu. Refer to your on-line help to use this program.

☑ **CHECKPOINT**

✓ Describe the different techniques that can be used to copy or move files.
✓ Launch My Computer and open the main folder window of your data disk.
✓ Copy all your files and folders into the folder with your name (created in the previous checkpoint.)

FIGURE WIN2-22 ■ RECYCLE BIN OPERATIONS

When invoking the Delete command to remove a file(s) from your hard-disk folder, the selection's reference is moved from its current position to the Recycle Bin. At this point, you can either restore or permanently delete the file(s) from the Recycle Bin.

Restoring Files	Deleting Files from the Recycle Bin
1. If Needed, minimize all windows 2. Double-click the *Recycle Bin* icon 3. Select the desired file(s) to restore 4. Click *File, Restore* 5. Close the *Recycle Bin*	1. If needed, minimize all windows 2. Double-click the *Recycle Bin* icon 3. Select the desired file(s) to delete 4. Click *File, Delete*

Emptying the Recycle Bin

Because each file deleted from your hard-disk folder is automatically moved to the Recycle Bin, the quantity of files stored there can grow over time if not deleted. The Empty Recycle Bin command can be used to delete the bin's entire contents.

1. If needed, minimize all windows
2. Right-click the *Recycle Bin* icon
3. Click *Empty Recycle Bin*

Note: When deleting a folder from your hard-disk folder, the files deleted within the folder are listed individually in the Recycle Bin.

✓ Create a *Shortcut* icon for the folder with your name in your main folder and then close My Computer.
✓ Describe the Recycle Bin.

CONTROLLING YOUR ENVIRONMENT

You can adjust the default settings of most items in your Windows environment. **Default settings** are the normal settings of your environment. An item's **properties** include the way information and other attributes (characteristics) are displayed or set. The Change Properties command can alter most objects' default characteristics. The **Control Panel** contains tools to set various parts of your system, including adding and removing hardware drivers (programs that help a piece of hardware communicate with your computer), screen displays, fonts, and so forth. These tools are also in the form of *Properties* dialog boxes. Another folder that can be accessed through My Computer is called **Printers.** This folder allows you to add a new printer, switch printers (if you have installed more than one printer), and check and control the status of your current print jobs.

> **Tip:** As seen in Chapter 1, you can also use the *Settings* submenu (*Start* menu) to access the Control Panel, Printers program, and *Taskbar Properties* dialog box.

CHANGING PROPERTIES

You can view and adjust almost any object's properties in Windows. The quickest way to open an object's *Properties* dialog box is to right click it and then click *Properties*. To better understand this topic, you will examine a disk's properties, file and folder properties, and the taskbar and *Start* menu properties.

DISK PROPERTIES.   To examine the properties of a disk,

STEPS

1 **Start Windows and remove the "Welcome" screen if necessary**

2 **Launch My Computer**

3 **Insert your data disk into Drive A if needed**

4 **Right-click the *3½ Floppy* drive icon and then click *Properties***

A *3½ Floppy (A:) Properties* dialog box similar to Figure WIN2-23a should appear. It displays the name, type of disk, used and free space in bytes, and total capacity of the disk (your dialog box may differ). At this point you can change the label (name) of the disk. Try this:

5 In the *Label* text box type your last name (maximum of 11 characters without spaces)

6 Click the *Apply* button

The *Apply* button invokes your latest adjustment and keeps the dialog box open, where-as the *OK* button invokes your latest adjustments and exits the dialog box.

A *Disk's Properties* dialog box also offers a variety of diagnostic tools in its *Tools* tab. For example,

7 Click the *Tools* tab

The *Tools* tab should appear as in Figure WIN2-23b. Examine the options presented in the tab. At this point, you can launch any of these diagnostic programs by clicking their respective buttons. These diagnostic programs should be used as needed. For now,

8 Click the *Cancel* button to exit the dialog box

FILE AND FOLDER PROPERTIES. File and folder properties are similar. To illustrate their *Properties* dialog boxes,

STEPS

1 Double-click the *3½ Floppy (A:)* drive icon

FIGURE WIN2-23 ■ **THE 3½ FLOPPY (A:) PROPERTIES DIALOG BOX**

(a) The *General* tab can be used to name (label) a disk. It also provides used/free space and total disk capacity information.

(b) The *Tools* tab can be used to launch diagnostic and backup programs.

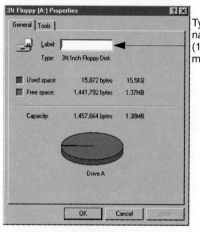

(a)

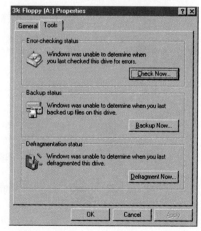

(b)

Word Processing

2 **Right-click the *Word Processing* folder and then click *Properties***

Your dialog box should appear similar to Figure WIN2-24a.

3 **Click the *Cancel* button**

NOTE1

4 **Right-click the *NOTE1* icon and then click *Properties***

Your dialog box should appear as in Figure WIN2-24b. Note that the information in both dialog boxes (refer to Figures WIN2-24a and 24b) are similar. In addition, you may change the attributes of the folder or file to Read-only, Hidden, Archive, or System (if available). The *Read-only* check box will protect a folder or file from being written on. The *Hidden* check box will hide the folder or file from the current Folder window display. The *Archive* check box will provide a backup of the folder or file, and the *System* check box will save the file as a systems file. Clicking an empty check box places a "✓" in it, indicating that the feature is on. Clicking it again will turn the feature off.

5 **5.   Close all windows**

TASKBAR AND START MENU PROPERTIES.   The *Taskbar Properties* dialog box can be used to change the properties of the taskbar and the *Start Menu Programs* menu.

STEPS

1 **Right-click an empty area of the taskbar and then click *Properties***

FIGURE WIN2-24 ■ *FOLDERS* AND *FILE PROPERTIES* DIALOG BOXES

(a) The *Word Processing Folder Properties* dialog box.
(b) The *NOTE1 File Properties* dialog box.

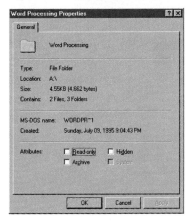

(a)   (b)

Your *Taskbar Properties* dialog box should appear as in Figure WIN2-25a. It has two tabs: *Taskbar Options* and *Start Menu Programs*. As with any check box a "✓" in the box indicates that a feature is on. For example, the *Always on top* and *Show Clock* check boxes each have "✓". These are the default settings. To turn a feature on or off, simply click its check box.

2 **Click the *Start Menu Programs* tab**

As in Figure WIN2-25b, you can use this tab to add, remove, or edit programs from the *Programs* menu of the *Start* menu. If you desire, you can use this tab to customize your *Programs* menu. You can also use this tab to clear the contents of the *Documents* submenu. Remember, the *Documents* submenu lists the last 15 documents you worked on. For now,

3 **Click *Cancel* to exit the dialog box**

RESIZING AND MOVING THE TASKBAR. The taskbar can be enlarged to display Window Taskbar buttons in two rows. To enlarge it, point to its top border until the pointer appears as a double-headed arrow, and then drag up. To resize the taskbar to its original size, drag the top border down. To move the taskbar, simply point to an open area along the bar, and then drag and drop it into its new location.

USING THE CONTROL PANEL

The Control Panel is a program that can be used to change the settings on your computer. It operates similarly to any Folder window. To launch the Control Panel as in Figure WIN2-26,

---

FIGURE WIN2-25 ■ THE TASKBAR PROPERTIES

(a) The *Taskbar Options* tab can be used to change the appearance of the taskbar.
(b) The *Start Menu Programs* tab can be used to add, remove, or edit the *Programs* submenu. It can also be used to clear the *Documents* submenu.

Indicates features are on (the default)

Indicates features are off

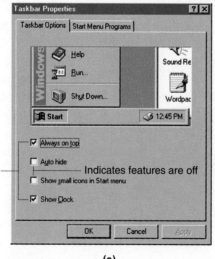

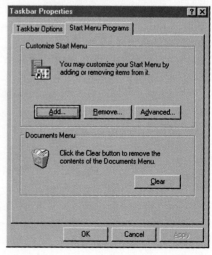

(a)

(b)

STEPS

1   **Launch My Computer**

Control Panel

2   **Double-click the *Control Panel* folder icon**

3   **If desired, click *View, Toolbar* to turn the toolbar on**

4   **Click the *Maximize* button of the Control Panel window**

> **Tip: The Control Panel can also be opened by clicking the *Start* button, pointing to *Settings*, and then clicking *Control Panel*.**

The *Control Panel* folder should appear as in Figure WIN2-26. Most icons in this window open to other windows that allow you to set the feature that you desire.

To better understand changing system settings, the following exercises provide procedures to change your system's date and time, alter its screen display, and add new hardware.

CHANGING DATE AND TIME.   To change your system's date and time,

STEPS

1   **Double-click the *Date/Time* icon**

FIGURE WIN2-26 ■ THE CONTROL PANEL

The Control Panel can be used to adjust the settings on a system.

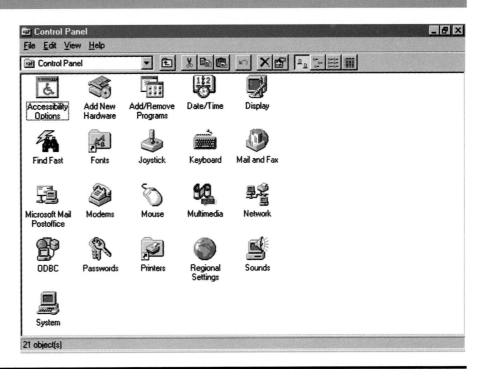

The *Date/Time Properties* dialog box should appear as in Figure WIN2-27. Your date and time will differ. This dialog box can be used to adjust your system's date and time if needed. For now,

2   **Click the *Cancel* button**

> **Tip:** To access this dialog box quickly, double-click the time message at the right side of the taskbar.

DISPLAY OPTIONS.   Four screen display properties can be set through the *Display Properties* dialog box. They include Background, Screen Saver, Appearance, and Settings. Background changes involve placing or replacing an image as the background screen of your desktop. Screen savers help prevent the "burning in" of a frequently used program's image on your monitor's screen. Appearance changes involve setting the color of items displayed in Windows. Settings choices pertain to the quality of the color and resolution of all displays in Windows. Each property has its own tab in the *Display Properties* dialog box. Only the *Background* tab is demonstrated next. Other tabs operate similarly. If you are operating your own computer, you may desire to use this dialog box to customize your screen displays. Check with your instructor before performing the next step.

STEPS

Display

1   **Double-click the *Display* icon**

Your dialog box should appear similar to Figure WIN2-28. The *Background* tab allows you to place a pattern or wallpaper as the background display of your desktop. Note that the default setting is "None." Your settings may differ.

FIGURE WIN2-27 ■ THE *DATE/TIME PROPERTIES* DIALOG BOX

This dialog box is used to adjust the system's date and time.

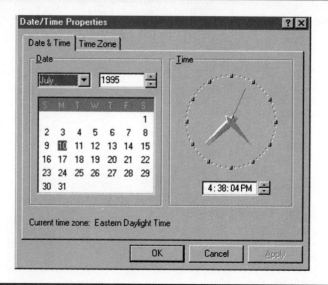

Like all tabs in this dialog box, the top portion displays a sample of the current setting section and the bottom portion contains the options to change the current settings. If this is your own computer, you can use the Background tab to change the desktop's appearance. Try this:

2   If needed, click *None* in the *Pattern* list box

3   Click *Arches* (or any other desired wallpaper) in the *Wallpaper* list box

Depending on your display settings (below the *Browse* button), a picture of an arch (the Center display option, which is the default), as in Figure WIN2-29a, or a full screen of arches (the Tile display option), as in Figure WIN2-29b, should appear in the display area (top portion) of the tab. If you selected a different wallpaper in Step 3, its picture should be displayed. You can place any of the available patterns or wallpaper as your desktop's background or even create your own. For now, cancel your selection:

4   Click the *Cancel* button to return to previous settings

ADDING NEW HARDWARE.   In the spirit of "plug and play," which is a move to simplify new hardware installation, Windows has developed the *New Hardware* wizard. A **wizard** is a program that helps make complicated tasks easier. **Plug and play** is the idea of simply plugging new hardware into your system and playing with (using) it immediately. Although Windows does not provide a 100 percent Plug-and-Play environment, the New Hardware wizard will make the installation of many hardware components simpler.

FIGURE WIN2-28 ■ THE *DISPLAY PROPERTIES* DIALOG BOX

This dialog box can be used to set the background screen, turn the Screen Saver program on and off, and set the Screen Saver program.

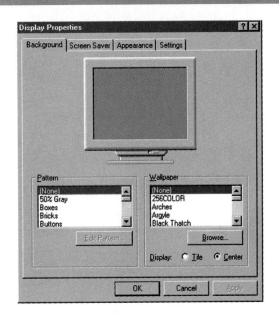

WIN

FIGURE WIN2-29 ■ CHANGING BACKGROUND DISPLAYS

(a) The Center Arches wallpaper display as it will appear on your desktop background if the *OK* or *Apply* button is clicked.
(b) The Tile Arches wallpaper display will fill the desktop background if selected and applied.

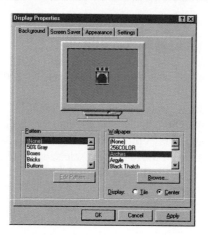

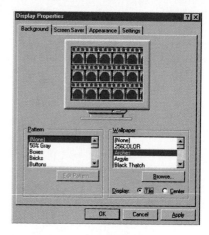

(a)   (b)

To use the New Hardware wizard, simply install your hardware with the power off, and then start Windows, launch My Computer, open the Control Panel, and then open the *Add New Hardware* icon. Next follow the New Hardware wizard instructions to complete the installation process.

USING PRINTERS

The *Printers* program is used to add a new printer to your system, switch the default printer, or view or control the status of current print jobs. A print job is simply documents sent to your printer to be printed. Windows allows you to send several print jobs to your printer. Although they are printed in the order sent, you can use the Printers program to change this.

STEPS

1   **Close the Control Panel and launch My Computer, if needed**

Printers

2   **Double-click the *Printers* folder icon**

> **Tip: The *Printers* folder can also be opened by clicking the *Start* button, pointing to *Settings*, and then clicking *Printers*.**

A Printers window should appear similar to Figure WIN2-30a. The printers available in your system may differ. Your window should also include an *Add Printer* icon, which can be used to launch the Add Printer wizard. This wizard helps you install a new printer into Windows after you have connected to your system. To see the status of your current print jobs,

3   **Double-click your printer's icon**

A window similar to Figure WIN2-30b should appear for your printer. The title bar displays the name of your printer. If you were printing any documents, they would first appear

FIGURE WIN2-30 ■ THE *PRINTERS* FOLDER

(a) The *Printers* folder can
be used to add a new printer,
set the default printer, or
open a Printer's status
window.
(b) The Printer's status
window displays current
print jobs and can also be
used to control the jobs.

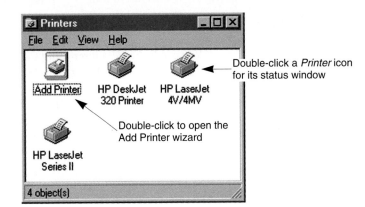

(a)

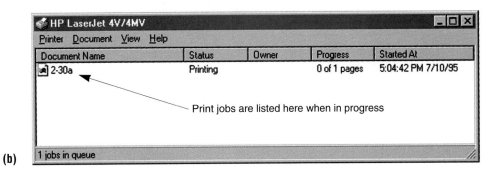

(b)

here. If you have several print jobs to process, they would be listed in this window with
their current print status. Refer to your on-line help to learn more about operating this window. For now,

[X] 4 **Close all windows**

☑ **CHECKPOINT**

✓ Define properties and default settings.
✓ Copy any document within your data disk and rename it as **Read Only.**
✓ Change the properties of the Read Only file to *Read Only.*
✓ Describe how to add a program to your *Start* menu
✓ Describe some of the settings that can be changed using the Control Panel.

UNDERSTANDING EXPLORER

Windows Explorer is another program that you can use to manage your computer.
The components of your system are listed in a hierarchal tree. Selecting a folder

WIN

(or other item) from the tree on the left side of the window will display its contents on the right side. Commands used with the My Computer program are also available through Explorer.

LAUNCHING EXPLORER

You can launch Explorer using the *Start* menu. Under this method, Explorer will open with its default display, which should be your hard disk. You can also launch Explorer from the My Computer (or a folder) window using a *Shortcut* menu, the *File* menu, or the toolbar. This method will directly display the contents of a desired disk or other folder.

The following exercises demonstrate both methods to launch Explorer.

BY THE *START* MENU. When launching Explorer by using the *Start* menu, it will open with your hard disk selected on the left and its contents displayed on the right. This is the default view.

STEPS

 ☐ Click the *Start* button   [**Ctrl** + **Esc**]

☐ Point to *Programs* and then click *Windows Explorer*

Explorer should display the contents of your hard-disk drive (or default disk drive).

 ☐ Close Explorer

BY MY COMPUTER. To launch Explorer by using My Computer,

STEPS

 ☐ Right-click My Computer for its *Shortcut* menu

☐ Click *Explore*

The Explorer window should now appear on your desktop.

 ☐ Close Explorer

Now, to launch Explorer through My Computer displaying the contents of your data disk,

STEPS

☐ Launch My Computer and insert your data disk into Drive A, if needed

BY *SHORTCUT* MENU

2 Right-click the *3½ Floppy (A:)* icon for its *Shortcut* menu

3 Click *Explore*

BY *FILE* MENU

2 Click the *3½ Floppy (A:)* icon to select it

3 Click *File, Explore*

4 If needed, click the *Maximize* button

[**Alt** + **Spacebar** , **X**]

> Note: Although it is not necessary to maximize the Explorer window, a maximized window is visually easier to work with.

5 If desired, click *View, Toolbar* to turn it on

6 If needed, click *View, Details* to display file details.

As in Figure WIN2-31, Explore opens with the *3½ Floppy (A:)* icon selected on its left side and the listing of its contents on its right. Note that Explorer and My Computer have

FIGURE WIN2-31 ■ WINDOWS EXPLORER

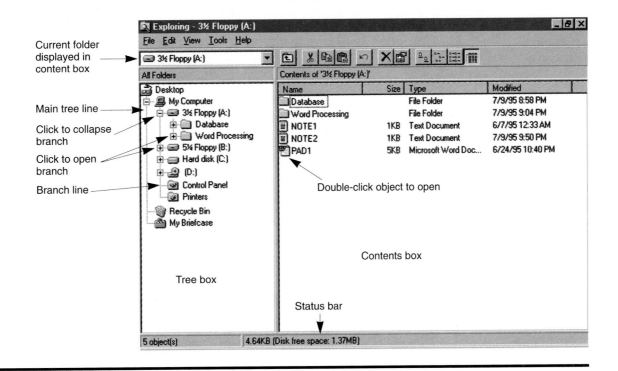

WIN

the same menu bar and toolbar. See Figure WIN2-4 for a description of its toolbar components.

Your Explorer window should resemble Figure WIN2-31. Leave this window open as you continue to the next section.

OPERATING EXPLORER

Explorer's commands operate similar to those of My Computer, however, the information in its workspace is displayed differently. As in Figure WIN2-31, the left side of the workspace displays a vertical hierarchical tree of all your system's components. This side will be referred to as the *Tree box*. The right side of the screen displays the contents of the item selected in the Tree box and will be referred to as the *Contents box*. It is similar to the workspace of a folder window. Items in both boxes are listed in alphabetical order.

VIEWING A TREE. The Tree box (left side of Explorer's workspace), as mentioned earlier, displays all your system's components in a vertical tree starting with the desktop icon on top. The left most vertical tree line is the **main tree line** and displays all items that appear on the desktop, including My Computer and the Recycle Bin. All lines extending from the main tree are called **branches.**

The *Go to a different folder* drop-down box (left side of toolbar) identifies the current folder selection—3½ Floppy (A:). Its contents are displayed in the Contents box (right side of window).

To select a different item on the tree, simply click it. Try this to select the desktop,

---

STEPS

 Desktop   **1** **Click the *Desktop* icon in the Tree box**

The *Desktop* icon now appears highlighted in the tree and its contents appear in the right side of the window. Now, select the Control Panel,

Control Panel   **2** **Click the *Control Panel* icon**

The *Control Panel* icon is now highlighted and its contents displayed in the contents box.

> **Tip:** You can also use the *Go to a different folder* drop-down box to select an item on the tree.

The Home key will quickly move the selection highlight to the beginning of any list in a list box and the End key will move the selection to the end of the list. Try this,

3 **Press** `Home` **to select the desktop**

4 **Press** `End` **to select the last item on the tree**

 3½ Floppy (A:)   **5** **Click the *3½ Floppy (A:)* icon to select it**

Your Explorer window should again appear similar to Figure WIN 2-31. This time the *3½ Floppy (A:)* icon is highlighted. Note that when you originally launched Explorer, it displayed the 3½ Floppy (A:) without its icon being highlighted. This is because Explorer launches with a dotted selection rectangle (see the *Database* icon in the figure) on the first item in the Contents box.

EXPANDING AND COLLAPSING BRANCHES.   The " + " icon to the left of any icon in the Tree box indicates that the item can be expanded to display a tree branch of folder(s) below it. Clicking a   +   icon expands the current tree.

STEPS

⊞ 📁 Database   **1**   **Click the   +   icon to the left of the *Database* folder icon**

The *Database* folder icon now branches to display the folders it contains and the   +   changes to a   −   as in Figure WIN2-32a. Note that its subfolder, Consult, also has subfolders. To display its subfolders as in Figure 2-32b,

⊞ 📁 Consult   **2**   **Click the   +   icon to the left of the *Consult* folder icon**

To collapse the branches and return the display to Figure WIN2-31,

⊟ 📁 Database   **3**   **Click the   −   icon to the left of the *Database* folder icon**

FILE MANAGEMENT.   You can perform all commands discussed under the "Managing Your Files" and "Sharing and Removing Your Files" sections of this chapter using Explorer. Instead of selecting files from a Folder window, you select them from the Contents box. Once selected, you can use the *File* menu to open, rename, or print them.

FIGURE WIN2-32 ■   EXPANDING BRANCHES

(a) Clicking a [+] icon to the left of a *Folder* icon expands its branch by one level.
(b) All branches of the database folder have been expanded.

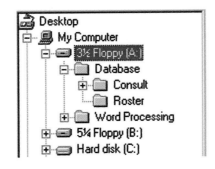

(a)

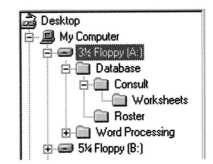

(b)

The Copy or Cut commands (*Edit* or *Shortcut* menu) can also be applied to any selection in Explorer's Contents box. The main difference between Explorer and My Computer is that you may need to scroll through your tree to locate the destination folder before invoking the Paste command. (Remember, in My Computer, you simply open the destination folder and click *Edit, Paste,* or right-click it and then click *Paste.*) The possible need to scroll to the destination folder makes the drag and drop sharing technique more cumbersome.

CONTROLLING THE ENVIRONMENT. Just as with My Computer, to change an object's properties in Explorer, simply invoke the Change Properties command from the item's *Shortcut* menu or *File* menu. To use Control Panel and Printers programs from Explorer, simply click its icon in the Tree box and then double-click the desired feature's icon in the Contents box.

VIEW OPTIONS. Explorer has view options similar to those of My Computer. You can access them by using the *View* menu or toolbar buttons. Icons can also be sorted as desired by using the *Arrange icons* submenu (*View* menu).

Before continuing to Chapter 3, complete the following steps to delete all folders (and any folders within them) that you created on your data disk for the exercises in this chapter. These folders include *Database* and *Word Processing:*

STEPS

🖙 3½ Floppy (A:)   **1** **If needed, click *3½ Floppy (A:)* drive icon in the Tree box**

📁 Database   **2** **Click the *Database* folder in the Contents box**

3 **Press and hold Ctrl while clicking the *Word Processing* folder icon**

4 **Click *File, Delete, Yes***

If you are using the Word Processing modules of the Mastering Today's Software series, you will need to create a folder called XWP: The *XWP* folder is also needed to perform the Application 1 problem at the end of this chapter.

5 **Click *File* and then point to *New***

6 **Click *Folder***

7 **Type XWP and press ↵**

☒ **8** **Close all windows**

9 **Shut down Windows**

☑ **CHECKPOINT**

✓ What is Explorer?

✓ Launch Explorer and select the Control Panel from the Tree box (left side).

✓ Select the *3½ Floppy (A:)* drive icon in the Tree box, use the Contents box to open NOTE1 and PAD1, and then close them.

✓ Copy PAD1 within the same main folder and then rename it PAD2.

✓ Delete PAD2 and then close Explorer.

SUMMARY

- My Computer is a program that can browse (view) and access all of the components of a computer system, manage files, and control computer settings and printing. It is normally launched by double-clicking its icon on the desktop. Its workspace is usually occupied by several drive icons, the *Control Panel* folder, and *Printers* folder.

- Storage media includes disks (hard disk and 3½″ or 5¼″ disks), CD-ROM (a special disk that has *read only memory*), tape, and system memory (RAM or ROM). This text assumes that you are using a hard disk and a 3½″ disk for data.

- A *file* is a program or document that is saved on a disk or other storage media and is represented in Windows by icons and titles (filenames). The number of files that can be stored on a particular storage media depends on its capacity.

- A *folder* is a group of related files. Subfolders are folders within folders. A disk (or other storage media) is also considered a folder and is referred to as the *main folder.*

- Filenames identify a document or program. Folder names identify a group of files. They can have up to 255 characters.

- A byte is equivalent to one alphanumeric character (A–Z, 0–9, and so forth). A kilobyte (KB) is one thousand bytes, a megabyte (MB) is one million bytes, and a gigabyte (GB) is one billion bytes.

- A drive is a device that reads and/or writes to a storage medium (such as a disk or a CD-ROM). In My Computer, drive icons and letter titles are used to identify each drive in the system. The letter *C* normally represents the hard drive; the letters *A* and *B* represent the disk drives, and the letter *D* generally identifies the CD-ROM. Other letters may be used to identify a network.

- *Formatting* prepares a disk for use on the computer. It sets up the disk's folder and file allocation table and divides the disk into addressable storage locations. It also checks for defective tracks on the disk and seals them off from further use.

- The Find feature can be used to locate any file in a folder and then open it.

- Drive and folder icons can be used to open Folder windows that display their contents.

- The My Computer program offers two ways to browse through folders: separate windows for each folder (the default) or a single window that changes to display each folder that is opened. These settings are changed through the *Options* dialog box (*View* menu).

- The My Computer and Folder windows status bar (at the bottom of the window) displays the number of objects (drive, file, or folder icons) in the workspace and the amount of bytes that those objects occupy on the disk. All items in a folder or the My Computer window are referred to as *objects*. The status bar is also able to display other messages when using this program.

- The workspace in a Folder window (or My Computer window) can be adjusted to display the icons in a smaller size, in a list, and with more or less detail by using the *View* menu or toolbar buttons. The sort order of objects can also be changed using the *View* menu.

WIN

- More advanced *View* options such as folder browsing choices, displaying hidden files, and MS-DOS file extensions and file association settings can be controlled by using the *Options* dialog box.

- File management involves organizing and maintaining files (including folders) within the computer environment.

- Double-clicking a *Drive* icon in the My Computer window opens a Folder window that displays the main contents of the disk in its drive. Double-clicking a folder within a Folder window displays its contents in another Folder window.

- The Folder command of the *New* submenu (*File* menu) can be used to create a new folder or subfolder.

- A new saved document can be created without first launching its program by clicking the desired file type in the *New* submenu (*File* menu).

- Selecting is the process of marking items. To select a file, click it. To select additional files, press and hold the Ctrl key while clicking each additional file (or other objects). Files may also be selected in a block. A block is a set of contiguous files (or other objects). To select a block of files, click the first file and then press and hold the Shift key while clicking the last file in the block. A block can be selected alone or with other selected files.

- Most documents created and saved with Windows programs are automatically associated (have a special connection) to their program and can be opened from a Folder window without first launching their individual programs. Files include documents, programs, and folders. To open (or launch) folders or multiple documents and programs, select their icons and then click *File, Open* (menu bar).

- Any file or folder can be easily renamed by using an object's *Shortcut* menu or *File* menu.

- To print document files from a Folder window, select the desired file icon(s) and then invoke the Print command from the *File* menu.

- Sharing files involves copying or moving documents, programs, and folders within the same folder or between folders.

- A *Shortcut* icon has a link (special connection) to the original file or folder and can be used to open the original document or folder or to launch the original program from the desktop or another folder. To create a *Shortcut* icon use the Copy and Paste Shortcut commands of the *Edit* menu.

- The Undo command (**Ctrl** + **Z**) is available in most programs and will undo your last action.

- Copy and move techniques include using the Copy, Cut (to move), and Paste commands of the *Edit* menu or *Shortcut* menus as well as drag and drop techniques. The folder from which a selection is copied or cut (moved) from is called the *source folder.* The folder to which it is pasted (placed) is called the *destination folder.*

- When copying within the same folder, the source and destination folders are the same. Windows automatically adds the words *"Copy of"* to the copy's title.

- Files or folders copied between folders are assigned their original names.

- Drag and drop techniques involve copying or moving a selection by pressing and holding the left mouse button while moving the pointer with the selection to a new location, sometimes with the use of other keys. The source folder and destination folder windows must be in view to use the drag and drop technique.

- The *Copy Disk* dialog box copies the contents of an entire disk to another disk. It is accessible through Copy Disk command of the My Computer *File* menu (after you have selected the desired drive icon) or the desired drive icon's *Shortcut* menu.

- The *Send* submenu (*File* menu) copies a selection to another disk, fax, or electronic mail.

- The Delete command removes a selection from its current place and is invoked from the *File* menu, an object's *Shortcut* menu, or by pressing the Delete key. When deleting a selection from your hard disk or network disk, the file's reference is normally relocated to the Recycle Bin (a Windows program that stores file references as a result of invoking the delete command) without actually deleting the file. Once there, you can either permanently delete the selection or restore it. Deleting a *Short* icon will not affect the original file.

- Default settings are the normal settings of your environment. Properties include the way information and other attributes (characteristics) of an item are displayed or set. The Change Properties command alters any object's default characteristics.

- The Control Panel contains tools to set various parts of a system, including adding and removing hardware drivers (programs that help a piece of hardware communicate with the computer), screen displays, fonts, and so forth.

- The Printer program is used to add a new printer, switch printers (if more than one printer is installed), and check and control the status of current print jobs.

- A wizard is a program that helps make complicated tasks easier. Plug and play is the idea of simply plugging new hardware into your system and playing with (using) it immediately.

- Windows Explorer is another program that can be used to for managing a computer. The system components are listed in a hierarchal tree. Selecting a folder (or other item) from the tree on the left side will display its contents on the right side, which is similar to a Folder window. Commands used with the My Computer program are also available through Explorer.

KEY TERMS

Associated (WIN83)	File management (WIN78)	Recycle Bin (WIN87)
Block (WIN83)	Find (WIN70)	Send to (WIN93)
Branches (WIN110)	Folder windows (WIN73)	Sharing files (WIN87)
Byte (WIN70)	Label (WIN69)	Shortcut icon (WIN87)
Control Panel (WIN99)	Main tree line (WIN110)	Subfolders (WIN69)
Copy disk (WIN93)	My Computer (WIN68)	Undo (WIN96)
Default settings (WIN99)	Plug and play (WIN105)	Windows Explorer
Delete (WIN97)	Printers (WIN99)	(WIN107)
Drive (WIN70)	Properties (WIN99)	Wizard (WIN105)

QUIZ

TRUE/FALSE

____ 1. Both My Computer and Windows Explorer are programs that have file management features.

____ 2. My Computer is normally launched from the *Start* menu

____ 3. The status bar of the 3½ Floppy (A:) window displays disk storage information.

____ 4. A folder may only contain document and program files.

____ 5. Folder windows can be used to perform file management operations.

____ 6. The Shift key must be used to select a group of files by mouse.

____ 7. Sharing files involves copying or moving files.

____ 8. The Settings program is used to change the default settings of your system.

____ 9. Deleting a file from your data disk (3½″ disk) moves it to the Recycle Bin.

____ 10. Explorer displays the hierarchy of your system in a tree.

MULTIPLE CHOICE

____ 11. A folder may include all of the following except
    a. A taskbar
    b. Other folders
    c. The *Program* file icon
    d. The *Document* file icon

____ 12. Double-clicking a drive icon will
    a. Start the drive wizard
    b. Reformat the disk
    c. Open the main folder window of a disk or other storage media
    d. Launch My Computer

____ 13. A group of related files is a
    a. Folder
    b. File
    c. Window
    d. Drive

____ 14. A device that reads and/or writes to a disk is called a
    a. Folder
    b. File
    c. Window
    d. Drive

____ 15. Which item(s) of a Folder window can be used to create a new folder?
    a. Toolbar
    b. *File* menu
    c. *Edit* menu
    d. *Folder* menu

____ 16. A set of contiguous files is a(n)
    a. Icon
    b. Block
    c. Menu
    d. Toolbar

____ 17. Before performing any file management commands on a file, you must
    a. Format it
    b. Recycle it
    c. Rename it
    d. Select it

____ 18. Dragging and dropping a selection between folders will ____ the selection.
    a. move
    b. open
    c. copy
    d. recycle

___ 19. Which of the following contains features to change the settings of your computer?
   a. Printers
   b. *Shortcut* menu
   c. Toolbar
   d. Control Panel

___ 20. An icon that can be used to open a file or folder stored in a different folder is a
   a. *Shortcut* icon
   b. *Smart* icon
   c. *Toolbar* button
   d. *File* icon

MATCHING

Select the lettered item from the figure that best matches each phrase below.

___ 21. Double-click this icon to open a Folder window displaying your hard disk's main folder.

___ 22. Click this button to display the details of all objects listed in the window.

___ 23. Use this menu to sort the objects in the window's workspace.

___ 24. Use this menu to move or copy a selection.

___ 25. This icon is created by using a command in the *New* submenu.

FIGURE WIN2-33 ■ MATCHING FIGURE

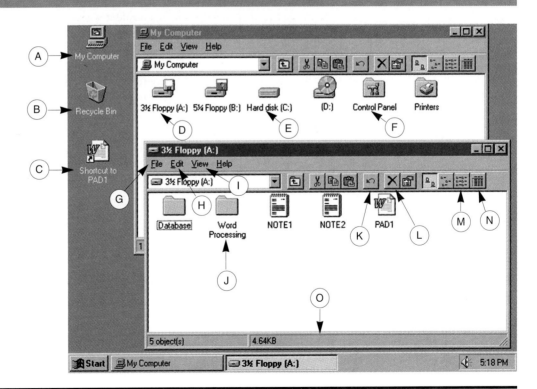

___ 26. This icon has a link to the file it represents.

___ 27. Click this button to undo your last action

___ 28. May hold items deleted from your hard disk.

___ 29. Can be used to change the settings of your computer.

___ 30. A bar used to display information about the contents of a window.

ANSWERS

True/False: 1. T; 2. F; 3. T; 4. F; 5. T; 6. F; 7. T; 8. F; 9. F; 10. T
Multiple Choice: 11. a; 12. c; 13. a; 14. d; 15. b; 16. b; 17. d; 18. c; 19. d; 20. a
Matching: 21. e; 22. n; 23. i; 24. h; 25. j; 26. c; 27. k; 28. b; 29. f; 30. o

EXERCISE

I. OPERATIONS

Provide the Windows commands necessary to complete each of the following operations. For each operation, assume a hard-disk system with a disk in Drive A. You may want to verify each command by trying it on your computer.

1. Launch My Computer.

2. Insert your data disk and open its main folder window.

3. Create a folder called WORD and then a subfolder within it called TEXT on your data disk.

4. Open the *Text* folder window and create a text document with the title OPERATIONS.

5. Open the OPERATIONS document, type in your name, and resave it.

6. Copy the icon for the OPERATIONS file to your data disk's main folder.

7. Rename the copy of the OPERATIONS file to SHARING

8. Create a *Shortcut* icon for the SHARING file in the *Text* folder.

9. Close My Computer and then launch Explorer to view your data disk.

10. Expand all branches of the *Word* folder and then collapse them. Close Explorer.

II. COMMANDS

Describe fully, using as few words as possible, what command is initiated or what is accomplished in Windows by the actions described below. Assume that each exercise part is independent of any previous parts.

1. Double-clicking the *My Computer* icon.

2. Double-clicking the *3½ Floppy (A:)* drive icon after inserting your data disk into Drive A.

3. Right-clicking an object in a Folder window.

4. Clicking the first object in a Folder window and then pressing and holding the Shift key while clicking the last object in the folder.

5. Dragging and dropping a selection from one folder to another.

6. Pressing the Delete key on a selection of files in your *Hard-disk* folder.

7. Clicking the right most toolbar button in a Folder window.

8. Right clicking the *My Computer* icon and then clicking *Explore*.

9. Clicking a *Shortcut* icon.

10. Clicking a − icon in the Tree box of Explorer.

WIN

III. APPLICATIONS

Perform the following operations, briefly tell how you accomplished each operation, and describe its results.

APPLICATION 1: UNDERSTANDING MY COMPUTER

1. Start Windows and launch My Computer.

2. If needed, use the steps on page WIN112 to create the *XWP* folder.

3. Use the Find feature to search for the NOTE1 file on your data disk.

4. Perform a new search to locate the *XWP* folder.

5. Open the *XWP* folder and then close it.

6. Open the main folder window of your data disk.

7. Turn on the toolbar and then use it to change the display to show file details.

8. Change the display back to large icons.

9. Close the 3½ Floppy window.

10. Close the My Computer window.

11. Shut down Windows.

APPLICATION 2: MANAGING YOUR FILES

1. Start Windows and launch My Computer.

2. Insert your data disk and open its main Folder window.

3. Create two folders named PERSONAL and BUSINESS.

4. Open the *Personal* folder and create two subfolders named CHECKING and SAVINGS.

5. Open the *Business* folder and create subfolders for SALES and PURCHASES.

6. Close the *Business* and *Personal* folder windows.

7. Create two text documents named ACCT #101 and INVOICES in the main folder.

8. Select and then open the ACCT#101 and INVOICES documents together.

9. Type **1/1/XX Balance $1,000** in the ACCT#101 document and then resave and close it.

10. Type **INV#354 Windows $5,000** in the INVOICES document and then resave and close it.

11. Select and print the ACCT #101 and INVOICES documents from the Folder window.

12. Close all windows and shut down Windows.

APPLICATION 3: SHARING YOUR FILES: COPYING AND MOVING

This problem requires first completing Application 2.

1. Start Windows and launch My Computer.

2. Insert your data disk and open its main Folder window.

3. Open the *Business* and *Personal* folders.

4. Minimize all windows and then open only the 3½ Floppy (A:) and Business windows.

5. Tile the windows horizontally and then move the INVOICES file from the *3½ Floppy (A:)* folder to the *Sales* subfolder in the *Business* folder.

6. Open the *Sales* subfolder and copy the INVOICES file to the *Purchase* folder.

7. Rename the INVOICES file in the *Purchase* folder to ORDERS.

8. Close the *Sales, Purchase,* and then *Business* folder windows.

9. Using similar techniques, move the ACCT #101 file to the *Checking* subfolder of the *Personal* folder, and then copy it to the *Savings* subfolder and rename as ACCT #202.

10. Close all windows and then shut down Windows.

APPLICATION 4: ADVANCE SHARING TECHNIQUES

This problem requires first completing Application 3.

1. Start Windows and launch My Computer.

2. Insert your data disk and open its main Folder window.

3. Open the *Business* folder and then the *Sales* subfolder.

4. Copy the INVOICES file three times within the Sales folder window.

5. Rename the files as INVOICE1, INVOICE2, INVOICE3, and INVOICE4.

6. Select and copy INVOICE1, INVOICE3, and INVOICE4 to the *Savings* folder.

7. In the *Savings* folder, rename the files BONDS, MUTUAL FUNDS, and MONEY MARKET.

8. Delete the ACCT #202 file in the *Savings* folder.

9. Create a *Shortcut* icon to open the MONEY MARKET file from the main folder window.

10. Open the MONEY MARKET file using its *Shortcut* icon and then close it.

11. Delete the MONEY MARKET file shortcut.

12. Close all windows and shut down Windows.

APPLICATION 5: CONTROLLING YOUR ENVIRONMENT

1. Start Windows and launch My Computer.

2. Insert your data disk and open the disk's properties.

3. Change the label of the disk to MY DISK.

4. Open the main folder for your data disk.

5. Change the properties for the PAD1 file to read-only.

6. Open the *Taskbar Properties* dialog box, clear your *Documents* menu contents, and then close it.

7. Open the Control Panel and examine, but do not change, the system's date and time.

8. Use the *Display* dialog box to add wallpaper of your choice to your desktop's background.

9. Use the *Display* dialog box to turn on or change your screen saver.

10. Close all windows and shut down Windows.

APPLICATION 6: OPERATING WINDOWS EXPLORER

This problem requires first completing Application 4.

1. Start Windows, launch My Computer, and insert your data disk.

2. Launch Windows Explorer to display the contents of the 3½ Floppy (A:) drive.

3. Expand all branches of the *Business* and *Personal* folders.

4. Create another folder in the *Business* folder called INVENTORY. (Hint: First select the *Business* folder in the tree and then use the *File* menu.)

5. Copy INVOICE2 and INVOICE4 from the *Sales* folder to the *Inventory* folder and then rename them ITEM1 and ITEM2.

6. Open the ITEM1 and ITEM2 documents using Explorer and then close them.

7. Select the *Checking* folder in the tree and create two new folders called NOW and REGULAR.

8. Expand the new branches of the *Checking* folder.

9. Collapse all branches in your *3½ Floppy (A:)* folder.

10. Close all windows and shut down Windows.

MASTERY CASES

The following mastery cases allow you to demonstrate how much you have learned about this software. Each case describes a fictitious problem or need that can be solved using the skills that you have learned in this chapter. Although minimum acceptable outcomes are specified, you are expected and encouraged to design your own response (files, data, lists) in ways that display your personal mastery of the software. Feel free to show off your skills. Use real data from your own experience in your solution, although you may also fabricate data if needed.

These mastery cases allow you to display your ability to

- Launch My Computer and Windows Explorer.
- Use My Computer to browse in folders.
- Perform a variety of file management techniques.
- Share and remove files.
- Control your computer environment.

CASE 1. USING WINDOWS AT SCHOOL

You have been asked to create a folder for each class that you are taking this semester. Create two text documents in one of the new folders, naming them REPORT 1 and REPORT 2. Copy those files to each new folder. Rename the REPORT 2 files to HOMEWORK 2. Close all windows and shut down Windows.

CASE 2. USING WINDOWS AT HOME

You have just installed Windows on your computer and desire to customize your screen display. Use the Control Panel and *Taskbar Properties* dialog box to accomplish this. Also select and turn on a desired screen saver. Close all windows and shut down Windows. (This case requires your own computer or the ability to change settings on the system that you are using. Check with your instructor before doing this case.)

CASE 3. USING WINDOWS AT WORK

You have been assigned to organize the customer files in your office. Create folders for five customers. Next, create two subfolders within one of the customer folders and name them *Receivables* and *Sales*. Create two text documents in the *Sales* folder and copy them to the *Sales* folders of the other customers. Launch Explorer and open all the branches of your data disk. Create a *Shortcut* icon for the *Sales* folder of one of the customers and place it in the main folder. Use the *Shortcut* icon to open the folder. Close all windows and shut down Windows.

3

OTHER WINDOWS FEATURES

OUTLINE

WORDPAD
Getting Started
Inserting New Text
Selecting Text
Deleting Text
Undoing an Action
Changing Text Appearance
Changing Text Layout
Moving and Copying a Selection

PAINT
Getting Started
Selecting a Drawing Tool
Drawing Objects
Moving and Copying Objects
Inserting Text
Capturing a Screen

LINKING AND EMBEDDING
Linking
Embedding

OTHER WINDOWS PROGRAMS
Accessibility Options
Accessories
Communications

OBJECTIVES

After completing this chapter, you will be able to

1 Use the editing features of WordPad (a word processing program).
2 Create and edit objects and text with Paint (a graphics program).
3 Perform object linking and embedding operations, including editing a linked or embedded object.

4 Use Windows accessibility options to adjust keyboard, display, sound, and mouse controls to individual preference.
5 Describe other Windows Accessories programs and communication features.

OVERVIEW

This chapter provides tutorials on using WordPad (a word processor) and Paint (a graphics program). It also examines how to share information between programs by using object linking or embedding techniques and the communication features of Windows.

The chapter concludes with an overall look at operating other Windows programs, including accessibility options, accessories, and communications software.

WORDPAD

WordPad is a simple word processing program that can help you create and edit documents. Both text and objects (graphic) images may be placed into a WordPad document. Only text entry and editing are discussed in this section. For object linking, embedding, and editing, see the "Linking and Embedding" section of this chapter.

WordPad allows you to edit (change) the content, text appearance, and format (layout) of your document. Content changes include inserting, deleting, modifying, copying, and moving text in your document. **Text appearance** changes include alterations to font type, style (regular, bold, or italic), and size. **Layout (format)** changes concern the way text is arranged in a document—for example, changing margin or tab settings.

GETTING STARTED

As demonstrated earlier, commands to launch and close WordPad (or any program), create, save, open, and print a document are common for most Windows programs. Although these commands are reviewed as needed in the following exercises, you should review the "Basic Document Management" section in Chapter 1 before continuing.

LAUNCHING WORDPAD.   Like most Windows programs, WordPad can be launched from the *Start* menu.

STEPS

1 Click the *Start* button   [Ctrl + Esc]

2 Point to *Programs* and then *Accessories* for its submenu

3 Click *WordPad* to launch it

4 If needed, click WordPad's *Maximize* button to maximize it [Alt + Spacebar , X]

Your WordPad window should resemble Figure WIN3-1.

> Tip: Remember, as illustrated in the "Document Approach" section in Chapter 2, you can also create and name a new document for any program in a Folder window.

THE WORDPAD WINDOW.   As identified in Figure WIN3-1, the WordPad window has a variety of common Windows features including a title bar (with program icon, program and document name, resizing buttons, and a close button), menu bar, toolbars (including a Format bar), workspace, and status bar. The operation of each component

FIGURE WIN3-1 ■ WORDPAD

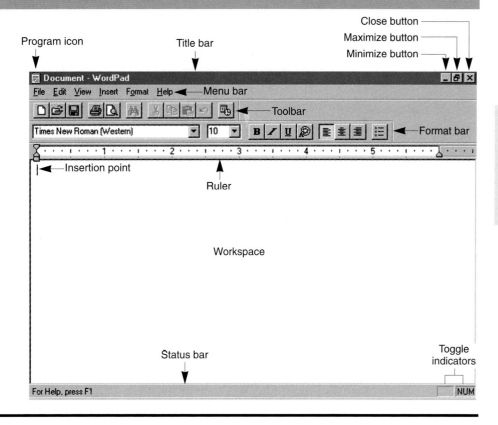

WIN

will be discussed as needed. WordPad also opens with a ruler just below its toolbars. This feature will be used later to set margins and adjust tab settings.

ENTERING TEXT.   As seen earlier, the average Windows program opens with a new blank document in its workspace. This is called the *default document.* You will now use WordPad's default document to create the document in Figure WIN3-2.

FIGURE WIN3-2 ■ ENTERING TEXT

```
Your Name↵
↵
Windows is a graphical user interface (GUI) that uses pictures instead of typewritten commands to help
you communicate with your computer. It is like using a picture of a cigarette in place of a written "No
Smoking" sign.|
```

As you enter text, do not press the Enter (or Return) key unless indicated. Unlike a typewriter, pressing the Enter key is *not* required at the end of each line. Text automatically flows to the next line as you type. This word processing feature is called **wordwrap.**

In a word processor, the Enter key produces a line break at the point where it is pressed. A **line break** ends a line before it reaches the right margin. It also moves the insertion point to the beginning of the next line. Line breaks are generally needed at the end of a paragraph, each line of an address, a salutation, or to skip a line.

Create a short document by entering text as follows:

STEPS

1   **Type your name**

2   **Press ↵ three times**

(Remember, do not press the Enter key as you type the following paragraph. Word-Pad's wordwrapping feature will automatically flow your text to the next line.)

3   **Type the paragraph shown in Figure WIN3-2**

> **Tip: If you make a mistake while typing, press the Backspace key to remove the error and type the correct text.**

DOCUMENT MANAGEMENT.   Basic document management commands include saving to disk, clearing the workspace, opening, and printing.

As demonstrated earlier, you can use the Save or Save As command to save a document. Invoking the Save command on a new document will open the *Save As* dialog box so that you can assign the document a filename. Remember, Windows 95 programs can accept filenames with up to 255 characters. Try this:

STEPS

1   **Click *File*, *Save***   [**Ctrl** + **S**]

2   **In the Filename box, type 1WORDPAD**

If needed, use Steps 3 and 4 to set the default drive to Drive A.

3   **Click the "▼" button of the *Save in* drop-down box for its list**

⊑ 3½ Floppy (A:)   4   **Click *3½ Floppy (A:)* to set the default drive to Drive A**

5   **Click the *Save* button**   [↵]

WIN

> **Tip:** Instead of Steps 3 and 4, you can change the default drive by typing A:\ before 1WORDPAD (for example, type [A:\1WORDPAD]) in Step 2. Also, if your data disk is not formatted, Windows will ask you whether you want to format it.

Your mouse pointer briefly changes to an image of a time bottle indicating " Please Wait" and the message "Saving File. Please wait." appears in the status bar (at the bottom of the window).

Invoking the Save command on a document previously saved will resave it under its original name. Try this:

 6 Click *File*, *Save*   [**Ctrl** + **S**]

Later, you will use the Save As command to save a revised copy of the document under another name. For now, clear your workspace for a new document.

 7 Click *File*, *New*, *OK*   [**Ctrl** + **N** , **↵**]

> **Note:** WordPad and many other programs offer several document types for a new document. If available, you can generally select the document type before clicking *OK* in Step 7.

Your workspace is now blank and ready for a new document. At this point you can create a new document. For now, however, you will practice opening the 1WORDPAD document. Remember, *opening* a document retrieves it from a disk.

 8 Click *File*, *Open*   [**Ctrl** + **O**]

9 Type **1WORDPAD** in the Filename box or click it in the list box

10 Click the *Open* button

Your 1WORDPAD document should again occupy WordPad's workspace.

> **Tip:** The *Save As* and *Open* dialog box can also be used for a variety of file management tasks similar to operating a Folder window. For example, to perform file management commands on a specific file, right click it in the *Files* list box for its *Shortcut* menu. This menu contains the same commands if the file had been right-clicked in a Folder window. Right-clicking a blank area of the *Files* list box will also open the same *Shortcut* menu as in a Folder window. See Chapter 2 for instructions on how to use these *Shortcut* menus.

Now, to print preview and then print the document:

 11 Click *File*, *Print Preview* to view the full page

The Print Preview feature displays a full page view of your document as it will appear when printed. This allows you to view text alignment and other format settings. You can zoom in to view different portions of your document by pointing and clicking the desired area. For now, to close the Print Preview feature, return to the document and then print it:

12 Click the *Close* button on the toolbar

13 Turn on your printer

 14 Click *File, Print, OK*   [**Ctrl** + **P** , **↵**]

Basic document management commands are summarized in Figure WIN3-3.

CLOSING WORDPAD.   As practiced earlier, WordPad (or any other program) can be closed by any method listed in Figure WIN1-26 in Chapter 1. Remember, closing exits the program. For now, to close WordPad,

 1 Click WordPad's *Close* button   [**Alt** + **F4**]

INSERTING NEW TEXT

WordPad allows you to insert (add) new text to material previously typed. Once inserted, WordPad automatically reformats the document. Practice inserting the new text shown in Figure WIN3-4a:

1 Launch WordPad

 2 If needed, click its *Maximize* button

 3 Click *File, Open* for its dialog box   [**Ctrl** + **O**]

If needed, do Steps 4 and 5 to set the default drive to Drive A.

4 Click the "▼" button of the *Look in* drop-down box for its list

🖴 3½ Floppy (A:) 5 Click *3½ Floppy (A:)* to set the default drive to Drive A

6 Click the *File name* box and type   1WORDPAD   or click it in the list box

7 Click the *Open* button

WIN

	Operation	Menu	Shortcut Keys
💾	Saving a Document to a disk[1]		
	With the Same Name	Click *File, Save*	Ctrl + S
	With a New Name	Click *File, Save As*	Alt + F, A
📂	Opening a Document from a Disk	Click *File, Open*	Ctrl + O
🖨	Printing a Document		
	To paper	Click *File, Print*	Ctrl + P
	To the screen	Click *File, Print Preview*	Alt + F, V
📄	Creating a New Document[2]	Click *File, New*	Ctrl + N

[1]When saving a document for the first time, both the Save and Save As commands will open the *Save As* dialog box for entering the document's name. All other times, the Save command will re-save a document under its original name and the Save As command will open the *Save As* dialog box. This offers you the option to save a revised document under a new name.

[2]In a program that allows only one document in its workspace—such as WordPad, Paint, and Notepad—the New command clears the program's workspace of a previous document so that you can create a new document. With a program that allows for multiple documents in its workspace, the New command opens a new document window over the current one. Refer to your specific program's on-line help to determine the maximum number of documents that can be opened and other document format options that may be available using the New command.

Tip: Double-clicking 1WORDPAD in place of Steps 6 and 7 will also open the document.

Again your document should resemble Figure WIN3-2. Now you are ready to insert new text.

8 **Move the insertion point to just before "instead"**
(To move the insertion point by mouse, simply click the desired position. With the keyboard, use the arrow keys.)

FIGURE WIN3-4 ■ ENTERING TEXT

```
Your Name                                        and menus ─────┐
                                                                 ▼
Windows is a graphical user interface (GUI) that uses pictures  instead of typewritten commands to help
you communicate with your computer. It is like using a picture of a cigarette  in place of a written "No
Smoking" sign.                                                               ▲
                          with a red slash through it ─────────────┘
```

(a) Inserting new text into a document.

```
Your Name
M/D/YY  ◀─────────── Click Insert, Date and Time, OK

Windows is a graphical user interface (GUI) that uses pictures and menus instead of typewritten commands
to help you communicate with your computer. It is like using a picture of a cigarette with a red slash
through it in place of a written "No Smoking" sign.
```

(b) The WordPad document with new text inserted.

---

9 Type   **and menus**

Notice that the words to the right of your insertion point have moved over to make room for the new words.

10 Press   **Spacebar**   to separate "menus" and "instead"

11 **Move your insertion point before the "i" in "in" on the second line**

12 Type   **with a red slash through it**

13 Press   **Spacebar**

WordPad also has a feature that allows you to insert the system's date and time. Try this to insert your system's date (which should normally be the current date):

14 **Move to the line below your name**

15 **Click *Insert, Date* and Time, OK**

Note that the default date format is mm/dd/yy. You can select a different format before clicking *OK* in Step 15.

Your document should resemble Figure WIN3-4b. To save this revised document as 2WORDPAD,

16 **Click *File, Save As* for its dialog box**

17 Type   **2WORDPAD**   in the Filename box

18 **Click the _Save_ button**   **[↵]**

Your revised document has now been saved as 2WORDPAD. Your original document, 1WORDPAD remains unmodified on your disk.

SELECTING TEXT

Selecting text involves marking (highlighting) it for editing. A selection of text is simply a contiguous segment of text. Text must be selected in order for you to perform appearance and format changes on it.

Mouse and keyboard selection techniques are summarized in Figure WIN3-5a. Some of these selection techniques will be demonstrated in the exercises to follow. WordPad's mouse selection area is illustrated in Figure 3-5b.

To cancel a selection by mouse, simply click the selection. With the keyboard, press any arrow key.

WIN

FIGURE WIN3-5 ■ SPECIAL SELECTION TECHNIQUES

(a) Summary of special selection techniques.
(b) The selection area of a WordPad document and mouse pointer. When using a mouse, you must first point to the selection area. This area is located on the left margin of the document. Notice that the mouse pointer will change to a right-slanted arrow.

Selecting a(n)	By Mouse	By Keyboard
Line	Point to the line from the selection area and click.	Move the insertion point to the beginning of the line and press the Shift and End keys.
Paragraph	Point to any line of the paragraph from the selection area and double-click	Move the insertion point to the first line of the paragraph and then press and hold the Shift key while pressing the Arrow key to the last line of the paragraph.
Entire document	Point to any part of the document from the selection area and then press and hold the Ctrl key while clicking.	Move the insertion point to the beginning of the document and then press the Ctrl, Shift, and End keys together.
Block of lines	Point to the first line of the block from the selection area and click. Point to the last line of the block from the selection area and then press and hold the Shift key while clicking.	Move the insertion point to the first line of the block and then press and hold the Shift key while pressing the Arrow key to the last line of the block.

(a)

Your Name
M/D/YY

Windows is
to help you
through it in

(b)

DELETING TEXT

Deleting text involves removing it from your document. When you delete text in a Word-Pad document, the remaining text automatically reformats. As mentioned earlier, to delete single characters to the left, press the Backspace key. To delete individual characters to the right, press the Delete key. To delete a selection (block) of text, use either the Clear command (*Edit* menu) or the Delete key.

Only a selection deletion is illustrated next. Try using the Backspace and Delete keys for individual character deletions on your own.

Delete the entire second line of your paragraph, beginning with "to" by doing the following:

STEPS

BY MOUSE

  1 Slowly point to the beginning of the second line from the left margin as in Figure WIN3-5b (your pointer should be pointing right)

  2 Click to select the line

  3 Click *Edit, Clear*

BY KEYBOARD

  1 Move the insertion point to the beginning of the second line

  2 Press **Shift** + **End** to select the line

[**Delete**]

The second line of your paragraph should now be deleted and the remaining text reformatted.

> **Tip:** To delete an entire paragraph, use the select command in Figure WIN3-5a and then click *Edit, Clear* or press the Delete key.

UNDOING AN ACTION

Many Windows programs contain an *Undo* command which you can invoke through the *Edit* menu, toolbar, or Shortcut keys. This command undoes your last action. To undo your deletion,

---

STEPS

  1 Click *Edit, Undo*

  2 Click the selection to remove the highlight

[**Ctrl** + **Z**]

[Any arrow key]

CHANGING TEXT APPEARANCE

If your printer has the capability, you can change the overall type face (**font**), style, and size of your text to improve the appearance of your document. You can also add strikeout and underline effects or change text color. All text appearance changes may be made prior to or after typing text.

In the following sections, you will type new text with a different font and then make other text enhancements to your document. Use Figure WIN3-6 as a guide.

FONT CHANGES.   Windows comes with several Truetype (TT) fonts that can be accessed by using the Format bar or the *Font* dialog box (*Format* menu). In the next exercise, you will change the font to Arial and font size to 14 points and then type in new text. (Note: A *point* is a typesetting unit of measure equivalent to about ½ of an inch.)

WIN

STEPS

1 Open the 2WORDPAD document

2 Press Ctrl + End to move to the end of the document

3 Press ↵ twice to skip two lines

BY FORMAT BAR

4 Click the "▼" button of the *Font* drop-down box (left side of Format bar) for its list as in Figure WIN3-7a (Your system's fonts may differ.)

BY *FONT* DIALOG BOX

4 Click *Format, Font* for its dialog box as in Figure WIN3-7b (Your system's fonts may differ.)

FIGURE WIN3-6 ■ TEXT ENHANCEMENTS

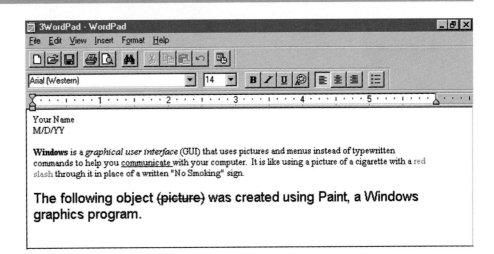

FIGURE WIN3-7 ■ CHANGING FONTS

(a) The *Font* drop-down list
(Format bar) can be used to
select an available font
(typeface).
(b) The *Font* dialog box
(*Format* menu) can also be
used to select a font.

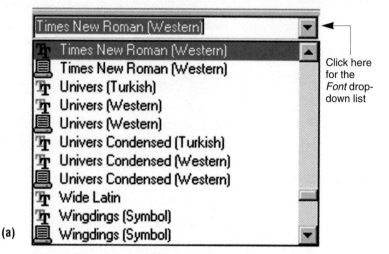

Click here
for the
Font drop-
down list

(a)

(b)

5 Press A to move the selection highlight to the beginning of the list

**Tip: Pressing a letter in a list will move the selection highlight to the first item be-
ginning with that letter in the list.**

BY FORMAT BAR

6 If needed, click the ▼ button of the *Font* drop-down list's scroll bar until *Arial* is visible

7 Click *Arial* to select it

8 Click the ▼ button of the *Font Size* drop-down box (Format bar)

9 Click *14* for font size

BY *FONT* DIALOG BOX

6 If needed, click the ▼ button of the *Font* list box's scroll bar until *Arial* is visible

7 Click *Arial* to select it

8 Click *14* in the *Size* list box

9 Click *OK*

10 Type   The following object (picture) was created using Paint, a Windows graphics program.

The font change is in effect from the point of change forward.

11 Save your document as 3WORDPAD *(File, Save As)*

OTHER TEXT ENHANCEMENTS.   As mentioned earlier, you can also change font style (which includes bolding or italicizing text), strikeout, underline, and change the color of text. Again, as you perform the exercises in this section use Figure WIN3-6.

Two ways to emphasis text is to bold or italicize it. **Bolding** darkens text, whereas **italicizing** slants text. Try this:

STEPS

1 Move the insertion point before "Windows" in the first paragraph (Either click it or use the arrow keys.)

2 Select the word *"Windows"*

Remember, either drag across the text with your mouse or press and hold the **Shift** key while pressing the → key.

Tip: Double-clicking a word will select it quickly.

3 Click *Format, Font, Bold* (in the *Font Style* list box), *OK*   [**Ctrl** + **B**]

Now, italicize "graphical user interface":

4 Select *"graphical user interface"*

I   **5** Click *Format*, *Font*, *Italic* (in the *Font Style* list box), *OK*   [**Ctrl** + **I**]

You can also emphasize text by underlining or striking it out (putting a line through it). Do the following to underline "communicate" and strikeout:

6 Select *"communicate"* from the second line of your paragraph

U   **7** Click *Format*, *Font*, the *Underline* check box, *OK*   [**Ctrl** + **U**]

8 Select *"(picture)"* in the last sentence

9 Click *Format*, *Font*, the *Strikeout* check box, *OK*

WordPad has options to change text color for further emphasis. Do not do Steps 10 and 11 if you do not have a color monitor or printer.

10 Select *"red slash"* at the end of the second line of the first paragraph

    11 Click *Format*, *Font*, the "▼" button of the *Color* drop-down box, *Red, OK*

12 Press any arrow key to unselect

Compare your document to Figure WIN3-6.

13 Resave this document as 3WORDPAD

14 Print the document and then open a new document

CHANGING TEXT LAYOUT

Layout (format) refers to the format of text in a paragraph or in an entire document. It includes indentation, alignment, bullet style, and tab changes. You can make layout changes using the *Format* menu, ruler, or toolbars.

INDENTATION.   In WordPad, **indentation** relates to the way a paragraph is indented or set from the left or right margin. You can also set the indentation for just the first line of a paragraph. Use the ruler or *Paragraph* dialog box (*Format* menu) for indentation changes. In the next exercises, you will indent only the first line of the first paragraph and then change the indentation of the second paragraph as in Figure WIN3-8.

STEPS

1 Open the 3WORDPAD document

2 Move the insertion point before the "W" in "Windows" in the first paragraph

FIGURE WIN3-8 ■ CHANGING TEXT LAYOUT

Your Name
M/D/YY

        Windows is a *graphical user interface* (GUI) that uses pictures and menus instead of typewritten commands to help you <u>communicate</u> with your computer. It is like using a picture of a cigarette with a red slash through it in place of a written "No Smoking" sign.

The following object (picture) was created using Paint, a Windows graphics program.

WIN

3 Click *Format, Paragraph* for its dialog box

4 Double-click the *First line* text box to highlight its contents

5 Type **.5** and then click *OK*

The first line of your first paragraph should now be indented as in Figure WIN3-9a.

> **Tip: Instead of performing Steps 3 through 5, you can drag the First Line Indent marker from the top left of the ruler to its current position above the .5″ marker (See Figure WIN3-9a).**

6 Move the insertion point before "The" in the second paragraph

7 Click *Format, Paragraph* for its dialog box

8 Type **1.5** in the Left text box and then press **Tab**

9 Type **2** in the Right text box and then click *OK*

> **Tip: Instead of Steps 7 through 9 you can drag the Left and Right Margin Indent markers on the ruler to the desired settings.**

    The entire second paragraph is now indented 1.5" from the left margin and 2" from the right margin as in Figure WIN3-9b. Note again that the corresponding markers on the ruler have also moved.

FIGURE WIN3-9 ■ INDENTATION ADJUSTMENTS

(a) You can indent the first line of a paragraph by dragging the First Line Indent marker on the ruler or by using the *Paragraph* dialog box (*Format* menu). (b) You can indent the left or right margins of a paragraph by dragging their respective markers on the ruler or by using the *Paragraph* dialog box (*Format* menu).

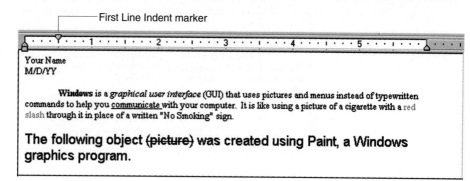

First Line Indent marker

(a)

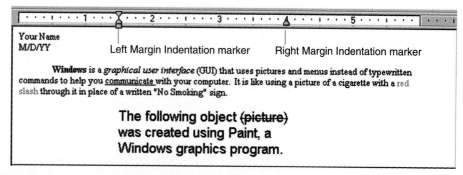

Left Margin Indentation marker   Right Margin Indentation marker

(b)

Tip: To indent an entire document before typing, open a new document, use the *Paragraph* dialog box or ruler to set the indentation and then begin typing. To indent an entire document after typing, click *Edit, Select All* (or press [Ctrl] + [A]) and then use the *Paragraph* dialog box or ruler to set the indentation.

10 Save this document as 4WORDPAD

11 Print the document

ALIGNMENT CHANGES. **Alignment** is how text aligns against a margin. The default alignment of WordPad and many word processors is *left*. Left aligned text has a *ragged right edge* as in Figure WIN3-10a. WordPad offers three alignment settings: left, center, and right. The next exercise will demonstrate the latter two alignments using the first paragraph of your 3WORDPAD document.

FIGURE WIN3-10 ■ **ALIGNING TEXT**

(a) Left aligned paragraph
(the default).
(b) Center aligned paragraph.
(c) Right aligned paragraph.

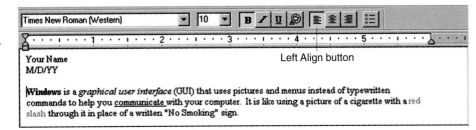

(a)

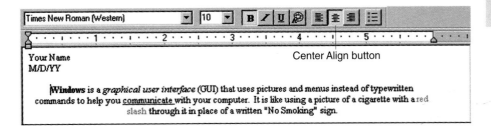

(b)

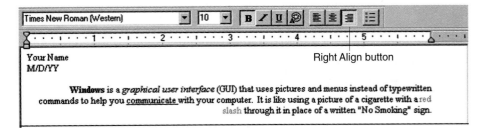

(c)

STEPS

1　Open the 3WORDPAD document

2　Move the insertion point before the "W" in "Windows" in the first paragraph

　3　Click the *Center Align Format bar* button

Your text is now center aligned as in Figure WIN3-10b.

4　Click the *Right Align Format bar* button

WIN

Your text in now right aligned as in Figure WIN3-10c.

5 **Click the *Left Aligned Format bar* button**

Your paragraph is now back to left aligned.

6 **Click *File, New, OK, No* for a new document without saving the current one**

BULLET STYLE. WordPad has a **bullet style** format that automatically inserts a bullet at the beginning of each line after pressing the Enter key. Try this to create the document in Figure WIN3-11:

STEPS

1 **On a new document, type** **New Features of Windows 95 include**

2 **Press ↵ twice**

3 **Click *Format, Bullet Style* to turn it on**

4 **Press** **Ctrl** **+** **B** **to turn on the bold feature**

5 **Type** **Start Button** **and then press** **Spacebar**

6 **Press** **Ctrl** **+** **B** **to turn off the bold feature**

7 **Type** **for quickly launching a program and accessing other features.**

8 **Press ↵ to move to the next bullet**

Tip: To delete an unwanted bullet, press the Backspace key.

FIGURE WIN3-11 ■ BULLET STYLE FORMAT

Bullet Style button

New Features of Windows 95 include:

* **Start Button** for quickly launching a program and accessing other features.
* **Taskbar** for easy switching between opened programs.
* **My Computer** for managing the components of your computer.
* **Close Button** for quickly exiting a window.

WIN

9 Repeat Steps 4 through 8 for the remaining three bullets using Figure WIN3-11 as a guide (Be sure to press Enter after typing the last bullet. You must add a blank bullet before turning off the feature.)

10 Click *Format, Bullet Style* to turn it off

11 Save this document as 5WORDPAD

12 Print the document

TAB CHANGES. **Tabs** are used to place text in specific positions on a line. These positions are called *tab stops*. WordPad's default tab stops are preset at one-half inch apart. As seen earlier, pressing the Tab key before beginning a paragraph will start your text one-half inch from the left margin. You can customize tab positions so that pressing the Tab key once will move you to a desired location. You can change tab stops using the ruler or *Tab* dialog box (*Format* menu). To create the document in Figure WIN3-12 using different tab stop settings:

STEPS

1 Click *File, New, OK,* (if needed, *No*) for a new document   [**Ctrl** + **N** , ⏎ , **N**]

2 Click the *Center Align* button (Format bar)

3 Press **Ctrl** + **B** to turn on the bold feature

4 Type Standard Shortcut Keys

FIGURE WIN3-12 ■ CHANGING TAB SETTINGS

Clicking the ruler will place a Tab marker at the location clicked. Tab markers can also be set using the *Tab* dialog box (*Format* menu).

Standard Shortcut Keys	
Open the Start Menu	Ctrl+Esc
Close a Program	Alt+F4
Create a New Document	Ctrl+N
Save a Document	Ctrl+S
Open a Saved Document	Ctrl+O
Print a Document	Ctrl+P
Undo the Last Action	Ctrl+Z
Copy a Selection	Ctrl+C
Cut a Selection	Ctrl+X
Paste a Selection	Ctrl+V
Select All	Ctrl+A
Help	F1

B

5 Press **Ctrl** + **B** to turn off the bold feature

≡

6 Press ↵ twice and then click the *Left Align* button (Format bar)

Now to set tab stops at the one-inch and four-and-a-half-inch marks:

BY RULER	BY *FORMAT* MENU
7 Point beneath the one-inch mark on the ruler	**7** Click *Format, Tabs* for its dialog box
8 Click beneath the one-inch mark on the ruler (an "L" appears)	**8** Type **1** and click the *Set* button to set the first tab stop
9 Click beneath the four-and-a-half-inch mark on the ruler	**9** Type **4.5** , click the *Set* button to set the second tab and then click *OK*

10 Press **Tab** to move to the one-inch tab mark

11 Type **Open the Start Menu**

12 Press **Tab** to move the four-inch tab mark

13 Type **Ctrl + Esc** and then press ↵

(Remember, you are typing the Shortcut keys, not pressing them.)

14 Type in the rest of the Shortcut keys listed in Figure WIN3-12 using the same techniques as illustrated in Steps 10 through 13

15 Save this document as 6WORDPAD

16 Print the document

17 Click *File, New, OK* to clear the workspace   [**Ctrl** + **N** , ↵]

MOVING AND COPYING A SELECTION

As mentioned earlier, WordPad can accept text and objects (graphic images). These items can be selected and moved or copied within a document (or to another file). *Moving* involves changing a selection's location. *Copying* involves duplicating a selection in another location. The difference between moving and copying is that moving removes (cuts) a selection from its original position, but copying leaves the original unchanged.

Because procedures for moving and copying are similar, only moving commands are illustrated next. To move the first sentence of the first paragraph to the end of the document as in Figure WIN3-13:

WIN

FIGURE WIN3-13 ■ MOVING A SELECTION

The first sentence of the first paragraph has been moved to the end of the document using the Cut and Paste commands (*Edit* menu).

> Your Name
> M/D/YY
>
> It is like using a picture of a cigarette with a red slash through it in place of a written "No Smoking" sign.
>
> ### The following object (picture) was created using Paint, a Windows graphics program.
>
> **Windows** is a *graphical user interface* (GUI) that uses pictures and menus instead of typewritten commands to help you communicate with your computer.

STEPS

1 Open the 3WORDPAD document

2 Select the sentence beginning with "Windows" (include the space after the period)

 3 Click *Edit, Cut* to move the selection to the Clipboard   [**Ctrl** + **X**]

 (To copy instead of cut, Click *Edit, Copy* or press **Ctrl** + **C** , for Step 3)

Remember, the Clipboard is a Windows program that temporarily holds copied or cut selections for future pasting.

4 Move your insertion point to the end of the document   [**Ctrl** + **End**]

5 Press ↵ twice

 6 Click *Edit, Paste*   [**Ctrl** + **V**]

Remember, the Paste command places a selection from the Clipboard into a desired location. Your document should resemble Figure WIN3-13.

7 Close WordPad without saving this document

8 If desired, shut down Windows

Tip: You can also move a selection by dragging and dropping it.

☑ CHECKPOINT

✓ Launch WordPad and type the first paragraph in this module.
✓ Change the font (including style and size) of some of the text in the paragraph.
✓ Underline, strikeout, boldface, and italicize some of the text in the paragraph.

✓ Center align the paragraph.

✓ Copy the last sentence to the beginning of the paragraph and then close WordPad without saving the document.

PAINT

Paint is a graphics program that you can use to create and save color images (pictures). It can also be used for editing graphic images created with other programs and for editing and saving screen captures. *Screen captures* are similar to what would result if you took a photograph of your current screen.

GETTING STARTED

Like WordPad, commands to launch and close Paint, save, open, print, and create a new document are common for most Windows programs. Although these commands are reviewed as needed in the following exercises, you should review the "Basic Document Management" section in Chapter 1 before continuing.

As with most graphics programs, Paint uses the mouse pointer as its drawing tool in its workspace. Drawing tool selection and operation techniques are discussed later.

LAUNCHING PAINT. Like most Windows programs, Paint can be launched from the *Start* menu.

STEPS

1 Click the *Start* button   [**Ctrl** + **Esc**]

2 Point to *Programs* and then *Accessories* for its submenu

3 Click *Paint* to launch it

4 If needed, click Paint's *Maximize* button to maximize it   [**Alt** + **Spacebar** , **X**]

5 If needed, click *View*, *Status Bar* to turn it on

Your Paint window should resemble Figure WIN3-14.

> **Tip: Remember, as illustrated in Chapter 2 "Document Approach," you can also create and name a new document for any program in a Folder window.**

MOUSE ACTIONS BY KEYBOARD. Freehand drawing with a mouse is generally easier than with a keyboard. Drawing with a keyboard, however, allows you to be more accurate in moving the mouse pointer. Before drawing in Paint with a keyboard,

FIGURE WIN3-14 ■ **THE PAINT WINDOW**

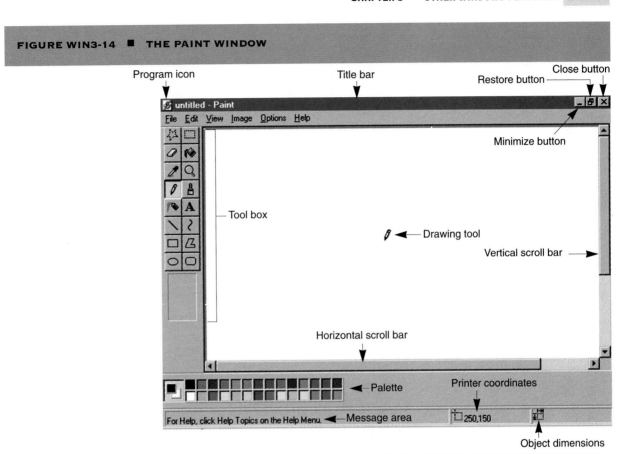

WIN

you will need to turn on the Use MouseKeys feature. This feature is part of the Accessibility Properties feature, which can be accessed through the Control Panel. If you desire to use the MouseKeys, see the "Mouse and Keyboard Operations" section in Chapter 1 and Figure WIN1-2b.

THE PAINT WINDOW.   As identified in Figure WIN3-14, the Paint window has a variety of common Windows features including a title bar (with program icon, program and document name, resizing buttons, and a close button), menu bar, workspace, and status bar. Each component operation is discussed as needed. Paint also opens with a tool box at the left side of its workspace and a palette just above the status bar. When the mouse pointer is in the workspace, it becomes the selected drawing tool. In this case, it is a pencil—the default drawing tool. This feature will be used shortly to select a drawing tool and color.

STATUS BAR.   As identified at the bottom of Figure WIN3-14, the status bar has three sections: a messages area (left side), pointer coordinates (position), and object dimensions (right side). The pointer coordinates area displays the horizontal (x-axis) and vertical (y-axis) coordinates of your pointer in Paint's drawing area (workspace). This is expressed in terms of pixels. A **pixel** is equivalent to one small dot. All objects drawn with your computer are composed of pixels.

STEPS

1 **Move your pointer around the drawing area until you are at the coordinates 100, 150 (horizontal or x=100, vertical or y=150)**

2 **Move your pointer to the coordinates 400, 100**

The width × height dimensions of an object in pixels appear at the far right end of the status bar when drawing. As a guide, both the pointer coordinates and width × height dimension pixels are supplied in the exercises to follow.

DOCUMENT MANAGEMENT.   Basic document management commands include saving to disk, clearing the workspace, opening, and printing. These commands are reviewed throughout the exercises in this section and are common to most Windows programs. See Figure WIN3-3 in the WordPad section for a summary.

CLOSING PAINT.   As with all programs, Paint can be closed by any of the methods listed in Figure WIN1-26 in Chapter 1. Remember, closing exits the program. For now, to close Paint,

STEP

  1 **Click Paint's *Close* button**   [**Alt** + **F4**]

SELECTING A DRAWING TOOL

A **drawing tool** is the instrument that you use to create a drawing. Selecting a drawing tool involves not only selecting the tool itself but also selecting its drawing width or fill style and its color. These items are normally selected from Paint's tool box and palette.

When you first launch Paint, the default drawing tool is a pencil. To draw with the pencil or any drawing tool, simply drag it. This will be demonstrated shortly.

The selections in the next exercises are required for the object that you will draw in the following section.

STEPS

1 **Launch *Paint***

  2 **If needed, click Paint's *Maximize* button to maximize it**    [**Alt** + **Spacebar** , **X**]

3 **If needed, click *View, Status Bar* to turn it on**

SELECTING A TOOL.   The **tool box,** as in Figure WIN3-15a, provides a variety of tools that can be used to create a drawing. Remember, the pointer becomes the selected drawing tool when in the workspace (drawing area). Procedures for tool selection are the same for each tool. Many tools offer options as to drawing width, shape, opaqueness, and fill style. If available for a tool, these options appear at the bottom of the tool box when the tool is selected. To see some of these options and practice selecting different tools, select the Line and then Ellipse tools.

> **Tip: Pointing to many buttons in the Windows environment without clicking will display their titles.**

To select the Line tool,

STEPS

1 **Click the *Line* tool box button**

Note that a variety of line widths appear below the tool buttons in the tool box as in Figure WIN3-15b. The default line width setting is the thinnest width. *The drawing width selected for the line or curve tool becomes the drawing width for any other tool selected afterward.* For the first drawing exercise in the next section, select the widest drawing width now:

2 **Click the *Thickest* drawing width in the tool box (bottom width)**

FIGURE WIN3-15 ■ SELECTING A DRAWING TOOL

(a) The tool box provides a variety of drawing tools. To select a tool, simply click its button. The lower portion of the tool box displays a tool's options (if any).
(b) Selecting the Line or Curve tool will display these drawing width options at the bottom of the dialog box.
(c) The Ellipse, Rectangle, Polygon, and Rounded Rectangle tools offer these fill style options when selected.

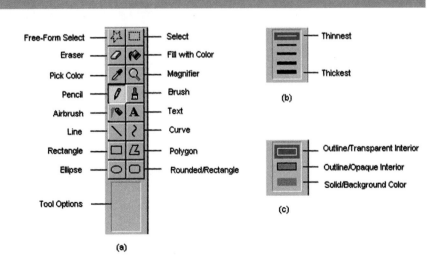

WIN

Tip: Drawing width options also appear when the Curve tool is selected.

To select the Ellipse tool:

 3 **Click the *Ellipse* tool**

As in Figure WIN3-15c, three fill style options appear at the bottom of the tool box: outline with a transparent interior, outline with an opaque interior, and solid with the background color. This tool can be used to draw ellipses or perfect circles. Wait until you are ready to complete the first drawing exercises in the next section before making this selection.

Tip: Fill styles are also available when using the Rectangle, Polygon, and Round Rectangle tools.

SELECTING A PALETTE COLOR. The **palette**, as in Figure WIN3-16, has a Select Colors box and a Paint Palette. The **Select Colors box** displays the currently selected foreground (black) and background colors (white). The color used by a tool when drawing is the foreground color. The background color is the drawing area's color. The **drawing area** is the workspace of Paint's window, which is like a piece of canvas or paper.

This text assumes that you are using a color monitor and that your palette has a variety of colors. If you have a black-and-white monitor, just pick a different pattern from the palette when performing the next exercises.

To select another foreground color, simply click the desired color in the palette. For example, to select red,

FIGURE WIN3-16 ■ THE PALETTE

Clicking a color in the paint palette will select the foreground color, which is used by the selected drawing tool. Right-clicking a color in the paint palette will select the background color.

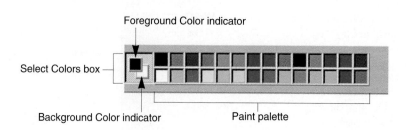

STEP

1 Click the *Red* palette box

Note that the foreground color in the Select Colors box is now red. Leave this selection for the first drawing exercise.

Tip: To change the background color, right-click the desired color.

DRAWING OBJECTS

Once you have selected a drawing tool, width, and color, you are ready to draw an object. An *object* is a picture that may include a graphic image or text. For example, the *My Computer* icon on the desktop is an object that includes a picture of a computer and the title "My Computer." To learn how to use Paint's features, you will create the "No Smoking" symbol in Figure WIN3-17. As you draw, take special note of the techniques that are used to draw each part of this picture. This text assumes that you have completed the previous section "Selecting a Drawing Tool."

DRAWING A SHAPE.   In this section you will use the Ellipse, Line, and Rounded Rectangle tools to draw a "don't" symbol (circle with a slash) and a cigarette. Horizontal and vertical (x, y) pointer position coordinates and width × height object dimensions are provided for drawing each shape. You do not have to be exactly at each set of coordinates or dimensions for the shapes that you create next. They are provided only as a guide.

To draw a red circle as in Figure WIN3-18a:

STEPS

1 Point to the position 30, 160 (horizontal, vertical)

FIGURE WIN3-17 ■ A DRAWING OF A "NO SMOKING" SYMBOL

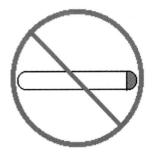

2 Press and hold ▯ **Shift** ▯ while dragging diagonally southeast to the dimensions 140 × 140 (width × height) and then release your mouse.

Holding the Shift key while dragging creates a perfect circle instead of an ellipse. Your circle should resemble Figure WIN3-18a.

Tip: If you make a mistake, click *Edit*, *Undo* to undo your last action.

To save this drawing as 1PAINT:

 3 Click *File, Save*

4 Type ▯ **1PAINT** ▯ in the Filename text box

 5 Click the "▼" button of the *Save as type* drop-down box and then click *16 Color Bitmap*

The default file type is 256 Color Bitmap. Although this is the highest quality file, it requires a lot of disk space when saved. The exercises in this manual will use 16 Color Bitmap to conserve disk space.

 6 If needed, click the "▼" button of the *Save in* drop-down box and then click *3½ Floppy (A:)* to change the default drive to Drive A

7 Click the *Save* button

To draw a line across the circle as in Figure WIN3-18b:

8 Click the *Line* tool on the tool box

FIGURE WIN3-18 ■ DRAWING SHAPES

(a) To draw a circle, press and hold the Shift key while dragging the Ellipse tool diagonally.
(b) To draw a straight line, press and hold the Shift key while dragging the Line tool.
(c) The Rounded/Rectangle, Line, and Fill With Color tools were used to create this picture of a cigarette.

(a)   **(b)**   **(c)**

9 Move to position 50, 182

10 Press and hold Shift while dragging southeast diagonally to the dimensions 95 × 95 and then release your mouse (As with drawing a circle, holding the Shift key while dragging the Line tool will draw a perfect line.)

Your "don't" symbol should resemble Figure WIN3-18b.

11 Resave your drawing as 1PAINT

Now to draw a cigarette as in Figure WIN3-18c.

12 Click the thinnest line width in the bottom section of the tool box

13 Click the *Rounded Rectangle* tool to select it

14 Click the color *Black* in the palette

15 Move to position 245, 220

16 Without releasing your mouse until the shape is completed, drag down to the dimensions 1 × 20, and then drag right horizontally to the dimensions 125 × 20

17 Release your mouse

18 Click the *Line* tool again

19 Move your pointer to position 358, 220

20 Press and hold Shift while dragging down vertically to the dimensions 1 × 20 and then release your mouse

Your cigarette drawing should resemble Figure WIN3-18c. Unlike the figure, the tip of your cigarette should be blank.

21 Resave the document as 1PAINT

FILLING IN AN AREA.   The Fill with Color tool can be used to *fill in* an area with a color or pattern. In the next exercise, you will use the Fill with Color tool to fill in the tip of the cigarette with gray and the open space of the drawing area with yellow.

STEPS

1 If needed, open the 1PAINT document

2 Click the *Fill with Color* tool to select it

3 Click the color *Gray* in the palette

4 Move the *Fill with Color* tool within the cigarette tip and then click it to fill

5 Resave the drawing as 1PAINT

Now, to fill in the drawing area with yellow,

6 Click the color *Yellow* in the palette

7 Point to any open space in the drawing area and click

The area around your "don't" symbol and cigarette are now yellow. Continue to the next section without saving, keeping the screen as is.

UNDOING.   Like other Windows programs, Paint has an undo command that will undo your last action. *Undo* does not work if you have resaved your document or selected another drawing tool.
To undo the yellow fill,

STEPS

1 Click *Edit, Undo*   [**Ctrl** + **Z**]

The yellow now disappears from your drawing area.

2 Click *File, New, No* to clear your drawing area   [**Ctrl** + **N** , **N**]

MOVING AND COPYING OBJECTS

When drawing, the ability to move or copy an object can save time and help create other objects. For instance, in the next exercise you will move the "don't" symbol over the cigarette to create a "No Smoking" symbol.
The process of moving or copying a selection in Paint is the same as in WordPad. However, as you will soon see, the selection procedure is different.
Remember, moving a selection involves changing its location. Copying a selection involves duplicating it in another location. The difference between moving and copying is that moving removes (cuts) the selection from its original position.

SELECTING AN OBJECT.   To select an object in Paint, you must use either the *Select* or the *Free-Form Select* tool. The **Select tool** is used to select an object with a dashed rectangular box. The **Free-Form Select tool** is used to custom or precision select an object with a dash line by its contour. Only selecting with the Select tool is demonstrated next:

WIN

1 **Open the 1PAINT document**

2 **Click the *Select tool* (top right tool)**

3 **Move your pointer to position 15, 150 and click**

4 **Drag diagonally southeast to the dimensions 165 × 165 and then release your mouse**

Your "don't" symbol should now be selected with a rectangular dashed box. If it is not fully selected, repeat Steps 3 and 4 and adjust your coordinates and dimensions as needed.

Tip: To select an object with the Free-Form Select tool, simply drag your mouse around the object.

Once an object is selected, it can be moved or copied within the drawing area or to another document. Because these procedures are similar, only moving techniques are demonstrated next:

5 **Click *Edit, Cut* to move the selection to the Clipboard**   [**Ctrl** + **X**]

(To copy instead of cut, click *Edit, Copy* or press **Ctrl** + **C** in Step 5.)

Remember, the Clipboard is a program that temporarily holds a cut or copied selection for future pasting.

6 **Click *Edit, Paste***   [**Ctrl** + **V**]

Your selection now appears at the top left corner of the drawing area. At this point, it can be moved to any position within the drawing area by dragging and dropping.

7 **Point anywhere within the rectangular selected area**

8 **Drag and then drop the "don't" symbol (red circle with a slash) over the cigarette as in Figure WIN3-19**

9 **Click anywhere outside the selection area to deselect**

Your "No Smoking" symbol should resemble Figure WIN3-17.

10 **Resave this drawing as 1PAINT**

Tip: A quick way to move a selected object around the drawing area is to drag it. To copy using this technique, you must hold the Ctrl key while dragging.

FIGURE WIN3-19 ■ **SELECTING AN OBJECT**

To select an object, click the Select tool and drag diagonally across the object. The selected object will appear with a dashed line around it. The dots on the dashed line are handles that can be dragged to resize the selection.

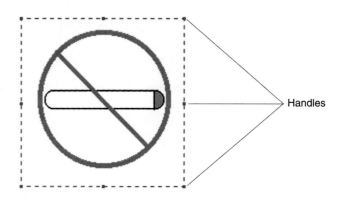

Handles

INSERTING TEXT

The **Text tool,** denoted by "A," allows you to place text into your drawing. As with other tools, you may select its color by using the palette. In addition, a **Text toolbar** is available when using the Text tool for other text appearance changes including font, font size, and style changes.

To add the caption "NO SMOKING" above the "No Smoking" symbol in your 1PAINT document as in Figure WIN3-20,

STEPS

1 **If needed, open the 1PAINT document**

FIGURE WIN3-20 ■ **THE COMPLETED "NO SMOKING" SIGN**

NO SMOKING

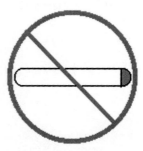

2 Click the *Text* tool in the tool box

You must now define the *text area,* as in Figure WIN3-21a. This is the area where your text will appear in the document:

3 Move to the position 235, 110 and click

4 Without releasing your mouse button, drag right horizontally to the 145 × 1 width and height and then drag down vertically to 145 × 35 as in Figure WIN3-21a

5 Release your mouse button

6 If needed, click *View, Text Toolbar* (Font toolbar) to turn it on

7 Click the "▼" button of the *Font* drop-down box (Text toolbar)

8 Use the vertical scroll bar of the *Font* drop-down list to locate *Times New Roman* and click it

9 Click the "▼" button of the *Font Size* drop-down box and then click *14* for font size

10 Click the *Bold* button

FIGURE WIN3-21 ■ INSERTING TEXT

(a) To insert text, click the *Text* tool and then drag to define the text area.
(b) Clicking *View, Text Toolbar* after defining the text area turns on this toolbar.

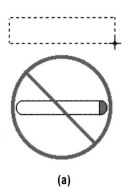

(a)

(b)

The selections in your Text (Font) toolbar should resemble Figure WIN3-21b.

11 Click the *Text Entry* box to move the insertion point there

12 Type NO SMOKING

13 Click outside of the *Text Entry* box to deselect it

 14 If needed, to better center the "NO SMOKING" text above the "No Smoking" symbol, click the *Select tool,* select the "NO SMOKING" text, and then drag and drop it as needed.

Your completed "No Smoking" sign should resemble Figure WIN3-20.

15 Resave this drawing as 1PAINT

16 Click *File, Print, OK* to print your 1PAINT document (If you do not have a color printer, your image will print with gray tones.)   [Ctrl + P , ↵]

 17 Close Paint

CAPTURING A SCREEN

Screen capturing is the process of taking a picture of your current screen. To capture a screen, simply press the *Print Screen* button on the keyboard. This copies the current image of your screen to the Clipboard for future pasting. Pasting this image to Paint allows you to edit, save, and print it.

> Tip: A screen capture can be pasted to any program that accepts it.

Try this to capture a screen of the Paint window with your 1PAINT document opened.

STEPS

1 Launch and maximize your Paint window

2 Open the 1PAINT document

3 Press Print Screen and wait a few seconds

4 Click *File, New* and if needed, *No* to clear the workspace

5 Click *Edit, Paste*   [Ctrl + V]

An image of the screen similar to Figure WIN3-22 appears selected in Paint's drawing area. You can now edit and save this image. For now, exit Paint without saving:

 6 Click Paint's *Close* button, *No*

7 If desired, shut down Windows

FIGURE WIN3-22 ■ SCREEN CAPTURING

Pressing the Print Screen key copies the image of the current screen to the Clipboard. Clicking *Edit, Paste* places the image into Paint for editing, saving, and printing.

WIN

> **Tip: To screen capture just the active window, press [Alt] + [Print Screen].**

 CHECKPOINT

✓ Launch Paint
✓ Draw a happy face with any line size and color you desire and save it as FACE.
✓ Copy the face image created in the previous checkpoint and change its expression to a sad face.
✓ Insert the text "Happy" above the happy face image and "Sad" above the other image.
✓ Resave the document as FACE and close Paint.

LINKING AND EMBEDDING

Earlier you learned how to copy and move information both between and within programs. Here you will explore two other techniques to share information between documents of different programs: linking and embedding.

In linking and embedding, an **object** is a set of information. The document with the original information is called the **source file.** The document receiving the information is called the **container file** or **compound document.**

The term **OLE** (short for "Object Linking and Embedding") refers to transferring information from one program to another as an object. When you OLE an object, it retains its source file's display format in the container file. For example, if you OLE a selection from Paint into a WordPad document, it will appear in Paint's format. This will be demonstrated shortly.

Objects may also be linked or embedded into a container file in formats that may differ from their source. Format options may differ for different programs. Only OLE (objects linked or embedded as objects) operations are demonstrated here. You may want to try the other format options on your own.

LINKING

Linking establishes an ongoing connection between the source file that provides the object and the container file that receives it. The object remains stored in the source file. The copy of the object in the container file is automatically updated whenever the source file's object is changed. For example, if a Paint object is linked with WordPad, changes in the Paint object will appear in the WordPad document.

EMBEDDING

Embedding inserts an object from the source file into a container file. The object then becomes part of the container file. Any changes in the source file do not appear in the embedded object.

You can, of course, change information in the embedded object. An embedded object is edited by using its source program without changing the source file. You might, for example, embed information from a Paint document into a WordPad document and then change only the information in the container file (WordPad document).

Because linking and embedding operations are similar, only an embedding operation is demonstrated next. Linking commands are supplied in brackets "[ ]" where different.

EMBEDDING AN OBJECT.   The following exercise embeds the "NO SMOKING" sign in the 1PAINT document into the 3WORDPAD document. Remember, embedding an object simply inserts it into the container file with the ability to edit the object using the source program. The following procedure assumes that you created the 3WORDPAD and 1PAINT documents from the previous modules in this chapter:

STEPS

1   Start your computer and Windows

2   Launch Paint and open the 1PAINT document

3   If needed, click *View, Status Bar* to turn it on

4   **Click the *Select* tool**

5   **Move your pointer to position 215, 100 (horizontal, vertical)**

6   **Drag the pointer diagonally southeast to position 210, 210 to select your drawing**

7   **Click *Edit, Copy* to copy the selection to the Clipboard**   [**Ctrl**   +   **C**   ]

> **Note: You must start with the source file to create a link.**

Remember, the Copy command copies a selection to the Clipboard, a program that temporarily holds the selection for future pasting, embedding, or paste linking into another location. Now you will use the *Paste Special* dialog box to embed your object into the 3WORDPAD document.

8   **Launch WordPad, maximize it (if needed) and open the 3WORDPAD document**

9   **Press**   **Ctrl**   +   **End**   **to move to the bottom of the document**

10   **Press**   ↵   **twice to skip two lines.**

11   **Click *Edit, Paste Special* for its dialog box as in Figure WIN3-23**

This dialog box lets you either paste (the default), which embeds an object, or paste link (if available). Several format options, if available, are listed in the *As* list box of the dialog box. To paste as an embedded bitmap object,

FIGURE WIN3-23 ■ THE PASTE SPECIAL DIALOG BOX

This dialog box is used for embedding or linking objects.

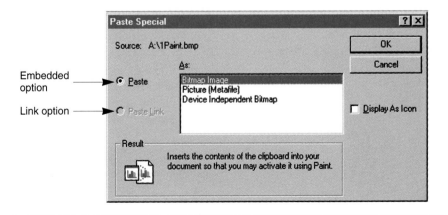

12 Click *OK*

(To paste link instead of embed, click the *Paste Link* option (if available), then click OK for Step 12.)

The 1PAINT image appears in the WordPad document as in Figure WIN3-24. It is also currently selected and can be moved by dragging it, or it can be resized by dragging one of its handles.

13 Click outside the embedded object to deselect it.

14 Save this document as 1EMBED

EDITING AN EMBEDDED OBJECT. To edit an embedded (or linked) object in its source program,

STEPS

1 Double-click the embedded (or linked) object in WordPad

The object is now displayed in its source program within the WordPad document as in Figure WIN3-24b. Note also the Paint's menu bar, tool box, palette, and status bar also appear in the WordPad window. This allows you to edit the object in Paint.

 2 Use the Rectangle tool to draw a rectangular box around the "NO SMOKING" text as in Figure WIN3-25

3 Click outside the object's window to deselect it

4 Resave your embedded document as 1EMBED and print it

> **Tip:** Some programs, upon saving the edited container file, give you the option to change the source file.

Your printed document now appears as in Figure WIN3-25. Because this object is embedded, only the container file was changed. Embedded objects are stored with the container file. Changes in the source file are not typically reflected in the container file. Complete the following steps to see that your source file has been unchanged.

> **Tip:** If this object were linked, the changes would be automatically reflected in the source and container files. Linked information is stored with the source file.

5 Click the *1Paint-Paint* taskbar button to switch back to Paint

FIGURE WIN3-24 ■ EMBEDDING AN OBJECT

(a) This object has been embedded from the 1PAINT document.
(b) Double-clicking an embedded object allows you to edit it in its source program without changing its source file.

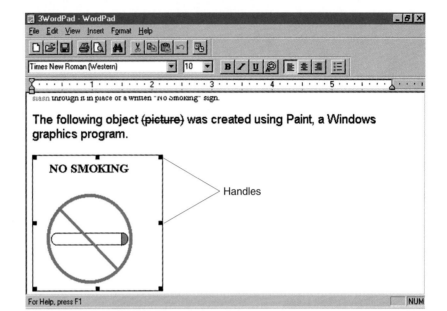

(a)

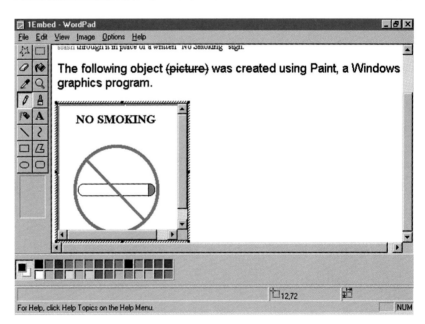

(b)

WIN

Examine the source document and note that the changes made in the 1EMBED document are not reflected there.

 6 **Close Paint and WordPad**

FIGURE WIN3-25 ■ THE PRINTED COMPLETED DOCUMENT

Your Name
M/D/YY

Windows is a *graphical user interface* (GUI) that uses pictures and menus instead of typewritten commands to help you communicate with your computer. It is like using a picture of a cigarette with a red slash through it in place of a written "No Smoking" sign.

The following object (picture) was created using Paint, a Windows graphics program.

7 **Shut down Windows**

Tip: If the object were linked and you later made changes to the linked Paint document while the WordPad document was not opened, the changes would appear the next time you opened it. Of course, this will only happen if both source and container files and programs are available in the same system.

Tip: To link or embed an entire document (file), use the Object command of the *Insert* menu. You can also use this command to embed a new object into a container file. For example, you can create a worksheet in Word using Excel. Once the new object is embedded, you can also link it. See your on-line instructions for details.

☑ CHECKPOINT

✓ Launch Paint and open the FACE document created in the Paint Checkpoint and resave it with the name SERVER.
✓ Select and copy the images to the Clipboard.
✓ Launch WordPad, type your name, and then save the document as CONTAINER.

✓ Embed the images from the Clipboard to the CONTAINER file beneath your name.
✓ Edit the embedded object from the CONTAINER document, adding a few things to the images and resave.

OTHER WINDOWS PROGRAMS

Windows comes with a variety of programs. To use many of these programs, you must first install them on your system. This section provides an overview of some of these programs and their key features. Check with your instructor before trying to access any of them.

STEP

1 Start Windows

ACCESSIBILITY OPTIONS

Windows **accessibility options** allows you to adjust keyboard, display, sound, and mouse controls based on individual preference. You can access the accessibility options through the Control Panel. Try this:

STEPS

1 Click the *Start* button   [**Ctrl** + **Esc**]

2 Point to *Settings* for its submenu and then click *Control Panel*

3 Double-click the *Accessibility Options* icon

As in Figure WIN3-26, the *Accessibility Options* dialog box has five tabs: Keyboard, Sound, Display, Mouse, and General. Each tab clearly defines its option.

4 Examine the Keyboard tab options

5 Click each of the other tabs to see their options

If you are working on your own system, you may want to select some of the options offered in the *Accessibility Options* dialog box. If you are on a network or other system, check with your instructor before making any changes.

FIGURE WIN3-26 ■ THE *ACCESSIBILITY PROPERTIES* DIALOG BOX

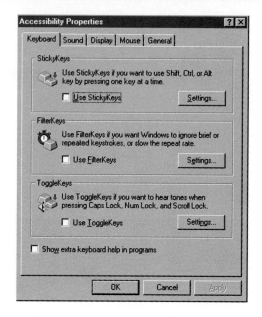

ACCESSORIES

The Windows **Accessories** group includes a variety of programs that can help you perform daily tasks. You have already worked with at least three of these programs, namely, Notepad, WordPad, and Paint. Figure WIN3-27 summarizes the Accessories programs. (Note: Your system's programs may vary.)

COMMUNICATIONS

Windows comes with a variety of **communications programs** that can be used for connecting to other computers, on-line services, electronic mail, and fax operations. Microsoft also has its own on-line service called Microsoft Network. **Electronic mail** allows users to send and receive electronic documents through a network or other forms of communication. Many of these programs require a modem, fax/modem, and/or network. See Figure WIN3-28 for a summary of these programs and their requirements.

A very popular source of on-line information service is the **Internet,** a group of international computer networks communicating by phone lines. It provides a variety of services including *electronic mail,* news, research information, and games.

You can use Windows Dial-Up Network to connect to the Internet or Microsoft Network. Both features require a modem and Microsoft Network also requires that you have Microsoft Exchange and have signed up as a user. See your on-line Help window for more information on accessing the Internet.

Accessory Program	Function
Calculator	On-line Calculator.
Calendar	For daily scheduling.
Cardfile	For creating electronic index cards.
Character Map	For inserting symbols and characters in a document.
Clipboard Viewer	For viewing the contents of Windows Clipboard.
Desktop Wallpaper	For inserting background images (pictures in the desktop background.
Document Templates	For creating new documents for your most common programs.
Games	Includes several games such as Solitaire, Minesweeper, Hearts, and FreeCell.
Mouse Pointers	For changing the size of your mouse pointer.
Notepad	For creating and editing text-only files.
Net Watcher	For monitoring your network.
Online User Guide	Windows 95 User Guide.
Paint	For creating, editing, and saving color images.
Quick View	For viewing a document without opening it.
Screen Savers	For preventing damage to your screen by displaying moving images while it is idle.
System Monitor	Monitor system performance.
System Resource Meter	For viewing system resource levels.
Windows 95 Tour	On-line tutorial for operating Windows 95.
WinPopup	For sending or receiving messages on a network.
WordPad	For creating simple documents.

WIN

STEPS

1 **Close any open window**

2 **Shut down Windows**

☑ CHECKPOINT

✓ What is available through the Windows accessibility options?
✓ Launch Calendar (Accessories group) and enter your class schedule for the current week. Save this file as SCHEDULE and then close the program.

FIGURE WIN3-28 ■ WINDOWS COMMUNICATION PROGRAMS

Program Group	Description
Dial-up Network	For connecting to other computers by modem.
Direct Cable Connection	For connecting to other computers by parallel or serial cable.
Hyper Terminal	For connecting to on-line services and other computers by modem.
Phone Dialer	For dialing a phone through a modem.
Microsoft Exchange	For managing and integrating electronic mail, MAPI, and other messaging programs. (Requires a network and/or modem.)
Microsoft Mail Services	For accessing Microsoft Mail Post Offices. (Requires a network and/or modem.)
Microsoft Fax Services	For sending and receiving faxes. (Requires a fax/modem.)
Microsoft Fax Viewer	For viewing Microsoft Fax images. (Requires a fax/modem.)
Microsoft Network	Microsoft's on-line service. (Requires Microsoft Exchange and a modem.)
Multilanguage Support	For creating documents in other languages.
Multimedia	For using CD-ROM drives and sound cards to play sound and videos.

✓ Launch Cardfile and create index cards for five or more of your friends and family members. Include each person's name, address, and telephone number. Save this file as PHONE and then close the program.

✓ Describe a few communications programs that come with Windows.

✓ What is the Clipboard Viewer and how can you access it?

SUMMARY

■ *WordPad* is a simple word processing program that can create and edit computer documents with text and objects (graphic) images.

■ Content changes include inserting, deleting, modifying, copying, and moving text in the document.

■ Text appearance changes include alterations to font type, style (regular, bold, or italic), and size.

■ Layout (format) changes concern the way text is arranged in a document, such as changes to the margin or tab settings.

■ Pressing the Enter key when using WordPad is *not* required at the end of each line. Text automatically flows to the next line as you type, which is called wordwrapping.

■ The Enter key produces a line break at the point where it is pressed ending a line before it reaches the right margin. It also moves the insertion point to the beginning of the next line. Line breaks are generally needed at the end of a paragraph, each line of an address, a salutation, or to skip a line.

- Selecting text involves marking (highlighting) it for editing. A selection of text is simply a contiguous segment of text. Text must be selected to perform appearance and format changes on it.

- Deleting text involves removing it from a document. When you delete text in a *Word-Pad* document, the remaining text automatically reformats.

- Paint is a graphics program that can create and save color images (pictures). It can also edit graphic images created with other programs as well as edit and save screen captures.

- Screen capturing is similar to taking a photograph of your current screen.

- Paint uses the mouse pointer as its drawing tool in its workspace. In addition to common Windows features, Paint also has a tool box at the left side of its workspace and a palette at the bottom of its window.

- Paint's status bar has three sections: a messages area (left side), pointer coordinates, and object dimensions in pixels (right side). All objects drawn with a computer are composed of pixels (small dots).

- In linking and embedding, an object is a set of information. The document with the original information is called the source file. The document receiving the information is called the container file or compound document.

- Object Linking and Embedding (OLE) refers to transferring information from one program to another as an object.

- Linking establishes an ongoing connection between the source file that provides the object and the container file that receives it. The object remains stored in the source file. The copy of the object in the container file is automatically updated whenever the source file's object is changed.

- Embedding inserts an object from the source file into a container file. The object then becomes part of the container file. Any changes in the source file do not appear in the embedded object.

- Accessibility options allow you to adjust keyboard, display, sound, and mouse controls based on individual preference.

- The Windows Accessories group includes a variety of programs that are helpful in performing daily tasks and are listed in Figure WIN3-27.

- Windows Communication programs can be used for connecting to other computers, on-line services, electronic mail, and fax operations. Microsoft also has its own on-line service called Microsoft Network. Many of these programs require a modem, fax/modem, and/or network.

KEYTERMS

Accessibility options (WIN163)
Accessories (WIN164)
Alignment (WIN138)
Bolding (WIN135)
Bullet style (WIN140)
Communications programs (WIN164)
Container file or compound document (WIN158)
Drawing area (WIN148)
Drawing tool (WIN146)
Electronic mail (WIN164)

Embedding (WIN158)
Font (WIN133)
Free-Form Select tool (WIN152)
Indentation (WIN136)
Internet (WIN164)
Italicizing (WIN135)
Layout (format) (WIN124)
Line break (WIN126)
Linking (WIN158)
Object (WIN158)
OLE (WIN158)
Paint (WIN144)
Palette (WIN148)

Pixel (WIN145)
Screen capturing (WIN156)
Select Colors box (WIN148)
Select tool (WIN152)
Source file (WIN158)
Tabs (WIN141)
Text appearance (WIN124)
Text tool (WIN154)
Text toolbar (WIN154)
Tool box (WIN146)
Wordwrap (WIN126)

QUIZ

TRUE/FALSE

____   1. Most Windows programs can be launched from the *Start* menu.

____   2. Only text can be placed into a WordPad document.

____   3. Selecting text or an object involves marking it for editing.

____   4. Only the Open and *Save As* dialog boxes can be used for file management.

____   5. WordPad's ruler can be used for text appearance changes.

____   6. Paint can be used to create color drawings with text and objects.

____   7. The Cut command will move any selection to the Windows Clipboard for future pasting.

____   8. Changes in a linked source file do not affect the container file.

____   9. Double-clicking an embedded object will allow you to edit using its source program.

____ 10. Communications programs can only be used with a modem.

MULTIPLE CHOICE

____ 11. All of the following can be used to open a saved document except,
   a. Clicking *Open, File*
   b. Using My Computer
   c. Pressing **Ctrl** + **O**
   d. Clicking *File, Open*

____ 12. Which command will clear the workspace of WordPad, Paint, or Notepad?
   a. Clear
   b. New
   c. Exit
   d. Delete

____ 13. Which graphical WordPad feature can be used to set indentation by mouse?
   a. Toolbar
   b. *Edit* menu
   c. Ruler
   d. Indent bar

____ 14. The Copy command will copy a selection to
   a. Windows Clipboard
   b. A new location in the same document
   c. A new location in another document
   d. Paint

____ 15. To select a drawing tool in Paint
   a. Double-click its button in the tool box
   b. Click its button in the tool box
   c. Select it from the *Tools* menu
   d. Click its button in the palette

     16. To select the background color
   a. Click the color in the tool box
   b. Click the color in the palette
   c. Click the color in the *Color* menu
   d. Right-click the color in the palette

___ 17. The term OLE is short for
    a. Object Line and Edit
    b. Object Linking and Embedding
    c. Opening Linking and Embedding
    d. Opening Layout and Edit

___ 18. In an embedding operation the embedded object is stored in the
    a. Source file
    b. Original document
    c. Container file
    d. Source program

___ 19. In a linking operation the linked object is stored in the
    a. Source file
    b. Original document
    c. Container file
    d. Source program

___ 20. To edit a linked or embedded object from the container document
    a. Click *Edit, Linked, or Embedded*
    b. Click the *OLE* toolbar button
    c. Double-click the linked or embedded object
    d. Click *Edit, Paste Special*

FIGURE WIN3-29 ■ MATCHING

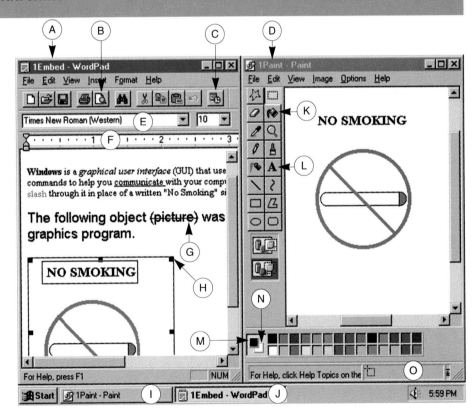

MATCHING

Select the lettered item from the figure on page WIN169 that best matches each phrase below.

___ 21. Indicates the active program.

___ 22. Dragging this item will resize the object.

___ 23. The selected foreground color.

___ 24. Can be used to adjust margins and tab settings by mouse.

___ 25. Used to insert text into a drawing.

___ 26. Can be used to insert the system date.

___ 27. The container document's name in an embedding operation.

___ 28. An effect created with the *Font* dialog box.

___ 29. The area where pointer coordinates are displayed when drawing an object.

___ 30. Used to fill an area with color.

ANSWERS

True/False: 1. T; 2. F; 3. T; 4. F; 5. F; 6. T; 7. T; 8. F; 9. T; 10. F
Multiple Choice: 11. a; 12. b; 13. c; 14. a; 15. b; 16. d; 17. b; 18. c; 19. a; 20. c
Matching: 21. j or a; 22. h; 23. m; 24. f; 25. l; 26. c; 27. a; 28. g; 29. o; 30. k

EXERCISE

I. OPERATIONS

Provide the commands to do each of the following operations. For each operation, assume a hard-disk system with a disk in Drive A. You may want to verify each command by trying it on your computer.

1. Launch WordPad and Paint and switch back to WordPad.

2. Type your name, address, and phone number on three separate lines.

3. Change the font type, size, and style of your name.

4. Center your name, address, and phone number

5. Save this WordPad document as MYLETTER.

6. Switch to Paint, draw a star, and fill it in with yellow.

7. Save the Paint document as STAR.

8. Embed the star from your Paint document into the WordPad document.

9. Edit the star from your WordPad document by adding a circle around it.

10. Resave the MYLETTER document and close all programs.

II. COMMANDS

Describe fully, using as few words as possible, what command is initiated or what is accomplished in Windows by the actions described below. Assume that each exercise part is independent of any previous parts.

1. Pressing **Ctrl** + **O** .

2. Pressing **Ctrl** + **S** .

3. Pressing **Ctrl** + **A** .

4. Clicking WordPad's ruler.

5. Double-clicking a linked object in the container file.

6. Using the Paste Special command.

7. Turning on the MouseKeys in the *Accessibility Properties* dialog box.

8. Pressing **Print Screen** .

9. Pressing and holding the Shift key while dragging the Line tool in Paint.

10. Dragging the handle of a selected object.

III. APPLICATIONS

Perform the following operations, briefly tell how you accomplished each operation, and describe its results.

APPLICATION 1: USING WORDPAD

1. Start Windows and launch WordPad.

2. Maximize the WordPad window.

3. Type the paragraphs in the box that follows. Be sure to include text appearance and layout changes.

4. Save this document as OLE.

5. Close WordPad and shut down Windows.

Your Name

Object Linking and Embedding (OLE) is a technique of transferring information from one program to another as an object. An <u>object</u> is a set of information. The document with the original information is the *source file*. The document receiving the information is the *container file*.

Linking establishes an ongoing <u>connection</u> between the source file that provides the object and the container file that receives it. The object *remains* stored in the source file. Whenever the object is changed in the source file, its copy in the container file is automatically updated.

Embedding *inserts* an object from the source file into a container file. Embedded objects can be edited from the container document using its source program. Changes to the object in the container file normally *do not* affect the source file.

APPLICATION 2: USING PAINT

1. Start Windows and launch Paint.

2. Maximize the Paint window and turn on the status bar.

3. Click the Ellipse tool.

4. Draw the head of a male stick figure (make sure you leave enough room for the body).

5. Click the Line tool.

6. Draw the body of the stick figure.

7. Save this drawing as FIGURE.

8. Print the FIGURE document.

9. Close Paint and shut down Windows

APPLICATION 3: USING A SCREEN CAPTURE

1. Start Windows and launch Paint.

2. Press **Print Screen** to capture your current screen.

3. Select the tool box from the screen capture of the Paint Window.

4. Cut the selection to the Clipboard.

5. Clear your Paint workspace.

6. Paste the selection (tool box) into the new Paint document.

7. Move it to the center of the drawing area.

8. Label the tool box. (Use Figure WIN3-15 as a guide.)

9. Save this as TOOLBOX and print it.

10. Close Paint and shut down Windows.

APPLICATION 4: EMBEDDING AN OBJECT
(Complete Applications 1, 2, and 3 before proceeding with this problem.)

1. Start Windows, launch WordPad, and open the OLE document created in Application 1.

2. Launch Paint and open the FIGURE document created in Application 2.

3. Maximize both windows.

4. Embed the stick figure from the FIGURE Paint document into the OLE WordPad document.

5. Save the revised OLE document as COUPLE.

6. Double-click the stick figure object in the COUPLE document to edit it.

7. Draw another stick figure.

8. Resave the document as COUPLE.

9. Print the COUPLE document.

10. Close all programs and shut down Windows.

APPLICATION 5: USING MOUSEKEYS

Note: Although using the Windows MouseKeys feature is helpful in creating precision drawings, it can be used with any operations in place of a mouse. The accessibility options must be installed on to your system to do this problem.)

1. Start Windows and launch Paint.

2. Turn on the MouseKeys. (For instructions, see the "Mouse and Keyboard Operations" section and Figure WIN1-2 in Chapter 1.)

3. Try to draw your favorite icon using the keyboard.

4. Save the document as MYICON.

5. Print the document.

6. Close Paint and shut down Windows.

APPLICATION 6: USING OTHER WINDOWS PROGRAMS

1. Start Windows and launch Cardfile.

2. Use the following steps to create five index cards for four family members or friends and yourself. Include each person's name, address, and phone number.
   a. Click *Edit, Index* for its dialog box.
   b. Type last name, first name, (for example, Kee, Charles)
   c. Click *OK*
   d. Type first and last names (for example, Charles Kee) and press [↵]
   e. Type address and phone number on separate lines
   f. Click *Card, Add*
   g. Repeat Steps b through e for each new card.

3. Save this file as ADDRESSBOOK.

4. Launch WordPad and maximize its window.

5. Switch to Cardfile.

6. Click the Index (top portion of index card) to select your own card.

7. Select and copy only your name and address to the Clipboard.

8. Switch to WordPad and paste your selection there.

9. Save the WordPad document MYADDRESS and print it.

10. Close all programs and shut down Windows.

MASTERY CASES

The following mastery cases allows you to demonstrate how much you have learned about this software. Each case describes a fictitious problem or need that can be solved using the skills that you have learned in this chapter. Although minimum acceptable outcomes are specified, you are expected and encouraged to design your own response (files, data, lists) in ways that display your personal mastery of the software. Feel free to show off your skills. Use real data from your own experience in your solution, although you may also fabricate data if needed.

These mastery cases allow you to display your ability to

- Launch WordPad and Paint.
- Make text appearance and layout changes to WordPad documents.
- Create objects in Paint.
- Embed objects from Paint documents into WordPad documents.
- Edit embedded objects.

CASE 1: USING WINDOWS AT SCHOOL

You have been asked to create a graphical guide to help your classmates learn some of the key components of the Windows screen. Arrange your Windows screen as you see fit. Screen capture it into Paint and save it. Now, use Paint to add labels, boxes, arrows, and any other objects you feel will help other students. Print and then resave the document. Close all windows and shut down Windows.

CASE 2: USING WINDOWS AT HOME

You have been asked to create a family tree and place it in a letter to your parent(s). Use Paint to draw and label the tree. Save and print this document. Next, prepare a short WordPad document addressed to your parent(s) explaining that you used Windows Paint to create the family tree. Change the fonts and layout as you feel necessary. Embed the family tree from your Paint document into your WordPad document. Save and print it. Now, edit the embedded object to include each person's place of birth. Resave and print it. Close all windows and shut down Windows.

CASE 3: USING WINDOWS AT WORK

Your are in the real estate business and need to create a flyer that announces the sale of a building. Use WorddPad to create this flyer and be sure that it has your company's name and a description of the property being sold, including its address and selling price. Use different fonts and other text enhancements to make your flyer more appealing. Next, using Paint, draw a picture of a house and embed it into your flyer. Now, add a "For Sale" sign to the embedded object. Save all documents and print only the flyer. Close all windows and shut down Windows.

MICROSOFT WINDOWS 95
FEATURES AND OPERATION REFERENCE

MOUSE OPERATIONS

A mouse (or other pointing device) allows you to control a mouse pointer (graphical image). As you move your mouse, the mouse pointer moves in a similar fashion on your screen. Common mouse pointer images and commands are summarized on Figure WIN1-2a and b in Chapter 1.

COMMON MOUSE ACTIONS

POINT. Pointing involves moving the mouse pointer on the screen by moving your mouse on a flat surface. When pointing in a menu, the selection highlight moves with the pointer to the desired item. Pointing to an item with a "▶" at its far right will open its submenu.

CLICK. Clicking involves quickly pressing and releasing your left mouse button.

DOUBLE-CLICK. Double-clicking involves quickly pressing and releasing your left mouse button twice.

DRAG. Dragging involves pressing and holding the left mouse button while moving the mouse pointer to a new location. Dragging can be used to select (mark by highlighting) text. Dragging can also be used in moving and copying operations called *dragging and dropping.*

DRAG AND DROP. Dragging and dropping can be used to move or copy a selection by mouse. Dropping is releasing your mouse button and the selection after dragging. To move or copy a selection using drag and drop:

	Moving	Copying
Within the Same File	Drag and drop	Press and hold Ctrl while dragging and dropping
Between Files	Press and hold Alt key while dragging and dropping	Drag and drop

RIGHT-CLICK. Right-clicking involves quickly pressing and releasing your right mouse button.

SELECT. Selecting is the process of marking (highlighting) text or other objects in order to edit, move, copy, open, print, or delete the item. Selecting text by mouse generally involves dragging your pointer over it. Selecting an object or menu item generally involves clicking it. Graphic programs, such as Paint, require special selection techniques that involve first selecting a Selection tool and then dragging your mouse pointer.

KEYBOARD OPERATIONS

Windows and many Windows programs can also be operated by keyboard. Keys that provide quick access to commands are called *Shortcut keys*. Shortcut keys are generally available with most Windows programs. Many also follow Windows standard Shortcut keys structure. For example, pressing `Alt` + `F4` will exit any program or dialog box. Keys used to perform mouse actions such as clicking, right-clicking, double-clicking, and dragging and dropping are called *MouseKeys*. Windows Accessibility Options must be installed on your system to use MouseKeys.

Other keyboard options available with the Accessibility Options include StickyKeys, FilterKeys, and ToggleKeys. *StickyKeys* allows you to use the Alt, Ctrl, or Shift keys by pressing each key one at a time. *FilterKeys* is an option that instructs Windows to ignore repeated keystrokes. *ToggleKeys* provides a sound when the Num Lock, Caps Lock, or Scroll Lock is pressed.

COMMON SHORTCUT KEYS

ALT. Pressed alone, the Alt key activates the selection highlight on a program window's menu bar. Once activated, the highlight can open a pull-down menu by either pressing its underlined letter or using the arrow keys and then the Enter key. If used with other keys, press and hold the Alt key while tapping the other key(s).

- `Alt` + `F4` exits any Windows program or dialog box.
- `Alt` + `Spacebar` opens a program window or dialog box's control-menu.
- `Alt` + `−` opens a document window's control-menu.
- `Alt` + `Tab` switches to the last active program when operating multiple programs.
- `Alt` + `Esc` switches to the next running program when operating multiple programs.
- `Alt` + `Print Screen` copies an image of the active window to Windows for future pasting.

ARROW KEYS. The arrow keys can be used with other keys or alone. When used with the Shift key, they expand a selection in the direction of the arrow. When used alone, an arrow key

- Moves the selection highlight in the direction of the arrow in a menu, list box, or drop-down box.
- Moves the insertion point in the direction of the arrow in a document or text box.

BACKSPACE. The Backspace key erases single characters to the left of the insertion point.

CAPS LOCK. The Caps Lock key keeps the Shift key active so that characters can be typed in uppercase.

CTRL. The Ctrl key is generally used with other keys to invoke a command.

- **Ctrl** + **Alt** + **Delete** exits the current program if it stops responding to the system. It is also used to reboot the computer.
- **Ctrl** + **B** turns the bold feature on or off.
- **Ctrl** + **C** copies a selection to Windows Clipboard for future pasting.
- **Ctrl** + **Esc** opens the *Start* menu.
- **Ctrl** + **F4** closes the active document window.
- **Ctrl** + **F6** switches the active document window when using multiple document windows.
- **Ctrl** + **I** turns the italic feature on or off.
- **Ctrl** + **N** opens a new document.
- **Ctrl** + **O** opens a document.
- **Ctrl** + **P** prints a document.
- **Ctrl** + **S** saves a document to disk.
- **Ctrl** + **U** turns the underline feature on or off.
- **Ctrl** + **V** pastes the contents of Windows Clipboard to a desired location.
- **Ctrl** + **X** cuts a section from its position and moves it to Windows Clipboard for future pasting.
- **Ctrl** + **Z** undoes the last action.

DELETE. The delete key erases the following:

- Single character to the right of the insertion point when editing data.
- A selection.

END.

- Moves the insertion point to the end of a line when editing data.
- Moves the selection highlight to the last item in a menu, list, or drop-down box.

ENTER.   This key invokes a selected command from a menu or dialog box.

ESC.   This key cancels a menu or dialog box.

FUNCTION KEYS.   The function keys, numbered **F1** through **F12** , are used alone, or in combination with the **Alt** , **Ctrl** , and **Shift** keys, to invoke commands. Except for the **F1** key, which is generally used to invoke on-line help, each program often defines the use of the function keys differently.

HOME.

- Moves the insertion point to the beginning of the line of data in a document, text box, or drop-down box.
- Moves the selection highlight to the beginning of a list in a menu, list box, or drop-down box.

INSERT.   In certain situations, the Insert key allows you to insert characters at the insertion point, called a *typeover,* when editing data in a document, text box, or drop-down box.

NUM LOCK.   This toggle (on/off) key activates the keypad that is on the right side of most keyboards. Pressing the Num Lock key either turns the keypad on or off.

PAGE UP AND PAGE DOWN.   This key moves your screen diplay one screen page up or one down.

PRINT SCREEN (PRTSC).   This key captures an image of a screen to Windows Clipboard for future pasting.

SHIFT.   This key works similar to the Shift key on a typewriter. When you hold it down and then press a letter or number, an uppercase letter or symbol assigned to a number key is produced. Other common commands invoked with the Shift key include:

- **Shift** + **Arrow key** expands the selection highlight in the direction of the arrow.
- **Shift** + **Tab** moves the insertion point or the selection highlight (or dotted rectangle) back one choice in a dialog box.
- **Shift** + **End** expands the selection highlight to the end of a line.

TAB.   This key moves the insertion point or dotted selection rectangle to the next option in a dialog box.

MOUSE ACTIONS BY KEYBOARD—MOUSEKEYS

MouseKeys is a feature of Windows Accessibility Options that you can access through the Control Panel. It allows you to use the numeric keypad to invoke mouse actions such as clicking, right-clicking, double-clicking, and dragging and dropping. To use any accessibility options, the program must first be installed on your system. This can be checked through Windows Add/Remove Programs feature.

CHECKING FOR THE ACCESSIBILITY OPTIONS FEATURE.   If the *Accessibility Options* icon appears in the Control Panel, then it has been installed on your system and is ready for use. To check,

`STEPS`

1 Click the *Start* button   [**Ctrl** + **Esc**]

2 Point to *Settings*

3 Click *Control Panel*

4 Examine the Control Panel window for the *Accessibility Options* icon

If the *Accessibility Options* icon does not appear and you have the Windows 95 CD-ROM (you must also have a CD-ROM drive) or setup disks, go to the Installing Accessibility Options section for installation procedures. If you want to turn on the MouseKey option, see the Turning On/Off MouseKeys section. To exit the Control Panel,

5 Click the Control Panel's *Close* button

INSTALLING ACCESSIBILITY OPTIONS.   The accessibility options can be installed using the *Add/Remove Programs* dialog box.

`STEPS`

1 Click the *Start* button   [**Ctrl** + **Esc**]

2 Point to *Settings*

3 Click *Control Panel*

4 Double-click the *Add/Remove Programs* icon

5 Click the *Windows Setup* tab

6 Click the *Accessibility Options* check box

7 Click the *Apply* button

8 Insert the Windows 95 CD-ROM or appropriate disk as requested on the screen

9 Click the *OK* button

TURNING MOUSEKEYS ON OR OFF.   The MouseKeys feature can be turned on or off using the *Mouse* tab of the *Accessibility Properties* dialog box. When the MouseKeys feature is on, you can use the numeric keypad to invoke mouse actions. To turn on/off the MouseKeys feature,

STEPS

1 Click the *Start* button   [**Ctrl**   +   **Esc**   ]

2 Point to *Settings* for its submenu

3 Click *Control Panel* for its window

4 Double-click the *Accessibility Options* icon for its dialog box

5 Click the *Mouse* tab

6 Click the *Use MouseKeys* check box

7 Click the *OK* button to exit the dialog box

8 Click the *Close* button of the Control Panel window

When the MouseKeys feature is on, a *mouse* icon appears in the message area of the taskbar. Double-clicking this icon also opens the *Accessibility Properties* dialog box.

USING MOUSEKEYS.   When the MouseKeys feature is on, you can control the mouse pointer movement by using the numeric keypad. See Figure WIN1-2d in Chapter 1 for this type of operation.

SUMMARY OF COMMON WINDOWS FEATURES

As in Figure WIN1-1 of Chapter 1, the Windows screen has two main components: a taskbar (which appears at the bottom of the screen) and the desktop (which is the large area above the taskbar). The taskbar has a *Start* button on its left and a message area displaying the system's time (and other messages) on its right. The desktop has several icons (small pictures) on it, including *My Computer* and the *Recycle Bin.* The following is summary of common Windows operations.

ADDING NEW HARDWARE

Windows provides a *New Hardware wizard* (a *wizard* is a program that helps make complicated tasks easier) to help you install new hardware.

STEPS

1 Turn off power

2 Install the new hardware

3 Click the *Start* button   [Ctrl + Esc]

4 Point to *Settings* and then click *Control Panel*

5 Double-click the *Add New Hardware* icon for the New Hardware wizard

6 Follow the wizard's instructions

ADDING, REMOVING, AND CONTROLLING PRINTERS

The Printers program can be used to add a new printer to your system, switch the default printer, or view or control the status of current print jobs. A print job is simply documents sent to your printer to be printed. Windows allows you to send several print jobs to your printer. Although they are printed in the order sent, you can use Printers to change this order.

LAUNCHING PRINTERS.   To launch the Printers program,

STEPS

1 Click the *Start* button   [Ctrl + Esc]

2 Point to *Settings* and then click *Control Panel*

Printers

3 Double-click the *Printers* folder icon for its window

ADDING A NEW PRINTER.   To add a new printer,

STEPS

| 1 | **Launch the Printers program** |

| 2 | **Double-click the *Add Printer* icon in the Printers window** |

| 3 | **Follow the Add Printer wizard** |

REMOVING A PRINTER.   To remove a printer,

STEPS

| 1 | **Launch the Printers program** |

| 2 | **Click the desired printer icon to be removed** |

| 3 | **Press   Delete** |

| 4 | **Click *Yes*** |

CONTROLLING A CURRENT PRINT JOB(S).   To see the status or control your current print jobs immediately after invoking the print command,

STEPS

| 1 | **Double-click the *Printers* icon in the message area of the status bar** |

The title bar of your printer's window should display the name of your printer. If you were printing any documents, it would first appear here. If you have several print jobs, they would be listed in this window with their current print status.

| 2 | **Select the print job(s) for editing** |

| 3 | **Invoke the desired edit command** |

For example, if you desired to delete selected print jobs, simply press the Delete key in Step 3. You can also open your printer's window by double-clicking its icon in the Printers window.

ADDING OR REMOVING PROGRAMS

To add/remove programs from Windows,

1 Click the *Start* button   [**Ctrl** + **Esc**]

2 Point to *Settings* and then click *Control Panel*

3 Double-click the *Add/Remove Programs* for its *Properties* dialog box

You can also add or remove Windows setup programs by using this dialog box.

ARRANGING ICONS ON THE DESKTOP

To sort icons by name, type, size, or date or to turn the *Auto Arrange* option on or off,

1 Right-click an empty area of the desktop for its *Shortcut* menu

2 Click *Arrange Icons* for its submenu

3 Click the desired arrangement option

To line up icons on the desktop,

1 Right-click an empty area of the desktop for its *Shortcut* menu

2 Click *Line up Icons*

CASCADING WINDOWS ON THE DESKTOP

1 Right-click an empty area of the taskbar for its *Shortcut* menu

2 Click *Cascade*

CHANGING DATE AND TIME

To change your system's date and time,

1　Double-click the *Date/Time* icon

2　Make desired adjustments

3　Click *OK*

To access this dialog box quickly, double-click the time message at the right side of the taskbar.

CHANGING DISPLAY OPTIONS

You can set four screen display properties through the *Display Properties* dialog box. They include Background, Screen Saver, Appearance, and Settings. Background changes involve placing or replacing an image as the background screen of your desktop. Screen Savers help prevent the image of a frequently used program from "burning in" on your monitor's screen. Appearance changes involve setting the color of items displayed in Windows. Settings options vary the quality of the color and resolution of all displays in Windows. Each property has its own tab in the *Display Properties* dialog box.

1　Open the Control Panel

Display

2　Double-click the *Display* icon

3　Click the desired tab

4　Make the desired changes

5　Click *OK*

CONTROL PANEL

The Control Panel is a program that can be used to change the settings on your computer. It operates similarly to any folder window. To launch the Control Panel as in Figure WIN2-26,

1　Launch My Computer

Control Panel

2 Double-click the *Control Panel* folder icon

3 If desired, click *View, Toolbar* to turn the toolbar on

4 Click the *Maximize* button of the Control Panel window

Most icons in this window open to other windows that allow you to set the desired feature.

To view a description of an icon in the Control Panel in the status bar,

5 Click the desired icon

To access an icon's features,

6 Double-click the desired icon

You can also click the *Start* button, point to *Settings,* and then click *Control Panel* in place of Steps 1 and 2.

CREATING A NEW DOCUMENT ICON ON THE DESKTOP

STEPS

1 Right-click an empty area of the desktop for its *Shortcut* menu

2 Click *New* for its submenu

3 Click the desired document type

4 Type the document's name and then press ↵

5 Drag the document icon to its desired position on the desktop

CREATING A NEW FOLDER ICON

To create a new folder icon on the desktop,

STEPS

1 Right-click an empty area of the desktop for its *Shortcut* menu

2 Click *New* and then *Folder*

3 Type the folder's name and then press ↵

4 Drag the folder icon to its desired position on the desktop

CREATING A NEW *SHORTCUT* ICON

Shortcut icons provide quick access to a program or document.

1. Right-click an empty area of the desktop for its *Shortcut* menu

2. Click *New* and then *Shortcut* for the *Create Shortcut* dialog box

3. Type in the desired command line or click the *Browse* button and select from its dialog box

4. When back in the *Create Shortcut* dialog box, click the *Next* button

5. If desired, type in a name for the *Shortcut* icon, and then click the *Finished,* or *Next* button (whichever appears)

If no icon is associated with the shortcut, a *Select Icon* dialog box will appear. If so

6. Click a desired icon and then click the *Finished* button

7. Drag the *Shortcut* icon to its desired position on the desktop

DISPLAYING THE TITLE OF A COMMAND BUTTON

A command button invokes its feature when clicked. In general, to display the title of a command button,

1. Point to the desired button and wait for its title to appear

2. Point away from the button to remove the title

HELP

To access Windows main Help feature,

1. Click the *Start* button   [Ctrl + Esc]

2. Click *Help* for its dialog box

3 Click the desired tab

LAUNCHING A PROGRAM

To launch any program using the *Start* menu,

STEPS

1 Click the *Start* button   [**Ctrl** **+** **Esc**]

2 Point to *Programs* for its submenu

3 If needed, point to the desired program group (folder)

4 Click the desired program to launch it

LAUNCHING OR OPENING ICONS ON THE DESKTOP

STEPS

1 Double-click the desired icon

MINIMIZING ALL WINDOWS ON THE DESKTOP

STEPS

1 Right-click an empty area of the taskbar for its *Shortcut* menu

2 Click *Minimize All Windows*

PASTING TO THE DESKTOP

To paste the contents of Windows Clipboard to the desktop,

STEPS

1 Right-click an empty area of the desktop for its *Shortcut* menu

2 Click *Paste*

PASTING A *SHORTCUT* ICON TO THE DESKTOP

To paste the contents of Windows Clipboard to the desktop as a *Shortcut* icon,

STEPS

1 Right-click an empty area of the desktop for its *Shortcut* menu

2 Click *Paste Shortcut*

PROPERTIES OF THE DESKTOP

STEPS

1 Right-click an empty area of the desktop for its *Shortcut* menu

2 Click *Properties* for the *Display Properties* dialog box

PROPERTIES OF AN OBJECT

To change the properties of an object (drive, program, or document icon),

STEPS

1 Right-click the object for its *Shortcut* menu

2 Click *Properties* for its *Properties* dialog box

PROPERTIES OF THE TASKBAR

To access Taskbar properties by *Shortcut* menu,

STEPS

1 Right-click an empty area of the taskbar for its *Shortcut* menu

2 Click *Properties*

To access taskbar properties by *Start* menu

STEPS

    1   Click the *Start* button   [**Ctrl** + **Esc**]

            2   Point to *Settings* for its submenu

            3   Click *Taskbar*

RUN

You can use the Windows *Run* dialog box to launch or open a desired program or document by typing its command line. Use it also to install new software from a CD-ROM or disks.

STEPS

    1   Click the *Start* button   [**Ctrl** + **Esc**]

            2   Click *Run* for its dialog box

            3   Type in the desired command line or click the *Browse* button to use its dialog box to select

            4   Click *OK*

SHORTCUT MENU

To open any object's (including an icon's) *Shortcut* menu,

STEPS

            1   Right-click the object

To open the desktop's *Shortcut* menu,

STEPS

            1   Right-click an empty area of the desktop

To open the taskbar's *Shortcut* menu,

STEPS

> **1** Right-click an empty area of the taskbar

SHUTTING DOWN

Shutting down Windows exits the operating system. Other *Shut Down* options are generally available upon invoking the command. These options are displayed in the *Shut Down Windows* dialog box as in Figure WIN1-6. To shut down Windows,

STEPS

> **1** Click the *Start* button   [**Ctrl** + **Esc**]
>
> **2** Click *Shut Down* for its dialog box as in Figure WIN1-6
>
> **3** Click the *Yes* button
>
> **4** Wait for Windows to prompt you with "It's now safe to turn off your computer."
>
> **5** Turn off your computer

START MENU

To open the *Start* menu, Windows' main menu system,

STEPS

> **1** Click the *Start* button   [**Ctrl** + **Esc**]

Items on the *Start* menu (or any menu) with a "▶" to the far right open to a submenu. To select "▶" items from a menu,

> **2** Point to the item with a "▶" to the far right   [Underlined letter or use arrow keys]

To select other items from the *Start* menu,

> **3** Click the desired item   [Underlined letter or use arrow keys]

To exit the *Start* menu (or any menu) without selecting,

> **4** Click outside of the menu   [**Esc**]

See Figures WIN1-7 and WIN1-8 in Chapter 1 for examples of the *Start* menu.

SWITCHING BETWEEN RUNNING PROGRAMS

To switch between running programs by taskbar,

STEPS

1   Click the desired program's taskbar button

To switch between running programs by keyboard,

STEPS

1   Press   **Alt**   +   **Tab**   until you locate the desired program

To switch between running programs where the desired program window is visible on the desktop,

---

STEPS

1   Click any area of the desired program window to switch to it

TASKBAR *SHORTCUT* MENU

STEPS

1   Right-click an empty area of the taskbar

2   Click the desired choice

TILING WINDOWS ON THE DESKTOP

STEPS

1   Right-click an empty area of the taskbar for its *Shortcut* menu

2   Click either *Tile Horizontally* or *Tile Vertically*

TIME AND DATE DIALOG BOX

1 **Double-click the time message on the taskbar**

2 **Adjust settings as desired**

3 **Click the *OK* button**

SUMMARY OF COMMON WINDOW FEATURES

Most windows (programs, documents, or dialog boxes) have a variety of common Windows features. These features include

- *Title bar* with the program's icon at its left, the program's name in its center, and two resizing buttons and a *Close* button on its right. It is located at the top of a window. See Figure WIN1-10 in Chapter 1.
- A *menu bar* is available only on Program windows. It is located just below the title bar, providing mouse or keyboard access to a program's features through pull-down menus.
- A *toolbar* is a set of command buttons and drop-down boxes that provides mouse access to a program's features. It is normally located below the menu bar.
- A *workspace* is the large interior space within a window.
- A *status bar* is a line of information, generally located at the bottom of a program window.

CLOSING A WINDOW

Closing a window exits it. To close by using the *Close* button (the "X" button on the right side of the title bar)

[X] 1 **Click the *Close* button**   [**Alt** + **F4** for program windows and dialog boxes]

[**Ctrl** + **F4** for document windows]

To close a window by program or document icon (located on the left side of the title bar):

1 **Double-click the program or document icon**

To close a window by control menu,

STEPS

1 Either click the program or document icon or right-click the title bar for the window's control menu

2 Click *Close*   [**Alt** + **Spacebar** for program windows,
Alt + **–** for document windows]

CONTROL MENU

Use a window's *control menu* to resize, move, or close the window. To open any window's control menu,

STEPS

1 Right-click the title bar

2 Click the desired item

You can also open a program or document window's control menu by clicking its icon.

MAXIMIZING A WINDOW

To maximize (enlarge a window to its maximum size),

STEPS

1 Click the *Maximize* button on the right side of the window's title bar
[**Alt** + **Spacebar** , **X** for program windows and dialog boxes,
Alt + **–** , **X** for document windows]

MENU BAR OPERATIONS

To open a pull-down menu,

STEPS

1 Click the desired menu bar item   [**Alt** + Underlined letter of menu bar item]

To obtain a description of a pull-down menu item's function in the status bar,

2 Point to (do not click) the desired item   [Arrow keys]

To select an item from a pull-down menu,

3 Click it   [Underlined letter]

MINIMIZING A WINDOW

To minimize a program window,

STEPS

1 Click the *Minimize* button on the right side of a program window's title bar

[**Alt** + **Spacebar** , **N**]

For a document window,

STEPS

1 Click the *Minimize* button on the right side of the menu bar   [**Alt** + **-** , **N**]

RESTORING A WINDOW

To resize a maximized program window (one at its largest size) to a smaller window using the Restore command,

STEPS

1 Click the *Restore* button on the right side of a program window's title bar

[**Alt** + **Spacebar** , **R**]

For a document window,

STEPS

1 Click the *Restore* button on the right side of the menu bar   [**Alt** + **–** , **R**]

TOOLBARS

If available, Toolbars provide a set(s) of buttons and drop-down boxes that you can use to access a program's features by mouse.

TURNING A TOOLBAR ON OR OFF.   If a toolbar is not turned on (displayed below the menu bar) by default, you must use the *View* menu to turn it on. In general, to turn a toolbar on or off,

STEPS

1   Click _View_ for the *View* menu, and then _Toolbars_

2   Click the desired toolbar (if available)

3   Repeat Steps 1 and 2 if needed to turn additional toolbars on or off

USING A TOOLBAR.   Like most buttons in the Windows environment, you can point to a toolbar button for its title or click it to invoke its feature.

To receive a toolbar button's title in a caption and a description of its function in the status bar,

STEPS

1   Point to (do not click) the desired toolbar button and wait

To remove the title caption and description message,

2   Point away from the button

To invoke a command by toolbar,

STEPS

1   Click the desired toolbar button

SUMMARY OF COMMON FILE AND EDIT COMMANDS

The techniques to invoke many basic file and edit commands are the same for most Windows programs. They include File commands to save, open, close, or print a document. Edit commands include selecting, copying, moving, pasting, and undoing. These commands are available with most Windows programs and are summarized next.

CLOSING A DOCUMENT

Closing a document removes it from system memory. You should invoke this command whenever a document is not being used to free up system memory. To close a document,

STEPS

    ☐ 1   Click *File, Close*   [**Ctrl** + **F4**]

COPYING A SELECTION

The Copy command duplicates a selection to Windows Clipboard, a temporary holding area. The Paste command copies the current contents of the Clipboard to a desired location. The location can be within the same document or in another document of the same or a different program.

STEPS

☐ 1   Select the desired item or items

    ☐ 2   Click *Edit, Copy* to copy the selection to the Clipboard   [**Ctrl** + **C**]

☐ 3   Move to the desired destination

    ☐ 4   Click *Edit, Paste*   [**Ctrl** + **V**]

MOVING A SELECTION

The Cut command moves a selection from its current position to Windows Clipboard, a temporary holding area. The Paste command copies the current contents of the Clipboard to a desired location. The location can be within the same document or in another document of the same or a different program.

STEPS

☐ 1   Select the desired item or items

    ☐ 2   Click *Edit, Cut* to move the selection to the Clipboard   [**Ctrl** + **X**]

☐ 3   Move to the desired destination

    ☐ 4   Click *Edit, Paste*   [**Ctrl** + **V**]

OBJECT LINKING AND EMBEDDING

An *object* is a set of information. Object linking and embedding (OLE) is the transferring of information from one program to another as an object. The *source file* (document) contains the original object and the *container file* or *compound document* contains the copy.

Objects may also be linked or embedded into a container file in the same format or in a format that differs from its source. Format options may differ for different programs.

LINKING AN OBJECT. *Linking* establishes an ongoing connection between the source file that provides the object and the container file that receives it. The object remains stored in the source file. The copy of the object in the container file is automatically updated whenever the source file's object is changed.

STEPS

1 Launch the source program and open (or create) the source file

2 Select the object to be linked

3 Click *Edit, Copy*   [**Ctrl** + **C**]

4 If needed, launch the container program and open (or create) the container file

5 If needed, switch to the container file

6 Move to the position where you want the linked object to appear

7 Click *Edit, Paste Special* for its dialog box

8 Click the *Link* option

9 If desired, click a format

10 Click *OK*

EMBEDDING AN OBJECT. *Embedding* inserts an object from the source file into a container file. The object then becomes part of the container file. Any changes in the source file do not appear in the embedded object. To embed an object,

STEPS

1 Perform Steps 1 through 7 for linking an object

2 If needed, click the *Paste* option

3 If desired, click a format

4 Click *OK*

EDITING A LINKED OR EMBEDDED OBJECT. To edit a linked or embedded object in the container file,

STEPS

1 Double-click the object

If the object was linked, the source file and its program will appear (if running). Changes to the source file will automatically be reflected in the container file. If the object was embedded, the source program will appear in the container file. Edit changes will only affect the container file.

2 Edit the object

3 Click anywhere outside the object to turn off the edit mode

4 Save the document(s) (if linked, both source and container files must be resaved)

OPENING A DOCUMENT

STEPS

1 Click *File*, *Open* for its dialog box   [**Ctrl** + **O**]

2 If needed, change the default drive using the *Look in* drop-down box

3 Type in the desired file's name in the *File name* text box or click it in the *Files* list box

4 Click the *Open* button

PRINTING A DOCUMENT

STEPS

1 Click *File*, *Print* for its dialog box   [**Ctrl** + **P**]

2 Select the desired print options

3 Click *OK*

SAVING A DOCUMENT

The *File* menu available in most programs offers two options for saving a document: Save and Save As. Invoking the Save command on a previously saved document will re-save it under its original name. Invoking the Save As command allows you to save the current document under a different name and will warn you if the name is the same as another file. This is helpful when updating documents because it allows you to save the updated version under a new name, thus keeping the original under its old name. Both the Save and Save As commands open the *Save As* dialog box when invoked on an un-saved document. This allows you to assign the document a filename. Filenames can have up to 255 characters.

To save a document for the first time,

STEPS

1 Click *File*, *Save* (or *File*, *Save As*) for the *Save As* dialog box   [Ctrl + S]

2 If needed, change the default drive using the *Save in* drop-down box

3 Type in the desired file's name in the *File name* text box or click it in the *Files* list box

4 Click the *Save* button

To resave a document under its previous name without confirmation,

STEPS

1 Click *File*, *Save* for its dialog box   [Ctrl + S]

To resave a document under its previous name with confirmation,

STEPS

1 Click *File*, *Save As* for its dialog box

2 Click the *Save* button

3 Click the *Replace* button

To resave a document under a new name,

STEPS

1 Click *File, Save As* for its dialog box

2 If needed, change the default drive using the *Save in* drop-down box

3 Type in the desired file's name in the *File name* text box

4 Click the *Save* button

UNDOING THE LAST ACTION

STEPS

   1 Click *Edit, Undo*   [**Ctrl** + **Z**]

SUMMARY OF COMMON MY COMPUTER AND EXPLORER FEATURES

My Computer and *Explorer* are programs that allow you to view and manage every part of your computer. My Computer displays the components of your system as icons in its workspace and uses separate windows to display the contents of those items. Explorer uses a single window to list the components of your system (left side) and display the contents of a selected component (right side). Explorer also lists your system's components in a hierarchical tree. Both programs have the same menu bar and toolbar options and their status bar displays similar information.

Generally, before using any My Computer or Explorer feature, you should launch the program.

LAUNCHING MY COMPUTER

The My Computer program is normally launched directly from the desktop, not the *Start* menu. To launch the My Computer program,

STEPS

   1 Double-click the *My Computer* icon at the top left corner of the desktop

The My Computer window contains a variety of common Windows features, including a title bar (with a program icon, resizing buttons, and a *Close* button), a menu bar, workspace, and status bar. These items operate the same as in other Program windows. Its workspace is normally occupied by several drive icons, the *Control Panel* folder, and *Printers* folder.

LAUNCHING EXPLORER

The way Explorer is launched determines its workspace's display. For example, if you launch Explorer using the *Start* menu, it will open with its default display which should be your hard disk. You can also launch Explorer from the My Computer (or a folder) window using a *Shortcut* menu, the *File* menu, or the toolbar. This method directly displays the contents of a desired disk or other folder.

LAUNCHING BY THE *START* MENU.   To launch Explorer by using the *Start* menu,

---
STEPS

1 Click the *Start* button   [**Ctrl** + **Esc**]

2 Point to *Programs* and then click *Windows Explorer*

Explorer now opens with your hard disk selected on the left and its contents displayed on the right. This is the default view.

LAUNCHING BY MY COMPUTER.   To launch Explorer by using My Computer,

---
STEPS

1 Right-click My Computer for its *Shortcut* menu

2 Click *Explore*

The Explorer window should now appear on your desktop

LAUNCHING BY *SHORTCUT* MENU OR *FILE* MENU.   To launch Explorer by *Shortcut* or *File* menu

---
STEPS

1 Launch My Computer and, if needed, open the desired drive window

BY *SHORTCUT* MENU

BY *FILE* MENU

2 **Right-click the desired *Drive* or *Folder* icon for its *Shortcut* menu**

2 **Click the desired *Drive* or *Folder* icon to select it**

3 **Click *Explore***

3 **Click *File*, *Explore***

Explorer now opens with the desired *Drive* or *Folder icon* selected on its left and the its contents displayed on the right.

Explorer commands operate similar to My Computer commands; however, the information in its workspace is displayed differently. The left side of the workspace displays a vertical hierarchical tree of all your system's components. This side will be referred to as the *tree box.* The right side of the screen displays the contents of the item selected in the tree box and will be referred to as the *Contents box.* It is similar to the workspace of a folder window. Items in both boxes are listed in alphabetical order.

The following techniques can be applied to My Computer or Explorer unless otherwise noted. The techniques can be invoked only after either one of the programs has been launched.

COPYING OBJECTS

Copying is the process of duplicating a selection into a new location. The folder from which a selection is copied is called the *source folder.* The folder to which it is pasted (placed) is called the *destination folder.* A summary of copying techniques is presented in Figure WIN2-12.

COPYING BY *EDIT* MENU. To copy a selection of files (and folders),

STEPS

1 **Open the source folder's window**

2 **Select the objects to be copied**

3 **Click *Edit*, *Copy*** [**Ctrl** + **C**]

4 **Move to the destination folder**

5 **Click *Edit*, *Paste*** [**Ctrl** + **V**]

COPYING BY DRAGGING AND DROPPING. Drag and drop techniques involve copying a selection by moving your pointer with the selection to a new location, sometimes with the use of the Ctrl key.

To copy a selection within the same folder or to another folder within the same disk,

1 **Open the source folder**

2 **If needed, open the destination folder, tile the folder windows, and then switch back to the source folder**

3 **Select the desired objects in the source window**

4 **Press and hold Ctrl while dragging the selection to the desired destination**

5 **Drop the selection in the desired location (release the mouse)**

To copy a selection to a folder in another disk, use the previous steps; however, do not press and hold the Ctrl key when performing Step 4.

COPYING AN ENTIRE DISK.   Use the *Copy Disk* dialog box (Figure WIN2-17) to copy the contents of an entire disk to another disk. It is accessible through Copy Disk command of the *My Computer* file menu (after selecting the desired drive icon) or the desired drive icon's *Shortcut* menu. When using this command, the *Copy from* disk must be the same as the *Copy to* disk.

CREATING A DOCUMENT

You can create a new saved document without first launching its program by using the *New* submenu, which you just used to create folders. (Note: The related program or document type must be listed in the submenu.) Try this to create a new text (Notepad) document:

BY *SHORTCUT* MENU

BY *FILE* MENU

1 **Right-click an empty area of the work-space for its *Shortcut* menu**

1 **Click *File***

2 **Point to *New* and then click the desired document type**

3 **Type the document's name and then press ↵**

CREATING A SHORTCUT ICON

A *Shortcut* icon can be created with a dynamic link to its original document, program, or folder. This link allows you to use the *Shortcut* icon to open/launch the file or folder it represents from any folder or the desktop.

To place *Shortcut* icons in a folder,

`STEPS`

1 Select the object(s) for the *Shortcut* icon

2 Click *Edit, Copy*   [**Ctrl** + **C**]

3 Move to the destination (open the destination folder if needed)

4 Click *Edit, Paste Shortcut*

To place *Shortcut* icons on the desktop,

`STEPS`

1 Select the object(s) for the *Shortcut* icon

2 Click *Edit, Copy*   [**Ctrl** + **C**]

3 Right-click an empty area of the taskbar for its *Shortcut* menu

4 Click *Minimize All Windows* for a better view of the desktop

5 Right-click the area to the right of the *My Computer* icon (or any desired empty area) on the desktop

6 Click *Paste Shortcut*

DELETING

Any selection in Windows can be deleted. The *Delete* command removes a selection from its current place and can be invoked from the *File* menu or an object's *Shortcut* menu.
The process of deleting a selection from a data disk and hard disk is the same.

`STEPS`

1 Select the objects to be deleted

2 Click *File, Delete*   [**Delete**]

A dialog box appears asking you to confirm the deletion. To delete these objects,

3 Click *Yes*

FINDING A FILE

Use the Find feature to locate any file in a folder. Once located, you can open the file from the lower section of the *Find* dialog box.

INITIAL SEARCH.   To locate a desired file,

STEPS

1 If needed, insert the desired disk or CD-ROM into the appropriate drive

BY *SHORTCUT* MENU   **BY *FILE* MENU**

2 Right-click the desired drive icon   2 Click the desired drive icon

3 Click *Find* for its dialog box   3 Click *File*, *Find* for its dialog box

4 Type the desired filename in the *Find* text box

5 Click the *Find Now* button

The results of your search will appear at the bottom of the dialog box.

To access the file from the bottom of the *Find* dialog box,

6 Double-click it

NEW SEARCH.   To perform another search using the *Find* dialog box

STEPS

1 Click the *New Search* button

The command will remove the results of the previous search prior to your entering a new find request.

2 If desired, use the *Look in* drop-down box to select a drive

3 Click the *Name* drop-down box to place the insertion point there

4 Type in the desired filename in the *Find* text box

5 Click the *Find Now* button

The results of your search should appear at the bottom on the dialog box. If desired, you can now open the document by double-clicking it.

FOLDERS

Folders are used to group files. A *Folder* icon is used to represent each folder created on a disk. *Drive* and *Folder* icons can be used to open Folder windows. *Folder windows* display the contents of a disk (or other storage media) or folders within the disk. Remember, a disk is also considered a folder and will be referred to as the *main folder*.

OPENING A FOLDER (OR DRIVE).   To open a folder (or drive) in My Computer or a Folder window,

STEPS

1 **Double-click the desired *Drive* or *Folder* icon to display its contents in another window**

In Explorer, clicking an icon on the hierarchical tree (left side) will display its contents on the right side of the window.

CREATING A NEW FOLDER.   To create the folders,

STEPS

1 **Click *File* for its menu as in Figure WIN2-8a**

This *File* menu appears when no objects are selected (marked) in the window.

2 **Point to *New* for its submenu and then click *Folder***

FOLDERS WITHIN FOLDERS.   To create a subfolder (a folder within a folder), first open the folder where you desire the subfolder to be placed, and then use Steps 1 and 2 for creating a new folder.

FOLDER DISPLAY OPTIONS.   The My Computer program offers two ways to browse through folders: separate windows for each folder (the default) or a single window that changes to display each folder that is opened. To check or change the browse settings of My Computer,

STEPS

1 **Click *View, Options* for its dialog box**

2 **If needed, click the *Folder* tab**

3 If the *Browse folders using a separate window for each folder* option is selected (a black dot will appear in the option circle), click the *Cancel* button

4 If the *Browse folders using a separate window for each folder* option is not selected, click it, and then click *OK*

When viewing folders through a single window that changes to display each open folder, you can click the *Up One Level* (see the left margin for the button) toolbar button to go back one level. The toolbar must, of course, be on.

SELECTING MULTIPLE FILES (OBJECTS)

Selecting is the process of marking items. Once marked you can invoke a variety of commands on an item. Refer to Figure WIN2-10 for a summary of object selection techniques.

SINGLE OBJECT. To select a single object,

STEPS

1 Click the object

GROUP OF OBJECTS. To select a group of objects (several objects),

STEPS

1 Click the first object of the group

2 Press and hold **Ctrl** while clicking each additional object

BLOCK OF OBJECTS. To select a block (a set of contiguous objects),

STEPS

1 Click the first object in the block

2 Press and hold **Shift** while clicking the last file in the block

A block can be selected alone or with other selected files.

REVERSE A SELECTION. To reverse a selection of files,

1 Click *Edit, Invert Selection* to reverse the items selected with those that are not

SELECT ALL. To select all files in a window,

1 Click *Edit, Select All*   [**Ctrl** + **A**]

OPENING FILES

Most documents created and saved with Windows programs are automatically *associated* (have a special connection) with their program. As such, they can be directly opened (with their program) from a Folder window without first launching their programs. If you know the folder your document was stored on, this method provides quicker access to it.

SINGLE FILE. The quickest way to open any object in a window is to double-click it. However, you can also use the object's *Shortcut* menu or the *File* menu.

BY *SHORTCUT* MENU

1 Right-click the desired *File* icon

2 Click *Open*

BY FILE MENU

1 Click the desired *File* icon to select it

2 Click *File, Open*   [↵]

GROUP OF FILES. To open (or launch) a group of files at once, first select the group and then use the Open command of the *File* menu.

1 Click the first object in the group

2   **Press and hold   Ctrl   while clicking each additional object of the group**

3   **Click *File, Open* to open the objects**   [↵]

BLOCK OF FILES.   Like opening a group of files, opening a block of files involves first selecting the block and then clicking *File, Open.*

STEPS

1   **Click the first object in the block**

2   **Press and hold   Shift   while clicking the last object of the block**

3   **Click *File, Open***

PRINTING FILES

To print document files from a Folder window,

STEPS

1   **Turn on your printer**

2   **Select the desired files**

3   **Click *File, Print***

To print a single document using its *Shortcut* menu,

STEPS

1   **Right-click the *File* icon for its *Shortcut* menu**

2   **Click *Print***

RECYCLE BIN

Selections deleted from a hard disk are removed from their folders, the desktop, or other locations and relocated to the Recycle Bin. Once there, you can either restore or permanently delete the files. See Figure WIN2-22 in Chapter 2 for Recycle Bin operations.

RENAMING FILES

You can easily rename any file or folder using the same techniques.
To rename an object by *Shortcut* or *File* menu,

STEPS

1 **If needed, open the desired Folder window**

BY *SHORTCUT* MENU

2 **Right-click the object's icon for its *Short-cut* menu**

3 **Click *Rename***

BY *FILE* MENU

2 **Click the object's icon to select it**

3 **Click *File*, *Rename***

4 **Type a desired filename and then press ↵**

To rename an object by clicking its title after it has been selected,

---

STEPS

1 **If needed, click the object's icon to select it**

2 **Click the object's title**

The folder's title is now selected and ready to be changed.

3 **Type in the new name and then press ↵**

SENDING FILES

Use the *Send* submenu to copy a selection to another disk, fax, or electronic mail.

STEPS

1 **Select the items that you desire to send**

2 **Click *File*, point to *Send To* for its submenu**

3 **Click the desired destination option**

The *Send To* menu can be customized to include destinations other than the default options. It is also available through *Shortcut* menus. Refer to your on-line help for these procedures.

TOOLBAR

Like other Windows programs, many menu commands can be accessed from a toolbar. The My Computer, Folder, and Explorer windows have the same toolbar as in Figure WIN2-4. To turn the toolbar on or off,

STEPS

1 Click *View, Toolbar*

As with many buttons and drop down boxes in the Windows environment, pointing to a toolbar item displays its title.

VIEWING OPTIONS

The Workspace in the My Computer window, Folder Window, or the right side of the Explorer window can be adjusted to display the icons in a smaller size, in a list, and with more or less detail. These view options are available through the *View* menu or toolbar. *View* menu options are listed and described in Figure WIN2-6 of Chapter 2.

STEPS

1 If needed, click *View, Toolbar* to turn it on

2 Click *View, Details* to display detailed information on each object

A *Details bar* now appears below the toolbar. Each object's name, size, type, and date and time last modified or created is displayed below this button bar. You can switch the display order from ascending to descending (or vice versa) by using any *Details* bar button's title. Other *View* options include the following:

3 Click *View, List* to list objects vertically as small icons

4 Click *View, Small Icons* to display objects as small icons horizontally

5 Click *View, Large Icons* to return objects to the default size

More advanced *View* options such as folder browsing, choices, displaying hidden files, and MS-DOS file extensions and file association settings can be controlled by using the *Options* dialog box. Refer to the dialog box's on-line help for these operations.

VIEWING OPTIONS—EXPLORER'S TREE DISPLAY

The left side of the Explorer window displays all the components of your system in a vertical tree starting with the *Desktop* icon on top. The left-most vertical tree line is the *main tree line* and it displays all items that appear on the desktop including My Computer and the Recycling Bin. All lines extending from the main tree are called *branches*.

The *Go to a different folder* drop-down box (left side of toolbar) identifies the current folder selection. Its contents are displayed in the *Contents* box (right side of window).

SELECTING AN ICON ON THE TREE.   To select a different item quickly,

STEPS

1   **Click the desired icon on the tree**

The selected icon now appears highlighted in the tree and its contents appear in the right side of the window.

GO TO TOP OF TREE.   To go to the top of the tree (the desktop),

STEPS

1   Press **Home**

GO TO END OF TREE.   To go to the end of the tree,

STEPS

1   Press **End**

EXPAND BRANCHES.   The "+" icon to the left of any icon in the tree box indicates that the item can be expanded to display a tree branch of folder(s) below it. To expand a branch of a tree to display folders that are within a folder,

STEPS

1   **Click its + icon to left of the desired icon on the tree**

COLLAPSE BRANCHES.   A "–" to the left of a folder on a tree indicates that its branches are displayed. To collapse the branches,

STEPS

1   Click the – icon to the left of the desired icon on the tree

UNDOING THE LAST ACTION

STEPS

   1   Click *Edit, Undo*   [**Ctrl** + **Z**]

SUMMARY OF DIALOG BOX FEATURES

A *dialog box* is a window that requests or gives information. A Dialog Box window operates similar to a program window; however, it cannot be resized. A dialog box has a title bar that displays its name, a *Help (?)* button, and a *Close* button. It also has a control menu (right-click the title bar to open).

Dialog boxes may also have *tabs,* which are different parts of a dialog box.

USING DIALOG BOX OPTIONS

To access Windows on-line help in using dialog box options,

STEPS

   1   Click the *Start* button   [**Ctrl** + **Esc**]

2   Click *Help*

3   Click the *Index* tab

4   Type   **DIALOG BOXES, USING**   or click it in the list box

5   Click the *Display* button

6   Click *The Basics* in the *Topics Found* dialog box

7   Click the *Display* button

8 Click the *Using dialog boxes* button

Your Windows Help window should appear as in Figure WINA-1. Dialog boxes may have one or more of these components. To learn how to operate them, simply click the desired component on the screen. When you are done,

9 Click the *Close* button of the window

PARTS OF A DIALOG BOX

Most parts of a dialog box are identified in Figure WINA-1. These and other dialog box components are described next.

CHECK BOX. A square box identified by its title to the right. A "✓" or "X" indicates that the option has been selected. More than one check box can be selected at a time.

COMMAND BUTTON. A command button directly invokes the item it represents when clicked.

DROP-DOWN BOX. A drop-down box initially appears as a single line box with a "▼" button on its right. Clicking the "▼" button opens a drop-down list. Some drop-down boxes allow text entry for selecting.

FIGURE WINA-1 ■ OPERATING DIALOG BOX OPTIONS

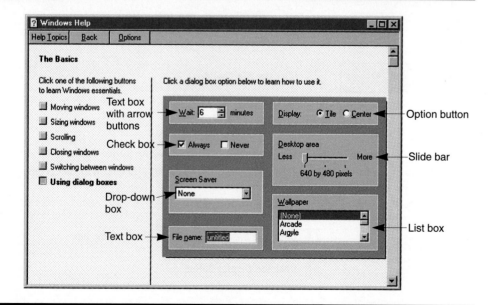

GROUP BOX. A group box is an area of a dialog box that contains related option buttons or check boxes.

INFORMATION BOX. An information box generally displays information about a current dialog box selection.

LIST BOX. A list box presents available options in alphabetical order.

OPTION BUTTON. An *Option* button is a small circle with its title to the right. When occupied by a "•" (dot), it indicates that the option is selected. Only one option can be selected in a group.

TAB. A tab identifies a section of a dialog box. Clicking a tab will display that section's format.

TEXT BOX. A text box allows text entry to communicate with the computer.

QUICK REFERENCE TO WORDPAD FEATURES

WordPad is a simple word processing program that you can use to create and edit documents with text and objects (graphic images). The following is a quick reference to Word-Pad's features). When invoking menu commands by mouse, simply click the item(s). With the keyboard, press the Alt key and the underlined letter of the menu bar item and then the underlined letter of the menu item. Otherwise perform the actions as indicated.

Feature	Commands	Shortcut Keys
Alignment Changes		
Left	*Left Align Format bar* button	Ctrl + L
Center	*Center Align Format bar* button	Ctrl + E
Right	*Right Align Format* bar button	Ctrl + R
Bold On/Off	*Bold Format bar* button	Ctrl + B
Bullet Style	*Format, Bullet Style*	
Copy a Selection		
From Source	*Edit, Copy*	Ctrl + C
To Destination	*Edit, Paste*	Ctrl + V

Feature	Commands	Shortcut Keys
Date and Time (insert)	*Insert, Date and Time*	
Delete a Selection	*Edit, Clear*	Delete
Deleting One Character		
Left		Backspace
Right		Delete
Edit a Selected Object	*Edit, Object* or double-click object if embedded or linked	
Embed an Object	*Edit, Paste Special, OK*	
Find a Text String		
Find Dialog Box	*Edit, Find*	Ctrl + F
Next Find	*Edit, Find Next*	F3
Font Changes	*Format, Font*	
Format Bar Off/On	*View, Format Bar*	
Indentation Changes	*Format, Paragraph*	
Link an Object	*Edit, Paste Special, Link, OK*	
Move a Selection		
✂ From Source	*Edit, Cut*	Ctrl + X
📋 To Destination	*Edit, Paste*	Ctrl + V
📄 New Document	*File, New*	Ctrl + N
Object Properties (Edit)	*Edit, Properties*	Alt + ↵
📂 Open a File	*File, Open*	Ctrl + O
Page Setup	*File, Page Setup*	
🖨 Print	*File, Print*	Ctrl + P
Print Preview	*File, Print Preview*	
Replace a Text String	*Edit, Replace*	Ctrl + H
Ruler Bar Off/On	*View, Ruler*	
💾 Save a Document	*File, Save*	Ctrl + S
Save As Dialog Box	*File, Save As*	
Select		
All	*Edit, Select All*	Ctrl + A
Text	Drag across text	Shift + Arrow key
Object	Click object	
Status Bar Off/On	*View, Status Bar*	
Tab Settings	*Format, Tabs*	
Toolbar Off/On	*View, Toolbar*	
U Underline	Underline *Format bar* button	Ctrl + U
↶ Undo	*Edit, Undo*	Ctrl + Z

QUICK REFERENCE TO PAINT FEATURES

Paint is a graphics program that can be used to create, open, edit, and save color images (pictures). You can also use it to edit graphic images created with other programs and to edit and save screen captures. The following is a quick reference to Paint's features. When invoking menu commands by mouse, simply click the item(s). With the keyboard, press the Alt key and the underlined letter of the menu bar item and then the underlined letter of the menu item. Otherwise perform the actions as indicated.

Feature	Commands	Shortcut Keys
Attributes of Document (width, height, unit of measure, and color)	*Image, Attributes*	Ctrl + E
Clear Image	*Image, Clear Image*	Ctrl + Shift + N
Color		
Background	Right-click the desired color in the palette	
Foreground	Click the desired color in the palette	
Color Box Off/On	*View, Color Box*	Ctrl + A
Copy a Selection		
From Source	*Edit, Copy*	Ctrl + C
To Destination	*Edit, Paste*	Ctrl + V
Copy a Selection to a File	*Edit, Copy To*	
Delete a Selection	*Edit, Clear Selection*	Delete
Display Options		
Normal Size	*View, Zoom, Normal Size*	Ctrl + PgUp
Large Size	*View, Zoom, Large Size*	Ctrl + PgDn
Custom	*View, Zoom, Custom*	
Full Window	*View, View Bitmap*	Ctrl + F
Draw Opaque	*Options, Draw Opaque*	
Drawing Tool	Click the desired tool in the tool box	
Flip/Rotate	*Image, Flip/Rotate*	Ctrl + R
Invert Colors	*Image, Invert Colors*	Ctrl + I
Move a Selection		
From Source	*Edit, Cut*	Ctrl + X
To Destination	*Edit, Paste*	Ctrl + V
New Document	*File, New*	Ctrl + N
Open a File	*File, Open*	Ctrl + O
Page Setup	*File, Page Setup*	
Palette Colors		
Edit	*Options, Edit Colors*	
Retrieve Saved Colors	*Options, Get Colors*	
Save	*Options, Save Colors*	
Paste an Object from a File	*Edit, Paste From*	
Print	*File, Print*	Ctrl + P
Print Preview	*File, Print Preview*	

Feature	Commands	Shortcut Keys
Repeat a Command	*Edit, Repeat*	F4
Select		
Object	*Select tool,* Drag diagonally across object	
All	*Edit, Select All*	Ctrl + L
Send a Document	*File, Send*	
Set as Wallpaper on Desktop		
Tiled	*File, Set As Wallpaper (Tiled)*	
Centered	*File, Set As Wallpaper (Centered)*	
Stretch/Skew	*Image, Stretch/Skew*	Ctrl + W
Text Toolbar On/Off	*View, Text Toolbar*	
Tool Box Off/On	*View, Tool Box*	Ctrl + T
Undo	*Edit, Undo*	Ctrl + Z

GLOSSARY

Accessibility options. A feature that allows you to adjust keyboard, display, sound, and mouse controls based on individual preference. It is accessible through the Control Panel. (WIN163)

Accessories. A group of programs that can help you perform daily tasks. They include Notepad, WordPad, Paint, and a variety of other programs. (WIN164)

Active (current) icon. The icon that is currently highlighted on your screen. Keyboard commands will affect this icon. (WIN11)

Active window. The window within which you are currently working. Its title bar is highlighted and taskbar button depressed. It accepts most keyboard commands. (WIN38)

Alignment. The way text aligns against a margin. The default alignment of WordPad and many word processors is left. Left aligned text has a ragged right edge. Other common alignment settings include center and right (ragged left edge). (WIN138)

Associated. A special connection between a document and its program that allows the document to be open in its program from a menu, My Computer, Explorer, and other parts of Windows. (WIN83)

Block. A set of contiguous files (or other objects or text). (WIN83)

Bolding. A command that darkens text for emphasis. (WIN135)

Booting up. The process of turning on your computer system. (WIN3)

Bullet style. A WordPad format feature that automatically inserts a bullet at the beginning of each line. (WIN140)

Byte. A binary unit of measure equivalent to one alphanumeric character (A–Z, 0–9, and so forth). A kilobyte (KB) is one thousand bytes, a megabyte (MB) is one million bytes, and a gigabyte is one billion bytes. (WIN70)

Cascade. A standard multiple-windows display that presents the windows overlapping each other. (WIN38)

Clicking. Rapidly pressing and releasing a mouse button (normally the left button). (WIN9)

Clipboard. A Windows program that temporarily holds a selection for future pasting. Data is copied or moved there by using the Copy or Cut commands of a program's *Edit* menu. (WIN43)

***Close* button.** An "X" button, located on the top right corner of most windows. Clicking it will close the window. (WIN12)

***Command* button.** Any button that when clicked directly accesses a program or window's feature. (WIN27)

Communications programs. Programs that can be used for connecting to other computers, on-line services, electronic mail, and fax operations. Windows comes with a variety of these programs. (WIN164)

Container file or compound document. The document receiving the information in a linking or embedding operation. (WIN158)

Control-menu. Clicking a window's Program or Document icon (left of the window name on the title bar) or right-clicking anywhere on the title bar will open its control menu. This menu contains commands to resize, move, or close a window. (WIN20)

Control Panel. A Windows feature that contains a variety of tools to set various parts of your system. These tools are also in the form of *Properties* dialog boxes. (WIN53)

Copy. The command that copies a selection to Windows Clipboard for future pasting. It can be accessed through the *Edit* menu, *Shortcut* menu, or *Toolbar* button (if available). (WIN43)

Copy disk. A command used to copy the entire contents of a disk to another disk of the same capacity. It is accessible through the My Computer *File* menu (after selecting the desired *Drive* icon) or the desired *Drive* icon's *Shortcut* menu. (WIN93)

Copying. The process of duplicating data to a new location. (WIN42)

Cut. The command that moves a selection from a document to the Clipboard for future pasting. It can be accessed through the *Edit* menu, *Shortcut* menu, or *Toolbar* button (if available). (WIN45)

Data. Text and graphic images (pictures) called objects. (WIN2)

Default document. The new blank document that appears in a program's workspace when it is launched. (WIN32)

Default drive. The drive to which a program is currently pointing. Files can be saved and opened from the disk or other storage media in this drive. (WIN33)

Default settings. The normal settings of your environment. (WIN99)

Delete. A command that removes a selection from its current place. It can be invoked from the *File* menu or an object's *Shortcut* menu. (WIN97)

Desktop. The large area above the taskbar in the Windows screen. Occupying the upper left side of the desktop are several icons, starting with the *My Computer* icon. (WIN5)

Dialog box. A window that either provides or requests information. (WIN5)

Disks. Storage media that can be used to hold computer-generated files. (WIN3)

Document. A file with data. (WIN2)

Document window. A window that contains a document. Document windows occupy a Program window's workspace. (WIN17)

Documents menu. A submenu of the *Start* menu that can be used to open any of the last 15 documents used with its program. (WIN52)

Double-clicking. Rapidly clicking your left mouse button twice. (WIN11)

Dragging. Pressing and holding your left mouse button while moving your mouse and the object to which it is pointing. (WIN11)

Drawing area. The workspace of Paint's window, which is like a piece of canvas or paper. (WIN148)

Drawing tool. The mouse pointer when in Paint's drawing area. It is used to create a drawing. (WIN146)

Drive. A device that reads or writes to a storage medium (such as a disk or CD-ROM). (WIN70)

Drop-down box. A one-line rectangular box that has a "▼" button on its right side. Clicking that button will open a drop-down list. (WIN27)

Dropping. Releasing your mouse and thus the object to which it is pointing after it has been dragged. (WIN11)

Electronic mail. A feature that allows you to send and receive electronic documents through a network or other forms of communication. (WIN164)

Embedding. The process of inserting an object from a source file into a container file. The object then becomes part of the container file. Any changes in the source file do not appear in the embedded object. The embedded object in the container file

can be edited using its source program without changing the source document. (WIN158)

File. A storage unit that may contain a program or document. (WIN3)

File management. The process of organizing and maintaining files (including folders) within your computer environment. (WIN78)

Filename. A name assigned to a document or program to identify it. A filename can have up to 255 characters. (WIN32)

Find. A feature that can be used to locate any file in a folder in your system. It is accessible through the *Start* menu, a drive, file, or folders *Shortcut* menu, or the *File* menu of the My Computer, Folder, or Explorer windows. (WIN70)

Find Menu. A submenu that can be used to locate files or folders within your system quickly. (WIN55)

Folder. A folder is a set of related files. (WIN3)

Folder windows. A window that displays the contents of a disk (or other storage media) or folders within the disk. (WIN73)

Font. A character type style. (WIN29)

Font size. The point size of the current font. A point is a typesetting unit of measure equivalent to $\frac{1}{72}$ inch. (WIN29)

Format bar. A set of command buttons and drop-down boxes that can be used to access features related to changing the appearance and alignment of a WordPad document's text. (WIN27)

Formatting. The process of preparing a disk for use on a computer. Formatting sets up the disk's directory and file allocation table and divides the disk into addressable storage locations. It also checks for defective tracks on the disk and seals them off from further use. (WIN33)

Function keys. Keys that are labeled F1–F12 on your keyboard. They may be located at the extreme left of your keyboard or across the top in one horizontal row. (WIN6)

Graphical user interface (GUI). Pronounced "gooey," this is any operating system that simplifies communication with a computer by using common symbols (called icons) and menus instead of typewritten commands. (WIN2)

Hardware. Any physical computer equipment. (WIN2)

Icons. Small graphical images or symbols used to represent a program, document, or other feature in the Windows environment. (WIN2)

Indentation. The way a paragraph is indented or set from the left or right margin. (WIN136)

Insertion point. A vertical blinking line that indicates where the next character you type will appear. The insertion point appears in any window or box that allows character entry. (WIN31)

Internet. A group of international computer networks communicating by phone lines. It provides a variety of services including electronic mail, news, research information, and games. (WIN164)

Italicizing. A command that slants text for emphasis. (WIN135)

Launching. Starting a program. (WIN14)

Layout (format). Changes that concern the way text is arranged in a document—for example, changing margin or tab settings. (WIN124)

Line break. A line break ends a line before it reaches the right margin. It is created by pressing the Enter key. It also moves the insertion point to the beginning of the next line. Line breaks are generally needed at the end of a paragraph, each line of an address, a salutation, or to skip a line. (WIN126)

Linking. A special feature that establishes an ongoing connection between the source file that provides the object and the container file that receives it. The object remains stored in the source file. The copy of the object in the container file is automatically updated whenever the source file's object is changed. (WIN42)

Maximize button. A resizing button resembling a small rectangular box. It is located to the right of the *Minimize* button on the title bar. Clicking it will enlarge a window to its maximum size. (WIN22)

Maximized. A window that is enlarged to its maximum size. (WIN17)

Menu bar. A feature available only in program windows. It provides mouse and keyboard access to a program's features through drop-down menus. The Menu bar is located just below a window's title bar. (WIN22)

Microsoft Windows 95. A Graphical User Interface operating system. (WIN2)

Minimize all windows. A multiple windows display that reduces all windows on the desktop to their taskbar buttons. (WIN38)

Minimize button. A resizing button that reduces a window to its taskbar button. (WIN21)

Mouse. A common pointing device used to control a mouse pointer (a small graphical image often in the form of an arrow) on your screen. (WIN5)

Mouse pointer or pointer. A small graphical image, often in the shape of an arrow, whose movements are controlled by a using a pointing device. It can be used to select features. (WIN5)

Moving. The process of relocating data. (WIN42)

Multitasking. The ability to work with two or more programs at the same time. (WIN37)

My Computer. A program that can be used to browse (view) and manage all of the components of your computer. (WIN68)

New. The *File* menu command that will clear a program window's workspace so that you can begin a new document. For programs that allow multiple documents, this command will open a new document window. (WIN35)

Notepad. A Windows Accessories program that can be used to create or edit text only files. (WIN43)

Object. In general, an object in Windows includes any icon, window, or set of information (linking and embedding). (WIN158)

Objects. Any graphical image (picture or symbol). They include icons and windows. (WIN2)

OLE. Short for "object linking and embedding," OLE refers to transferring information from one program to another as an object. (WIN158)

Open. A *File* menu command that can be used to retrieve a saved document from a disk. (WIN36)

Palette. Used to select foreground and background colors when using Windows Paint, a graphics program. The *Select Colors* box displays the currently selected foreground and background colors. The color used by a tool when drawing is the foreground color. The background color is the drawing area's color. (WIN148)

Paste. The *Edit* menu command that places a selection from the Clipboard to a desired location. (WIN43)

Pixels. Dots that make up a computer-generated picture or character. (WIN145)

Plug and play. The idea of simply plugging new hardware into your system and playing with (using) it immediately. (WIN105)

Pointing. A mouse action that involves moving your mouse on a flat surface, and thus moving the mouse pointer on your screen to a desired item or area. (WIN6)

Pointing device. A device used to control a mouse pointer (small graphical image often in the form of an arrow) on your screen. Pointing devices may include a mouse, trackball, trackpoint (pointing stick), track pad, or electronic pen. (WIN5)

Print. The *File* menu command that produces a hard copy of a document on paper. (WIN35)

Printers. A folder that can be accessed through My Computer or the *Settings* submenu (*Start* menu). It is used for adding a printer, switching printers (if you have installed more than one printer), and checking and controlling the status of current print jobs. (WIN55)

Printers. A Windows program that can be used to view the current printers installed and their activity.

Program. A set of computer instructions. (WIN2)

Program groups. Logical groupings of programs and files by categories on the *Programs* submenu for easier visual access. (WIN15)

Program window. A window that contains a program. Program windows occupy the desktop. (WIN17)

Properties. The way information and other attributes (characteristics) of an item are displayed or set. The Change Properties command can be used to alter any object's default characteristics. (WIN99)

Pull-down menu. A menu that drops down from its menu bar selection. (WIN22)

Recycle Bin. A program that stores references to files deleted from other places on your hard disk and desktop. (WIN87)

Resizing buttons. Located on the title bar, clicking a resizing button will quickly resize a window. Resizing buttons include *Minimize, Maximize,* and *Restore* button. (WIN21)

Restore. A window resizing command that reduces a maximized window to its previous size. (WIN21)

Restore button. A resizing button that appears on the right side of a window's title bar when a window is maximized. Clicking it will resize a window to its previous size. (WIN22)

Right-clicking. Pointing to an object and pressing and releasing the right mouse button. (WIN10)

Run dialog box. A dialog box accessed through the *Start* menu. It can be used to launch programs, or open folders or documents by typing its command line. It is often used to install new programs. (WIN55)

Save. A command that can be used to save a document for the first time and re-save a previously saved document under its original name without confirmation. (WIN32)

Save as. A command that opens the *Save As* dialog box for saving. It allows you to save an updated document under a different name, thereby keeping the original document under its old name. (WIN32)

Screen capturing. The process of taking a picture of the current screen by pressing the Print Screen key. This copies the current image of the screen to the Clipboard for future pasting. (WIN156)

Select colors box. A section of the palette in Windows Paint program that displays the currently selected foreground and background colors. (WIN148)

Selection. Data marked for editing. (WIN25)

Send to. A submenu that can be used to copy a selection to another disk, fax, or electronic mail. (WIN93)

Settings menu. A submenu of the *Start* menu that can be used to launch the Control Panel window, Printers window, and open the *Taskbar Properties* dialog box. (WIN53)

Sharing files. Copying or moving documents, programs, and folders within the same folder or between folders. (WIN87)

Shortcut icon. An icon created with a link (special connection) to the original file or folder. It allows you to open the original document or folder or to launch the original program from the desktop or another folder. (WIN87)

Shortcut keys. Keys that provide quick keyboard access to specific commands. They may involve pressing a function key alone or in conjunction with the Ctrl, Alt, or Shift keys. The Ctrl, Alt, or Shift keys may also be used in conjunction with other keys. (WIN6)

Shortcut menu. A menu that contains common commands that can be invoked on the related item. Right-clicking will open an item's *Shortcut* menu, if available. (WIN10)

Shut down. The *Start* menu command that can be used to exit Windows. (WIN13)

Source file. The document with the original information in a linking or embedding operation. (WIN158)

Start button. Located on the left side of the taskbar, the *Start* button can be used to open the Windows *Start* menu (main menu) by mouse. (WIN5)

Start menu. The Windows main menu. It can be used to start programs, find documents, adjust system settings, find a document (file), access help, or shut down Windows. It can be opened by clicking the *Start* button on the taskbar or pressing the Ctrl + Esc keys. Each option on the *Start* menu is listed with its corresponding icon to its left. (WIN5)

Subfolder. A folder within a folder. (WIN69)

Tab. A section of a dialog box, similar to tabs used in a manual filing system. (WIN47)

Tabs. A word processing feature used to place text in specific positions on a line. (WIN141)

Taskbar. The bar at the bottom of the Windows screen with a *Start* button on its left side. It is used to start programs and switch between running programs. (WIN5)

Taskbar Properties dialog box. A dialog box used to change the taskbar's display settings and add or remove programs from the *Programs* menu. (WIN55)

Text appearance. Changes to the physical appearance of text. It includes font type, style (regular, bold, italic), and size. (WIN124)

Tile. A standard multiple windows display that presents the windows next to each other either horizontally or vertically. (WIN38)

Title bar. The top row of a window. It identifies the window's name. It can also be used to resize or close a window. (WIN17)

Tool box. A Windows Paint feature that provides a variety of tools for creating a drawing. (WIN146)

Toolbar. A set of command buttons that relate to basic file management and editing commands in WordPad. (WIN27)

Undo. A command that can be used to undo your last action. It is available in many Windows programs. (WIN96)

Window. A rectangular box that may contain a *program* (a set of computer instructions) or *document* (a file with data, information, and/or graphics). It also is used to request or give information about a task or feature. (WIN2)

Windows Explorer. A program that can be used for managing your computer. The components of a system are listed in a hierarchical tree on the left side of the window. Selecting a folder (or other item) from the tree will display its contents on the right side. (WIN107)

Windows screen. The main screen of Windows 95. It has two primary parts: the taskbar and the desktop. (WIN5)

Wizard. A program that helps make a complicated task easier. (WIN105)

WordPad. A simple word processing program that comes with Windows. (WIN15)

Wordwrap. A word processing feature that automatically flows text to the next line as you type. (WIN126)

Workspace. The large interior space of a window. (WIN17)

INDEX

About dialog box, WIN24
About longer filenames, WIN48
About WordPad, WIN24
Accessibility options, commands,
    WIN163–WIN164, WIN167, WIN219
Accessibility Properties, WIN13, WIN188
    dialog box, WIN164
Accessories, WIN15, WIN164, WIN167,
    WIN219
    functions, WIN165
    group submenu, WIN15, WIN16
    program group, WIN15
Active (current) icon, WIN11, WIN219
Active window. *See* Window, active
Add New Hardware icon, WIN106
    commands, WIN181
Alignment, of text, WIN138–WIN140,
    WIN219
    commands, WIN139–WIN140
Always on top, WIN102
Apply button, WIN100
Archive check box, WIN101
Arrange icons, commands, WIN183
    submenu, WIN112. *See also* Explorer
Associated, WIN83, WIN114, WIN219

Backgrounds. *See* Displays, background
Block (set of files), WIN83, WIN219
Bold(ing), WIN135, WIN219. *See* also Font
Booting up (operating system), WIN3,
    WIN57, WIN219
Boot disk, WIN71
Branches. *See also* Main tree line
    expanding and collapsing, commands,
        WIN111
Browse. *See* View
Bullet style, commands, WIN140–WIN141,
    WIN219
Buttons. *See* Individual buttons
Byte(s), WIN70, WIN113, WIN219
    of information, WIN75

Calculator, WIN165
Calendar, WIN165

Cancel button, WIN34
Cardfile, WIN165
Cascade, WIN58, WIN219
    command, WIN38–WIN39
CD-ROM *(read only memory),* WIN69,
    WIN113
Changing properties. *See* Properties
Character Map, WIN165
Clicking, of mouse, WIN7, WIN9, WIN57,
    WIN175, WIN219. *See also* Pointing
    right, WIN10
Clipboard, WIN43, WIN89, WIN219
    Viewer, WIN165
Close (a window), WIN14
    button, WIN2, WIN12, WIN19, WIN22,
        WIN58, WIN219
    commands, WIN19, WIN47, WIN192–
        WIN193
    dialog box, WIN34
    Paint, WIN146
    techniques, alternative, WIN45–WIN46
    a window, WIN22
    windows. *See Exit,* windows; Shut
        Down Windows
    WordPad, commands, WIN31, WIN128
Command button, functions,
    WIN27–WIN29, WIN58, WIN219. *See
    also* Individual command buttons
Communications programs, WIN164,
    WIN166, WIN167, WIN219. *See also* In-
    dividual programs
Container file (compound document),
    WIN158, WIN219
Contents box, WIN110, WIN112. *See also*
    Explorer
Contents tab, WIN47, WIN58. *See also Help,*
    tabs
Control menu, WIN20–WIN21, WIN219
    for closing, WIN47
Control panel, WIN53–WIN54, WIN99,
    WIN115, WIN219
    commands, WIN184–WIN185
    folder, WIN103, WIN113
    launching, WIN102

commands, WIN103, WIN184–WIN185
Copy, WIN58, WIN75, WIN112, WIN114, WIN142–WIN143, WIN219
   commands, WIN43–WIN44, WIN45, WIN143
   between files, WIN175
   within same file, WIN175
Copy disk, WIN219
   dialog box, WIN93, WIN114
   command, WIN93
Copying, WIN42, WIN87–WIN96, WIN219
   data, WIN43–WIN44
   definition, WIN87
   a disk, WIN93
   documents, WIN87
   by dragging and dropping, commands, WIN91–WIN93
   files
     between folders, commands, WIN89–WIN91
     within same folder, commands, WIN88, WIN89
     send to submenu, WIN93, WIN94
   folders, WIN87
   and pasting, WIN43. *See also Edit,* menu commands, WIN45
   programs, WIN87
Create
   a document, WIN30
   commands, WIN35–WIN36
   a new folder, WIN34, WIN82. *See also* Folders
   button, WIN34
   a shortcut. *See* Shortcut
Custom window displays. *See* Windows, displays
Cut, WIN58, WIN75, WIN112, WIN219
   commands, WIN45
   and Paste commands. *See* Paste

Data, WIN2, WIN58, WIN219
   sharing, WIN42–WIN45
Database icon, WIN111
Date & Time, tabs, WIN54
   changing, commands, WIN103–WIN105, WIN184
   dialog box, WIN54
   properties dialog box, WIN104
Default document, WIN32, WIN58, WIN125, WIN219. *See also* WordPad
Default drive, WIN33, WIN219
Default settings, WIN99, WIN115, WIN219
Delete, WIN75, WIN97, WIN219. *See also* Undelete
   all folders, commands, WIN112

commands, WIN97, WIN115
   text, commands, WIN132, WIN167
Desktop, windows, WIN2, WIN5, WIN57, WIN188, WIN219
   select, commands, WIN110–WIN111
   wallpaper, WIN165
Destination folder, WIN88, WIN114
   tiling, WIN92
Details button, WIN34, WIN75
   view, WIN77
Dialog box, WIN5, WIN9, WIN220. *See also* Individual dialog boxes
   definition, WIN17
   help, WIN9, WIN59
   options, commands, WIN213–WIN215
Dial-up Network, WIN166
Direct Cable Connection, WIN166
Directory, WIN69. *See also* Folder
   subdirectory, WIN69
Disk(s), WIN220
   boot, WIN71
   capacity (size), WIN71
   floppy, disks, WIN69
   handling, WIN2–WIN3
   name, WIN71
   operations, WIN70
     diagnostics, WIN70
     formatting. *See* Formatting, a disk
     properties. *See Disk Properties,* dialog box
   for storing data, WIN68–WIN69
Disk Properties. See also Properties, changing
   dialog box, WIN70, WIN100
   Tools tab, WIN100
Display(s), background, WIN106
   options, commands, WIN184
   window. *See* Windows, display
Display Properties
   commands, WIN104–WIN105, WIN184
   dialog box, WIN104, WIN105, WIN184
Document(s), WIN2, WIN3, WIN220
   create. *See* Create, a document
   default. *See* Default document
   definition, WIN31
   icons, WIN185
   management, basic, WIN31–WIN36, WIN58, WIN167
   commands, WIN126–WIN128
   in Paint, WIN146
   menu, WIN52–WIN53, WIN220
   open. *See Open,* a document
   print. *See* Print(ing), a document
   saving. *See Save,* a document
   select, command, WIN131

Start menu, WIN52
submenu, WIN102
templates, WIN165
window, WIN17, WIN220
Documents menu. *See* Document(s), menu
Double-clicking, of mouse, WIN7, WIN12,
    WIN57, WIN220
    command, WIN11, WIN175
Dragging, WIN7, WIN11, WIN175,
    WIN220. *See also* Dragging and dropping
Drag and drop, WIN11, WIN12, WIN57,
    WIN114
    sharing files, commands, WIN88
Drawing. *See also* Paint
    area, WIN148, WIN220
    objects, WIN149
    a shape, commands, WIN149–WIN151
    tool(s), WIN146–WIN148, WIN220
        elipse tool, WIN148
        line tool, WIN147
        rounded rectangle tool, WIN151
Drive(s), WIN70, WIN113, WIN220. *See
    also* Storage, media
        icons, WIN73, WIN113, WIN114
Drop-down boxes, WIN27–WIN29, WIN58,
    WIN220
Drop-down list, WIN28
Dropping, WIN7, WIN11, WIN220. *See also*
    Dragging and dropping

Edit command, WIN45, WIN195–WIN200
    an embedded object, WIN160–WIN161
    menu, WIN23, WIN24, WIN25,
        WIN57, WIN58
        copying between folders, commands,
            WIN90
        sharing files, commands, WIN88
Electronic mail, WIN164, WIN220
Electronic pen, WIN57
Embedding, WIN158–WIN162, WIN220.
    See also Linking, and embedding
        commands, WIN197–WIN198
Enter, WIN178
Esc, WIN178
Exit command, WIN46, WIN47
    windows, commands, WIN13–WIN14.
    See also Shut Down Windows
Explorer, WIN107–WIN112, WIN115
    commands, WIN110–WIN112
    launching, WIN108–WIN110. *See also*
        Contents box
        by My Computer, commands,
            WIN108–WIN109
        by the Start menu, commands,
            WIN108

operating, WIN110–WIN112

Fields, category of data, text box, WIN33
File(s), WIN55, WIN69, WIN220. *See also*
    Folders
    block of, WIN83
    commands. *See* Individual commands
    definition, WIN69, WIN113
    find. *See* Find, a file
    list box, WIN34
    management. *See* File management
    menu(s), WIN23, WIN24, WIN25,
        WIN26, WIN32, WIN35, WIN36,
        WIN57, WIN80
    for closing, commands, WIN47
    create, a document, commands,
        WIN82
    examples, WIN80
    find, commands, WIN72–WIN73
    format a disk, commands, WIN71
    launch Explorer, commands, WIN109
    open, a file, commands, WIN84
    renaming files, commands, WIN85
    multiple, selecting, WIN83
    names. *See File Name*
    name box, WIN34
    opening, WIN83–WIN85. *See also* As-
        sociate
    properties. *See* Properties, file and folder
    sending. *See* Sending files
    of type box, WIN34
File management, WIN78–WIN86,
    WIN111–WIN112
    definition, WIN78, WIN114, WIN220
    with Explorer, WIN111–WIN112
    folders. *See* Folders
File Name (for documents), WIN32, WIN58,
    WIN69–WIN70, WIN113, WIN220
    number of allowable characters,
        WIN69–WIN70
Find, WIN59, WIN70, WIN72–WIN73,
    WIN113, WIN220
    a file, WIN70, WIN72–WIN73
        by file menu, commands, WIN72–
            WIN73
        commands, WIN72–WIN73
    menu, WIN55, WIN220. *See also*
        Files; Folders
    by shortcut menu, commands,
        WIN72–WIN73
    Start menu, WIN52
    tab, WIN47, WIN58. *See also Help,* tabs
Floppy (A:) window, WIN75
Folder(s), WIN3, WIN15, WIN55,
    WIN69–WIN70, WIN220. *See also*

Storage, media
  creating, new, WIN79
    commands, WIN79–WIN80
    document approach, commands,
      WIN82
  definition(s), WIN15, WIN55, WIN69
  delete all, commands, WIN112
  destination, WIN88
  display options, WIN74. *See also* My
    Computer
    commands, WIN74
  within folders. *See* Subfolder(s)
  icons, WIN73, WIN79, WIN80
    create, WIN185
    drive, WIN79
  looking in, WIN73–WIN76
  main. *See Main folder*
  names (for groups of files), WIN69–
    WIN70
  properties. *See* Properties, file and folder
  root or *main directory,* WIN69
  placing shortcuts in, commands,
    WIN94–WIN95
  source, WIN87
  subfolders. *See* Subfolders
  using, WIN79
  windows, WIN73, WIN220
    for printing files, WIN86
Font (typeface), WIN29, WIN220
  changes, commands, WIN133–WIN135
  dialog box, WIN133
  drop-down box, list, WIN28, WIN29
  size, WIN29
  style list box, WIN135
Format(s), WIN220
  a disk, WIN33–WIN34, WIN58,
    WIN70, WIN71
    commands, WIN71
    description, WIN113
    reformat, WIN71
  menu, WIN136. *See also* Layout
Format bar, WIN27, WIN58, WIN220
  font changes, commands, WIN133–
    WIN135
Free-Form Select tool, WIN152. *See also*
  Paint
Function keys, WIN6, WIN57, WIN178,
  WIN220

Games, WIN15, WIN165
Gigabyte (GB). *See* Byte
Go to a different folder, button, WIN75
  drop-down box, WIN110
Graphical user interface (GUI), WIN1,
  WIN2, WIN56, WIN135, WIN220

GUI. *See* Graphical user interface

Hard-disk drive, using, WIN4–WIN5. *See*
  also Storage, media
Hardware, handling, WIN2–WIN3, WIN220
  adding, WIN105–WIN106. *See also*
    Wizard
Help dialog box, WIN9–WIN10
Help feature, WIN9–WIN10,
  WIN46–WIN51
  button, WIN34, WIN51, WIN57
  commands, WIN48, WIN186–WIN187
  within a dialog box, WIN50–WIN51
    commands, WIN50–WIN51
  filenames, WIN48
    longer, WIN48–WIN49
  Index tab, commands, WIN47–WIN49
  main, WIN47–WIN50
    dialog box, WIN58
  menu, WIN23, WIN51
    open, commands, WIN24–WIN25
  within a program window, WIN51
  by selecting, WIN49–WIN50
  tabs, WIN47–WIN49
  What's New, WIN50
Help Topics: Windows Help
  dialog box, WIN47, WIN50
  tabs, WIN47
    Contents, WIN47
    Find, WIN47
    Index, WIN47
Hidden check box, WIN101
Home key, WIN178
Hyper Terminal, WIN166

Icons, WIN5, WIN19–WIN20, WIN56,
  WIN220. *See also* Individual icons
  create, commands, WIN185–WIN187
  Add New Hardware, WIN106
  Database, WIN111
  large and small
    toolbar button, WIN75
    view, default, commands, WIN77–
      WIN78
  shortcut. *See* Shortcut icon
Indentation, WIN136–WIN138, WIN220
  Paragraph dialog box, WIN136
Index tab, WIN47–WIN49, WIN58. *See also*
  Help, tabs
Input device, WIN6
Insert text, WIN128–WIN131, WIN178
  in Paint, commands, WIN154–WIN156.
    See also Paint
Insertion point, WIN30, WIN44, WIN220
Internet, WIN164

Italicize, WIN135–WIN136, WIN220. *See also* Font

Keyboard operations. *See* Individual commands
    deleting text, commands, WIN129
    selecting, a document, WIN129
      line(s), WIN129
      paragraph, WIN129
Kilobyte (KB). *See* Byte

Label (disk name), WIN69. *See also* Properties, changing
LAN (local area network), WIN4
Launching, a program, WIN14, WIN15–WIN17, WIN57, WIN220
    commands, WIN15–WIN16, WIN187
    control panel, commands, WIN102–WIN103
    multiple programs, WIN37–WIN38
      commands, WIN37–WIN38
    My Computer. See My Computer, launching
    Paint. *See* Paint
    WordPad. *See* WordPad
Layout (format), WIN124, WIN136, WIN166, WIN220
    menu, WIN136
Line selection, command, WIN131
Line break, WIN126, WIN220
Linking, WIN42, WIN158, WIN167
    definition, WIN158, WIN220
    and embedding, WIN157–WIN162, WIN167
      definition, WIN158
      an object, commands, WIN158–WIN160, WIN161
List,
    button, WIN34, WIN75
    view, WIN77
Long filenames, WIN48–WIN49
Look in box, WIN34
    drop-down box, WIN36

Main folder, disk, WIN69, WIN79, WIN113. *See also* Storage; Folders
    setting up. *See* Format, a disk
Main tree line, WIN110. *See also* Explorer
    branches, WIN110
      selecting, commands, WIN110–WIN111
Managing, the computer, WIN67–WIN115
    files. *See* File management
Maximize, WIN17, WIN22, WIN221
    button, WIN19, WIN22, WIN58

Megabyte (MB). *See* Byte
Menu(s), WIN56
    commands, WIN25–WIN26
    file, WIN23
    functions, WIN23
    indicators, WIN26–WIN27, WIN58
      summary of, WIN27
    pull-down, WIN23
    using, WIN23–WIN25
Menu bar, WIN22–WIN23, WIN57
    description, WIN22
    operations, WIN193–WIN194
Menu bar item, WIN58, WIN221
Microsoft Exchange, WIN166
Microsoft Fax Services, WIN166
Microsoft Fax Viewer, WIN166
Microsoft Mail Services, WIN166
Microsoft Network, WIN166, WIN167
Microsoft Windows 95, WIN2, WIN221. *See also* Windows
Microsoft Word, WIN31
Minimize, command, WIN21–WIN22
    button, WIN21, WIN58, WIN221
    a window, WIN22, WIN38
    all windows, WIN41, WIN58, WIN221
Modem, fax modem, WIN167
MouseKeys, WIN6, WIN13. *See also Use MouseKeys*
    commands, WIN179–WIN180
Mouse operations, WIN6–WIN14
    actions, common, WIN7, WIN175. *See also Use MouseKeys*
    delete text, commands, WIN132
    pointers. *See* Mouse pointers
    select, a document, WIN129
      line(s), WIN129
      paragraph, WIN129
Mouse pointer(s), WIN5, WIN7–WIN8, WIN57, WIN165, WIN221
Mouse symbols, WIN7
Move, WIN42, WIN87–WIN96, WIN114, WIN142–WIN143, WIN221
    commands, WIN45, WIN175
    data, WIN45
    definition, WIN87
    documents, WIN87
    by dragging and dropping, commands, WIN91–WIN93
    files
      between folders, commands, WIN89–WIN91
      within same folder, commands, WIN89
    folders, WIN87

programs, WIN87
the taskbar, WIN102
Multilanguage Support, WIN166
Multimedia, WIN166. *See also* CD-ROM
Multiple documents, WIN36
Multiple files. *See* Files, multiple
Multitasking, WIN2, WIN37–WIN46,
   WIN221
   definitions, WIN36, WIN58
My Computer, icon, WIN5, WIN11, WIN17,
   WIN57, WIN67–WIN68, WIN113,
   WIN221
   commands, WIN200–WIN213
   drives, WIN70
   launching, commands, WIN68
   program icon, WIN68

Name(s)
   section in title bar, WIN19, WIN20–
      WIN21
   using, commands, WIN4
Net Watcher, WIN165
Network, WIN95, WIN167
New, command, WIN35, WIN58, WIN221.
   See also File, menu
   dialog box, WIN35
   submenu, WIN114
New Text Document, icon, WIN82
Notepad, WIN37, WIN43, WIN165, WIN221
Num Lock, WIN178

Object(s), WIN2, WIN58, WIN113,
   WIN221. *See also* Icons
   selecting, WIN83–WIN84
OLE (object linking and embedding),
   WIN158, WIN167, WIN221. *See also*
   Linking, and embedding
Online User Guide, WIN165
Open (file), commands, WIN84–WIN85,
   WIN221
   a block of files, commands, WIN85
   dialog box, WIN36
   a document, WIN34, WIN36
      command, WIN36
   group of files, commands, WIN84
   Shortcut menu. *See* Shortcut menu,
      open
Options Properties dialog box, WIN7

Page up, Page down, WIN178
Paint, WIN144–WIN157, WIN165, WIN167
   area. *See* Drawing, area
   capturing, a screen, commands,
      WIN156–WIN157
   close, command, WIN146

copying objects, commands, WIN152–
   WIN154
definition, WIN144
document management, WIN146
drawing tools. *See also* Drawing
   selecting, commands, WIN146–
      WIN149, WIN152
features, quick reference, WIN217–
   WIN218
filling in an area, commands,
   WIN151–WIN152
inserting text, commands, WIN154–
   WIN155
launching, commands, WIN144
mouse actions by keyboard, WIN144–
   WIN145
moving objects, commands, WIN152–
   WIN154
palette. *See* Palette
Print Screen, commands, WIN156
selecting an object, WIN152–WIN154
status bar, WIN145
undoing, command, WIN152
window, WIN146
Palette, color, WIN148–WIN149, WIN221
   Select Colors box, WIN148
   selecting, command, WIN149. *See also*
      Drawing, area
Paragraph
   dialog box, WIN136–WIN138
   selection, command, WIN131
Paste, WIN43, WIN58, WIN75, WIN89,
   WIN112, WIN221
   commands, WIN45, WIN187–WIN188
   link, WIN58
   Special, WIN159. *See also* Linking, and
      embedding
      dialog box, WIN159
Phone Dialer, WIN166
Pixel, WIN145, WIN221. *See also* Paint
Plug and play, WIN105, WIN221. *See also*
   Hardware, adding
Pointer. *See* Mouse pointer
Pointing, WIN6, WIN7, WIN221
   and clicking, command, WIN8–WIN9
Pointing device. *See* Mouse pointer
Print(ing), WIN231
   commands, WIN35
   a document, WIN35, WIN162
   files, commands, WIN86, WIN114
   Help, information, WIN50
      commands, WIN50
   Topic, WIN50
      dialog box, WIN50
Print Preview, WIN167

Print Screen, WIN156, WIN178

Printers, program, WIN55, WIN59, WIN99, WIN106–WIN107, WIN115, WIN221

    adding, commands, WIN183

    folder, WIN68, WIN107, WIN113

    removing, commands, WIN183

    using, commands, WIN106–WIN107

Program(s), WIN2, WIN3

    menu, WIN55, WIN57

    starting, WIN18

    switching. *See* Switching, between programs

    submenu, WIN15, WIN16

    window, WIN17, WIN221

Program groups, WIN15, WIN221

Program icon, WIN45, WIN68

Properties (characteristics), WIN68, WIN99, WIN221

    changing, WIN69, WIN70, WIN99–WIN102, WIN115

    in Explorer, WIN112

    dialog box, WIN99, WIN100–WIN101

    of a disk, commands, WIN99–WIN100

    file and folder, commands, WIN100–WIN101

    dialog box, WIN100–WIN101

    taskbar. *See Taskbar Properties*

    toolbar button, WIN75

Pull-down menus, WIN22–WIN23, WIN57, WIN221. *See also* Menu(s)

    open, commands, WIN23

    select, a menu item, WIN23

Quick View, WIN165

RAM, WIN69, WIN113. *See also* Storage, media

Read-only check box, WIN101

Read only memory. See CD-ROM

Recycle Bin, WIN87, WIN97–WIN98, WIN115, WIN221

    operations, WIN98

      deleting files from, commands, WIN98

      emptying, commands, WIN98

      restoring files, commands, WIN98

Reformat, a disk. *See* Format, a disk

Renaming (files), commands, WIN85–WIN86, WIN114

Resizing

    buttons, WIN21–WIN22, WIN57, WIN221

    the taskbar, WIN102

    a window, custom, WIN42

Restore button, WIN19, WIN22, WIN58, WIN221

Right clicking, of mouse. *See* Clicking

ROM, WIN69, WIN113. *See also* Storing, media

Ruler. *See* Tab(s)

Run, WIN59

    command, WIN55–WIN56, WIN189

    dialog box, WIN55, WIN221

    Start menu, WIN52

Save, WIN26, WIN221

    button, WIN34

    commands, WIN33, WIN34–WIN35, WIN129

    a document, WIN32–WIN35

Save as, WIN32

    commands, WIN25–WIN26, WIN129

    dialog box, WIN32, WIN33, WIN34

    type box, WIN34

Save in, WIN33

    box, WIN34

Screen capturing, in Paint, commands, WIN156–WIN157, WIN167, WIN222

Screen Savers, WIN165

Scroll bar, WIN49

    box, WIN49

Select(ing), WIN25, WIN43. *See also* Copying; Move

    Colors box, WIN222

    command, WIN44

    definition, WIN83, WIN114

    by keyboard, commands, WIN131

    by mouse, commands, WIN131

    multiple files. *See* Files, multiple

    objects, (single, group, and block), WIN83

    in Paint, WIN152–WIN154. *See also* Paint

    techniques, WIN83, WIN131

    text, WIN131, WIN167

Send to, submenu, WIN93, WIN94, WIN115, WIN222

Sending files, WIN93

Setting(s), WIN52

    menu, WIN53

    Taskbar Properties dialog box. *See Taskbar Properties*

Sharing data. *See* Data, sharing

Sharing files, WIN87–WIN98, WIN222

    commands, WIN88

    copying documents, WIN87. *See also* Copying

    definition, WIN87, WIN114

    moving documents, WIN87. *See also* Moving

    within same folder, WIN88

Shortcut(s), creating, WIN93–WIN96
  commands, WIN94–WIN95
  on the desktop, commands, WIN95–WIN96
Shortcut icon, WIN87, WIN93, WIN114, WIN222
Shortcut keys (command keystrokes), WIN6, WIN129, WIN222
  creating, a new document, WIN129
  opening a document, WIN129
  printing, WIN129
  saving a document, WIN129
Shortcut menu(s), WIN10–WIN11, WIN29–WIN30, WIN38, WIN40, WIN41, WIN50, WIN57, WIN58, WIN87, WIN222
  for closing, command, WIN47
  commands, WIN29–WIN30
  copying between folders, commands, WIN90
  create, a document, commands, WIN82
  find, a file, commands, WIN72–WIN73
  format, a disk, commands, WIN71
  launch Explorer, commands, WIN109
  open, commands, WIN40, WIN84, WIN189–WIN190
  options, WIN29
  printing files, commands, WIN86
  reformat, a disk, commands, WIN71
  renaming files, commands, WIN85
Show Clock, WIN102
Shut Down Windows, WIN13–WIN14, WIN57, WIN222
  commands, WIN190
  dialog box, WIN14
Source file, WIN158, WIN222
Source folder, WIN87, WIN114
  tiling, WIN92
Start button, WIN5, WIN57, WIN222
Start menu, WIN1–WIN2, WIN5, WIN15, WIN19, WIN26, WIN52–WIN56, WIN57, WIN222
  commands, WIN52–WIN53, WIN59
  main Help, WIN47, WIN58
  tabs, WIN58. *See also* Individual tabs
  programs. *See Start Menu Programs* menu
Start Menu Programs menu, WIN101, WIN102
Starting
  a program, WIN18
  windows, WIN3
Status bar (bottom of window), WIN75–WIN76
  commands, WIN76

Storage
  documents, WIN68–WIN70
  files, WIN69
  folders, WIN69, WIN113. *See also* Folders
  main, WIN113
  media, WIN68–WIN69, WIN113
  CD-ROM. *See* CD-ROM
  disks. *See* Disks
  hard disk, WIN68–WIN69. *See also* Hard-disk drive
  system memory. *See* RAM; ROM
  tape, WIN69
  programs, WIN68–WIN70
  terminology, WIN70
Subdirectory. See Directory; Subfolders
Subfolders, WIN69, WIN80–WIN82, WIN113, WIN222
Submenus, WIN57
Switching
  between programs, WIN38
  command, WIN38, WIN191
  between windows, WIN38
System Monitor, WIN165
System Resource Meter, WIN165
System time, button, WIN38, WIN41
System Tools, options, WIN15

Tab(s), WIN141–WIN142, WIN178, WIN222
  changes, commands, WIN141–WIN142
  by *Format* menu, WIN142
  by ruler, commands, WIN142
Taskbar, WIN5, WIN55, WIN57, WIN188–WIN189, WIN222
  moving, WIN102
  options, WIN102
  resizing, WIN102
Taskbar Properties, dialog box, WIN53, WIN55, WIN59, WIN101, WIN222
  commands, WIN101–WIN102
Text, appearance, WIN124, WIN166, WIN222
  changing, WIN133
  entering. *See* WordPad
  layout (format). *See* WordPad
  tool, WIN154–WIN156
Tile, display, WIN38, WIN40–WIN41, WIN222. *See also* Window(s), display
  commands, WIN191
  horizontally, WIN58
  source and destination folders, WIN92
  vertically, WIN58
Time formats. *See Date & Time*
Time Zone, tab, WIN53–WIN54

Title bar, WIN17, WIN19, WIN58, WIN222
  description, WIN19, WIN34
Tool box, WIN222
Toolbar, WIN27, WIN58, WIN74,
  WIN194–WIN195, WIN222
    button titles, WIN75. *See also* Individual button titles
    display, command, WIN74–WIN75, WIN76
Trackball, WIN57
Track pad, WIN57
Tree box, WIN110, WIN112. *See also* Explorer
Typeface. *See* Font

Undelete, WIN98
Undo, WIN75, WIN96, WIN222
  commands, WIN96, WIN114, WIN132, WIN152
  Minimize All, command, WIN41
  using, WIN96
Up One Level button, WIN34, WIN75
Use MouseKeys, WIN13, WIN167
  commands, WIN7, WIN13

View, a tree, WIN110–WIN111. *See also* Explorer
View, menu, WIN75, WIN76, WIN78
  description, WIN78
  options, commands, WIN76–WIN78. *See also* Individual options
  dialog box, WIN113, WIN114
  in Explorer, WIN112

Window(s), WIN57, WIN222
  active, WIN38, WIN58, WIN219
  common features, WIN2, WIN14–WIN31. *See also* Individual features
  communications. *See* Communications programs
  desktop. *See* Desktop
  displays, standard, WIN38–WIN41
    Cascade, WIN38–WIN39
    Minimize All Windows. *See* Minimize
    Tile, WIN38
  custom, WIN41–WIN42
    commands, WIN42
  environment, WIN1–WIN59
  explorer. *See* Explorer
  features, WIN123–WIN167. *See also* Individual features
    common, WIN180–WIN192
  screen, WIN5, WIN222
  taskbar. *See* Taskbar
  types of, WIN17

Windows Explorer, WIN107–WIN112. *See also* Explorer
WinPopup, WIN165
Wizard, WIN105–WIN106, WIN115, WIN222
WordPad (word processor), WIN15, WIN20, WIN124–143, WIN165, WIN166
  aligning text, WIN138–WIN140
    commands, WIN139–WIN140
  bullets. *See* Bullet style
  close, WIN31, WIN128
  common operations, commands, WIN129
    shortcut keys, WIN129
  copy a selection, commands, WIN143
  delete text, WIN132
  document management, commands, WIN126–WIN128
  entering text, WIN125–WIN126, WIN130
    default document, WIN125
  features, quick reference, WIN215–WIN216
  font changes, commands, WIN133–WIN135
  insert text, commands, WIN128–WIN131
  launching, commands, WIN15–WIN16, WIN124
  moving a selection, commands, WIN142–WIN143
  selecting text, WIN131
  tab
    changes, commands, WIN141–WIN142
    dialog box, WIN141
    settings, WIN141
  text appearance, WIN124
    changing, WIN133
  text layout (format), commands, WIN136–WIN142
    indentation, commands, WIN136–WIN138
  undoing an action, command, WIN132
  window, WIN124–WIN125
Wordwrap, WIN126, WIN166–WIN167, WIN222
Workspace (work area), WIN17, WIN30–WIN31, WIN222
  adjusting, WIN113
  definition, WIN30
  in a folder window, WIN76
Workspace shortcut menu, WIN80